Library of
Davidson College

The Iowa Testing Programs

E. F. Lindquist
1901 – 1978

THE IOWA TESTING PROGRAMS

THE FIRST FIFTY YEARS

Julia J. Peterson

UNIVERSITY OF IOWA PRESS
IOWA CITY

University of Iowa Press, Iowa City 52242
©1983 by The University of Iowa. All rights reserved
Printed in the United States of America

Library of Congress Cataloging in Publication Data

Peterson, Julia J.
   The Iowa Testing Programs.

   Includes index.
   1. Iowa tests of educational development—History.
I. Title.
LB3052.I8P47 1983   371.2'62   83-10390
ISBN 0-87745-121-4

CONTENTS

ILLUSTRATIONS	
PLATES	ix
FIGURES	x
ABBREVIATIONS	xi
Foreword	xii

PART ONE: THE PIONEERING THIRTIES

1	The Original Iowa High School Testing Program	1
	First Years	1
	Growth	6
	Focus on Educational Values	12
	Continuing Evolution of the First Test Battery	15
	English Correctness	16
	Comprehension of Literature	18
	Contemporary Affairs	18
	Correction for Guessing	20
	The Separate Answer Sheet	21
	The Intelligence Testing Program	22
	Branching Out	23
	Research	24
	Fruition	24
2	The Early Elementary School Program	26
	Germination	26
	The Shape of the Program	26
	The 1935 – 39 Basic Skills Batteries	27
	Expectations for the Tests	30
	Originality in Reports and Norms	32
	The Pupil Profile Chart	32
	The Building Average Reports	32
	Norms for Many Needs	34
	Other Follow-up Aids	35
	Improved Service Systems	36
	Reception by the Schools	38
	Beyond Expertise	38

PART TWO: THE VIGOROUS FORTIES

3   The Extended Basic Skills Program   43
       The New Series of ITBS   43
          The Individual Cumulative Record   45
       Problems and Progress   45
       Appointment of Director Hieronymus   49
       Coast-to-Coast Clientele   50

4   The *Iowa Tests of Educational Development*   53
       Rationale   53
       Guidelines for the Fall Testing Program   55
       Salient Characteristics of the ITED   56
          Subject Area Testing   56
          The Reading Tests   57
          The English Test   59
          Uniform All-school Testing   61
          Scoring and Reporting Services   61
          The Standard Score Scale   62
       Administrative Highlights   64
          Rental of Test Booklets   65
          Test Security   65
          Other Innovations   66
          Pre-electronic Scoring   68
       The Take-Home Profile Leaflet   76
       Acceptance of the New Program   77
          Participation   77
          Comment   78
       The SRA Connection   79
       Military Service by the ITED   82
          The USAFI and the ITED   82
       The *Cooperative Test on Recent Social and
          Scientific Developments*   83

PART THREE: THE ELECTRONIC FIFTIES

5   The First Iowa Scoring Machine   89
       The Beginning   90
       The Announcement   106
       Struggle   108
       Victory   114
       Summary of the Lindquist Inventions   122

6	ITED Developments 1950–59	123
	Tests and Norms	123
	Appointment of Director Feldt	124
	New Services to the Schools	124
	Extent of Test Usage	125
7	ITBS Developments 1950–59	127
	Completion of the L-T Series	127
	The ITBS Self-Interpreting Profile	127
	The Multilevel Edition	129
	Development of the Battery	129
	Scales and Norms	136
	Service Improvements	137
	Expectations	138

PART FOUR: SPIN-OFFS FROM THE IOWA TESTING PROGRAMS

8	The Measurement Research Center (MRC)	143
	Genesis and Corporate Structure	143
	Financial Structure	147
	Plant and Personnel	150
	Engineering Developments	153
	Clientele	163
	The Sale of MRC	168
	The Iowa Measurement Research Foundation	173
9	The American College Testing Program (ACT)	177
10	University Related Spin-offs	181
	The Statistical Service Bureau	181
	The University Examinations Service	182
	The University Computer Center	184
	The Iowa Educational Information Center	187

PART FIVE: THE IOWA PROGRAMS IN RECENT DECADES (1960–80)

11	The Changing Environment	193
	The General Climate	193
	Within ITP	193
12	The ITED 1960–80	199
	Overview	199
	Specifics of Service Improvements	201
	The Local Norms and Distributions	201

	The Consultant Services	201
	The Numeric Grid	202
	The Item Analysis Service	204
	ITP Adaptations to Changing Values	204
	The Shortened ITED Battery	205
	The Two-Level Battery	209
	The Slide in Student Performance	212
	The Test Results and "Accountability"	216
	The Fall Program at 1980	217
13	The ITBS 1960 – 80	218
	Overview	218
	Individualized Testing With the ITBS	220
	The Latest Multilevel Edition	224
	The Tests for Primary Grades	224
	The Supplementary Tests in Social Studies and Science	226
	Iowa Performance on the Tests	227
	Achievement Trends in Iowa	227
	Comparisons With National Performance	230
	Growth in Program Services	232
	Achievement Versus Ability Data	233
	The State of the Program	235
	Recent Volume of Testing	235
	Increasing Complexities of Program Operations	236

Postword	241
APPENDIX	243
NOTES	251
INDEX	257

ILLUSTRATIONS

Plates

E. F. Lindquist		*Frontispiece*
1.	Contestants in 1931 State Scholarship Contest	7
2.	Awards banquet, State Scholarship Contest	8
3.	Key awarded to winning pupils	9
4.	Students at Iowa City High School taking the ITED in 1943	69
5.	Scoring crew at work, 1943 Fall Program	72
6.	Counting right answers, close-up view	72
7.	Bookkeeping machine used in test processing	74
8.	Scorers using special easels and tables	76
9.	Device for normalizing moisture content of answer sheet paper	110
10.	East Hall	111
11.	First electronic scoring machine	112 – 13
12.	ITP/MRC work areas in East Hall, 1958	120 – 21
13.	Measurement Research Center headquarters building	151
14.	MRC engineering shops and development areas	156 – 57
15.	Assembling and testing scanner components	160 – 61
16.	Group photo of four MRC engineers	162
17.	Test processing areas in the MRC building	166 – 67
18.	Five models of MRC document readers	169 – 70
19.	The Lindquist Center for Measurement	174
20.	E. F. Lindquist and Ted McCarrel	179
21.	The University Computer Center in 1961	185
22.	Dedication of the Lindquist Center for Measurement	195 – 98
23.	Leonard Feldt and Robert Forsyth	217
24.	Local meeting of test authors and publishers	221

Figures

1.	Confidential report of school results, 1935	11
2.	Procedure in scoring 1937 Reading Test	29
3.	Early pupil profile chart for ITBS	33
4.	Revised pupil profile chart for ITBS	33
5.	Profile chart of building averages on ITBS	34
6.	Individual cumulative record of ITBS scores	46
7.	Mark-sense card for reporting test scores	47
8.	Pupil profile card for ITED	62
9.	Confidential summary report for ITED	63
10.	Fanfold answer sheet for ITED	67
11.	Ad for test scorers	69
12.	Layout of scorer's desk	71
13.	Steps in production of an ITED pupil profile	73
14.	Double copy rack for typist	75
15.	Authorization for construction of first scoring machine	92
16.	Drawings by E. F. Lindquist for components of scoring machine	96 – 98
17.	Drawing by Lindquist of proposed basic electronic circuit	100
18.	Letter from Lindquist to Phillip Rulon	103 – 04
19.	Letter from Lindquist to Rulon	105
20.	Printout from first electronic scoring, 1955 ITBS	116
21.	Interpretive leaflet for ITBS	128
22.	Arrangement of items by grade in Multilevel ITBS	131
23.	Organization of content in old and new editions of ITBS	132
24.	Capitalization exercises in old and new editions of ITBS	134
25.	Flyer announcing the Measurement Research Center facilities	146
26.	The numeric grid	202
27.	Mean composite scores of Iowa pupils on the ITED	214

ABBREVIATIONS

ACT	American College Testing Program
ASTP	Army Specialized Training Program
CTS	Cooperative Test Service
DAT	*Differential Aptitude Tests*
ERC	Educational Research Corporation
ETS	Educational Testing Service
GATB	*General Aptitude Test Battery*
GE	grade-equivalent score
GED	*Tests of General Educational Development*
IBM	International Business Machines Corporation
ICRSA	Iowa Center for Research in School Administration
IEIC	Iowa Educational Information Center
IMRF	Iowa Measurement Research Foundation
ITBS	*Iowa Tests of Basic Skills*
ITED	*Iowa Tests of Educational Development*
ITP	Iowa Testing Programs
IQ	intelligence quotient
Mod	model
MRC	Measurement Research Center
NEDT	*National Educational Development Tests*
NMSQT	*National Merit Scholarship Qualifying Test*
R&D	research and development
RemRand	Remington Rand Corporation
RSSD	*Cooperative Test on Recent Social and Scientific Developments*
SCAT	*School and College Ability Tests*
SRA	Science Research Associates
STEP	*Sequential Tests of Educational Progress*
SVIB	*Strong Vocational Interest Blank*
UCC	University of Iowa Computer Center
UI	The University of Iowa
USAFI	United States Armed Forces Institute
WLC	Westinghouse Learning Corporation

FOREWORD

THERE ARE many stories within the story of the Iowa Testing Programs. There is the measurement story; the unfolding of an idea strong in its impact upon educational practice and research; the continuing evolution in the philosophies and techniques of testing. There is the development of facilities from manual to electronic; the growth of organizations from mini to major, spilling out into multibuilding complexes. There is the story of people, of lives and labors bound up in common enterprise; a cast that swelled from a few to many hundreds—clerks, educators, carpenters, engineers, janitors, printers, programmers, editors, secretaries, and others; a mix of personalities and interactions, leaders and followers. There are the interrelations with the university, the city, the state—as employer, consumer, supplier of service, training center, subsidizer, producer of income. There is the story of ambitions, drives, challenges, of renown hard-won in a single generation through individual and collective effort. These and more.

Not all the facets can be considered, and few can be treated in depth, in a limited history. This telling attempts to trace the main events of record, interwoven with fragments and hints of the many secondary themes.

I wish to thank the present and former staff associates who have assisted variously in the preparation and publication of the manuscript. I am indebted especially to program directors William E. Coffman, Leonard S. Feldt, and A. N. Hieronymus for information, reviews, and encouragement; to Charles S. Davidson for a chapter reading; and to the late E. F. Lindquist for shared recollections and for his interest in this writing. The fact that he read several portions of it in early draft form tempers only slightly my regret that he did not see it completed.

J. J. P.

PART ONE:
THE PIONEERING THIRTIES

1 The Original Iowa High School Testing Program

First Years

IN NOVEMBER 1928 a letter to all Iowa school superintendents called attention to a novel undertaking at The University of Iowa.

> As has been previously announced [at the Annual Conference on Administration and Supervision in October] the College of Education and the Extension Division of the University of Iowa are sponsoring an Academic Meet for every high school in the State of Iowa, to be held at the end of the present school year with a view to stimulating renewed interest on the part of pupils in the fundamental activities which enter into a high school education.[1]

Thus was seeded the project that later came to be known as the Iowa Testing Programs. It burgeoned surprisingly in the economic rubble of the thirties and has flourished without interruption ever since—through depression, prosperity, war, and peace.

The Iowa project was the first statewide testing program of its type and scope. Pocket programs for selected participants or for special purposes were functioning here and there before 1929—such as the Educational Records Bureau programs for private Eastern schools, the Iowa eighth-grade graduation examination conducted by the State Department of Education, and limited scholarship contests under various sponsors in a dozen states.[2] None of these exhibited all the salient features of the Iowa project, which were: the testing of every pupil in the courses for which tests were provided; statewide yet voluntary basis of school participation; annual editions of achievement tests for fundamental academic high school subjects; precise, complex program organization; highly controlled procedures for test administration; the computation of state (Iowa) norms for pupil scores and for school averages; comprehensive services to facilitate *both* pupil and school evaluation. In structural and service characteristics, professional purposes and quality, the Iowa program was a pioneer undertaking. It became the recognized prototype for subsequent developments in large-scale achievement testing.

This prairie venture in measurement at the high school level was a cooperative effort by the College of Education and the Extension Division of The University of Iowa. Professor Thomas J. Kirby, the head of secondary education, chaired the project the first two years. Assistant Professor E. F. Lindquist was responsible for test construction and administration during that time, becoming director in the third year. Dean of Education Paul C. Packer gave advice, encouragement, and widely influential support. The Extension Division, headed by Dr. Bruce E. Mahan, cooperated in certain logistics and liaison with the schools.

The prime objectives of the program were: *first*, the improvement of educational measurement, and *second*, the stimulation of scholarship, in Iowa public secondary schools. The latter goal was spotlighted at the outset by the competitive features of the project. In sports and music, Iowa high schools already had well-organized statewide tournaments and festivals, but there was no comparable arena for academic talent. The very bright youngster remained a strictly local light unless also a star at sprinting, dribbling, or fiddling. Some means was needed to marshal and reward Iowa's youthful intellectual resources. Dr. Lindquist and colleagues provided it. Exploiting the popular interest in track meets, the sponsors christened this parallel competition the Iowa Academic Meet.

Professor Kirby's rather quaint exclamation in a letter to Iowa superintendents expresses the mood and the hope of the early years.

> What a motivating force this series of contests should be, culminating as they will in the spectacle of almost eight hundred of the outstanding high school pupils of the state assembled in the final contest at the University of Iowa![3]

A related period piece appearing in 1929 and 1930 bulletins and convocation programs is the following homily:

> To keep cool in the excitement of contest
> To be poised when under strain
> To give one's best regardless of difficulty
> To lose without bitterness
> To win with modesty
> These are outcomes that make a contest worthwhile.

However, even in the very first (February 1929) announcement, participating schools were admonished that "the element of award should very decidedly be kept in the background making such element an accompaniment to a significant educational undertaking rather than an objective."

The early archives are fragmentary with respect to many details, particularly program statistics. It is evident, however, that in the first year at least 223 schools participated, testing 40,000 pupils; in the second, about 360 senior and junior high schools took part; and by the third year, some 395 schools, enrolling "well over half of all high school pupils in the state," registered for the testing.[4]

The structure of the project was initially three tiered, consisting of local, district, and state (final) contests. The first level of testing involved all pupils; the second and the third, only contestants who had qualified at the preceding level. In 1929, participating high schools were merely *encouraged* to administer a full slate of the tests available; in 1930 and 1931, they were *required* to do so to be eligible for competition. From the outset, participants were asked to measure *every pupil* in each class tested.

Recruiting of talent for test construction apparently posed no problems. As in later years, the enthusiasm of the program directors and the dean seemingly was infectious, and their colleagues no doubt recognized the importance and the possibilities of this link with Iowa public education. Committees of specialists, with Assistant Professor Lindquist the technical overseer, undertook preparation of the tests. These authors are named in Appendix Table A.

Tests for administration in twelve high school courses were offered in the 1929 program. The ten test titles were: English Mechanics for grades 9 and 10, English and American Literature for grades 11 and 12, World History, American History, First Year Algebra, Plane Geometry, General Science for grade 9, Physics, and—by popular request—Fourth Semester Typewriting, and Stenography. In 1930 the latter two were replaced by American Government (Civics) and Economics tests, a single English Correctness Test was administered in all four grades, and separate English Literature and American Literature tests, appropriate for grades 11 and 12, were offered.[5]

All tests were forty-five minutes in length, fitting the normal class period. In general, the test items dealt mainly with facts the specialists considered important to understanding of the subject. The content sampling was broad, and pupil responses were indicative at least of the pupil's familiarity with the subject matter then taught. Even in these earliest editions one finds items concerned with cause and effect relationships, literary qualities, and application of scientific principles. In this as well as later programs the test builders consulted not only the Iowa State Courses of Study and widely used textbooks but also classroom materials solicited from school administrators for analysis.

For the most part, the tests were multiple-choice, completion, matching, true-false, or combinations of these. The algebra items and some geometry items were computational, free-response. In the English test the pupil was asked to detect the mistakes in printed discrete sentences and to categorize them as grammar, punctuation, or spelling errors. Actual typing and dictation exercises were included in the two tests of commercial skills offered in 1929.

An interesting precursor of materials issued to Iowa school educators in later decades is a mimeographed eight-page pamphlet carrying no by-line but exhibiting the exactness of thought and rhetoric characteristic of Lindquist's writing. Besides describing the principal features and purposes of the Academic Meet, it discusses the construction, content, and standardization of the tests, arriving at the following summation:

> Because of the fact, therefore, that the contest examinations are constructed with at least as much care as that characteristic of the usual standardized test, because they are specifically adapted in content to what is being taught in the high schools in the State of Iowa, because the norms are established specifically for Iowa high schools and based on far greater numbers than any commercialized standardized test, and finally because of the way in which these norms are expressed, it may be safely asserted that they represent the best achievement measures now available for the Iowa high schools in the subjects for which they are constructed. They may be used for all of the purposes for which the usual standardized test might be employed, and because of these superiorities they can be so used with much greater effectiveness.[6]

Economy in production and operations was essential in a program launched without any reserve funds and intended to be self-supporting. The charges to participants also had to be modest in that era of lean school budgets. In the first years, the schools paid only for the tests administered locally, at an average of 3.6 cents per copy. This one charge had to cover all the costs of printing, postage, extra clerical help, and miscellaneous operating expenses in all three events of the series. Work space, office assistance, and the professional talent needed for test construction and program direction were supplied by The University of Iowa. The closing balance in the Academic Meet accounts was $361 in 1929 and $984 in 1930.[7] By such a fine fiscal margin, a tailored-for-Iowa testing service was placed within affordable reach of all Iowa schools.

The first contest was held on April 17, 1929. From each participating school, in each subject tested, the two pupils earning the highest raw scores were qualified to represent their school in that subject in their particular district contest on April 26. (The ten districts of the first meet were expanded to sixteen in the second year to reduce travel distance for the pupils.) In the district event, the two highest scoring pupils in each test in each of two enrollment divisions (large and small schools) were named eligible to compete for final honors at Iowa City on June 3–4. There the top ten scorers in each test subject were named. In addition, recognition was accorded to the schools ranking highest in each of the three events.[8]

Local school staffs administered and scored the first set of tests, computed local averages, and reported their results to Iowa City in nine days. Administration and scoring of the district tests were also done locally under supervision by the superintendent of the host school and assistants from nearby schools, duly approved by the central office. With up to 24 pupils qualifying from each school, 2,000 "whiz kids" might assemble in a single district—quite an invasion for the smaller towns to handle. The tests had to be scored the same day—or night—so that results could be announced promptly to anxious contestants. In the final contest in Iowa City, test scoring was done by the chairman's colleagues and staff; again, scoring was virtually curbside, to permit announcement of all winners at the banquet on the second evening.

The high-ranking pupils were publicized and feted at each step of the competition. In the initial testing, local schools were urged to "arrange some fitting recognition for the pupils who win these honors."[9] In the second event, entertainment and housing were provided by the host school and townspeople. In the final round, the contestants were guests of The University of Iowa. Lodging for the youngsters and their chaperons was scrounged in dormitories, the Field House, and private homes by the Extension Division staff; campus tours and other diversions were arranged to enliven the contestants' free hours; and a final banquet was staged in the ballroom of the Iowa Memorial Union, at which the winners were announced. (See Plates 1 and 2.)

The banquet was the climax of many tense weeks. Amid cheers and tears, the winning scholars in each subject were summoned in turn to the speakers' platform to receive their awards from the director or a colleague in the pertinent discipline. Medals, certificates, and a few modest scholarships for outstanding performance were given by The University of Iowa in the first two years of the program, but the scholarships were discontinued thereafter—for lack of funds, no doubt.

The Iowa Academic Meet was very well received by educators and laymen. Pupils, parents, and public seemingly enjoyed the competition. It was good press copy, too, making headlines under catchy nicknames such as Brain Derby and Cranium Contest. Beyond the immediate excitement, there were deeper outcomes. School administrators acknowledged an adrenalin effect on teaching and learning. A few of their favorable remarks cited in the third announcement[10] are:

> The tests increase pupil interest in school work more than any other single factor.
>
> Pupils are more critical of the way in which they are being taught, and are making a better effort toward thorough mastery of the things they think will be tested in the spring tests.
>
> The scholar has at last attained a prestige and importance equal to that of the athlete.
>
> Many pupils who ranked low last year are making a determined effort to make a better showing on this year's test.
>
> In all subjects pupils are cooperating wholeheartedly with their teachers in an attempt to do better work.

The experiences of the first two years proved the practicality of statewide achievement testing at nominal cost. They disclosed potentials for more extensive services to the schools and for both short- and long-range research. The revealed possibilities deserved the full attention of a single administrator and staff. In the summer of 1930, Professor Lindquist was named director, with complete responsibility and virtual autonomy for the development of the fledgling project. That role he was to play, with some variations, for thirty-nine years.

Growth

IDEAS FOR program improvements that had been maturing in the new director's mind during the first two years were promptly put into practice.

The district testing was dropped. Its elimination reduced the stress of the individual competition considerably and heightened attention to total-school accomplishment. It also simplified the administrative structure of the program, freeing staff time and energies for improving the main battery of tests and expanding the services.

The immensely popular final competition was retained at Dean Packer's urging. Renamed the State Scholarship Contest, it was repeated annually in Iowa City as long as the main program continued. Although no monetary scholarships could be awarded, the new name and the gold keys introduced in 1931 gave added luster to the scholastic achievements thus honored. The inscribed gold emblem (Plate 3), styled after the Phi Beta Kappa key, was presented to each first or second place winner. Each multiwinner received a key set with "jewels" (a "ruby" for each first place earned and a "pearl" for each second place) and reinscribed to show all of the pupil's high rankings in the contest. These emblems, especially the jeweled keys, were highly coveted and treasured. Doubtless many may still be found in old family jewelry boxes.

To emphasize the all-school aspect of the testing, the initial battery

The Original Iowa High School Testing Program 7

Plate 1. Contestants in 1931 State Scholarship Contest, assembled on steps of Old Capitol. (University Photo Service)

8   The Iowa Testing Programs

Plate 2. Presentation of awards at banquet in Iowa Memorial Union at conclusion of State Scholarship Contest. (Photo taken in 1931 or 1932. University Photo Service)

was renamed the *Iowa Every-Pupil Tests*. School awards based solely on the Every-Pupil results were made within size and geographical categories. Schools in three enrollment classes below 400 were ranked within their own districts and on a state-wide basis, while all larger schools competed against each other. Ten grand awards for highest composite achievement in the state were also made. In all, 102 school awards were given. In 1935 the number was reduced to twenty (first to fifth place in each enrollment class). From 1932 through 1935, testing in all subjects was required only of those four-year Iowa high schools that wished to compete for awards. A *noncompetitive* basis of participation provided an alternative for administrators who wanted the values of annual measurement but felt that competition had fulfilled initial purposes. From 1936 on, no awards or publicity were accorded to high ranking schools, school rankings being reported only to the school administrator in the Confidential Summary Report; all participating schools were permitted to select the subjects to be tested but agreed to test all pupils in those subjects.

Certain specific needs had surfaced during the first two years. School personnel needed and wanted detailed interpretative materials and suggestions for using the test results. More normative data were desirable, in conjunction with more comprehensive reports of results. Item analyses and other research data were needed in the construction of future tests. Furthermore, the program could become an important vehicle of direct

Plate 3. Key awarded to winning pupils in State Scholarship Contest.
(*Actual size:* $^9/_{16}$ x $1^1/_4$ *inches.*)

help toward improving the *content* of instruction. And so on.

In line with these perceptions, the major goals of the program were redefined in the announcement of the third annual contest[11] as:

— high quality measurement of achievement
— motivation of improved instruction and scholarship
— improvement of curriculum content
— exploitation of research possibilities

Modifications made in the organization and operation of the program fostered the attainment of these goals. Closer regulation and control of test administration in the schools, coupled with improved methods and accuracy in the clerical/statistical treatment of the test results in Iowa City, produced highly reliable norms of pupil and school performance. A very informative summary report was designed by the director to express the school's average results in three ways: numerical rank, percentile rank, and T-score value, in the distribution of all averages on each test. A composite measure for each school (the average of its T-scores) was also computed, and interpreted both by numerical position and by percentile rank. Frequency distributions and tables of Iowa percentile norms (for pupil scores and for school averages) were provided as well.

Such an adequate basis for interpretation of test results could not be obtained with any other standardized test published at that time. For many high school tests, only frequency distributions of raw scores, or at best pupil percentile norms, were available—and these were based on limited, often poorly defined populations.

Streamlining of tests, forms, and procedures was undertaken. After exploring various printing methods, the director decided that offset printing from camera copy prepared by his staff would yield the best quality at the lowest price. He then redesigned the tests into a two-column format that could be typed in sections on large sheets, to be combined and reduced photographically to an 8½-by-11-inch page. The film pages were then assembled on large printing plates, from which eight-page booklets were produced. Scoring keys were designed on 8½-by-11-inch sheets which could be cut into strips, each strip fitting a test page, with the answers positioned on the key to match the pupil's responses on the page. For the hand scoring of tests by teachers, no more efficient and convenient scoring key had yet been devised.

New forms to simplify reporting of scores in each subject were also developed. Each carried a chart of preprinted intervals for a grouped frequency distribution, in which the school administrator entered the frequencies of scores earned by the group tested. Simply combining the reported distributions, either by hand or by punched card method, was a quick and economical means of compiling tables of norms.

From 1935 on, the printed confidential report of results to each school carried also a bar diagram depicting in descending order its rankings on all tests taken (Fig. 1). The diagrams were drawn by hand.

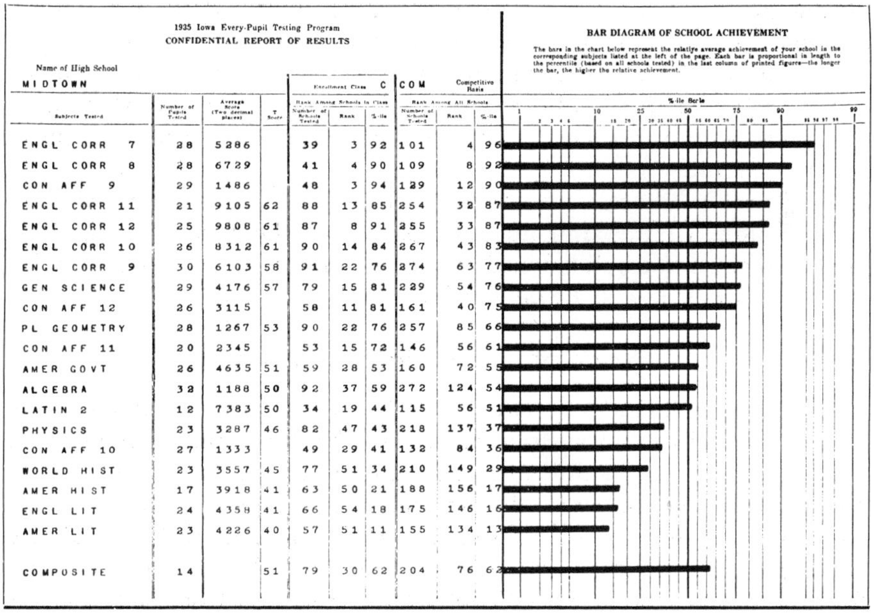

1935 Iowa Every-Pupil Testing Program
CONFIDENTIAL REPORT OF RESULTS

Name of High School: MIDTOWN

				Enrollment Class C			COM Competitive Basis		
				Rank Among Schools in Class			Rank Among All Schools		
Subjects Tested	Number of Pupils Tested	Average Score (Two decimal places)	T Score	Number of Schools Tested	Rank	%-ile	Number of Schools Tested	Rank	%-ile
ENGL CORR 7	28	5286		39	3	92	101	4	96
ENGL CORR 8	28	6729		41	4	90	109	8	92
CON AFF 9	29	1486		48	3	94	129	12	90
ENGL CORR 11	21	9105	62	88	13	85	254	32	87
ENGL CORR 12	25	9808	61	87	8	91	255	33	87
ENGL CORR 10	26	8312	61	90	14	84	267	43	83
ENGL CORR 9	30	6103	58	91	22	76	274	63	77
GEN SCIENCE	29	4176	57	79	15	81	229	54	76
CON AFF 12	26	3115		58	11	81	161	40	75
PL GEOMETRY	28	1267	53	90	22	76	257	85	66
CON AFF 11	20	2345		53	15	72	146	56	61
AMER GOVT	26	4635	51	59	28	53	160	72	55
ALGEBRA	32	1188	50	92	37	59	272	124	54
LATIN 2	12	7383	50	34	19	44	115	56	51
PHYSICS	23	3287	46	82	47	43	218	137	37
CON AFF 10	27	1333		49	29	41	132	84	36
WORLD HIST	23	3557	45	77	51	34	210	149	29
AMER HIST	17	3918	41	63	50	21	188	156	17
ENGL LIT	24	4358	41	66	54	18	175	146	16
AMER LIT	23	4226	40	57	51	11	155	134	13
COMPOSITE	14		51	79	30	62	204	76	62

Fig. 1. Example of reports of average results sent to schools in early Every-Pupil high school programs. *(From Bulletin No. 826 for 1936 Program, p. 15.)*

The many innovations of this period were not mere exercises in ingenuity. Efficiency and economy were vital to the continuing existence of the testing program. To help cover costs, the price of the Every-Pupil tests was raised, but only to a uniform four cents per copy, from which it never increased thereafter. This income from the sale of tests had to cover staff salaries, clerical wages, materials, and printing costs. Most of the administrative and editorial work was accomplished by the director and a staff of two. The shipping of test materials, billing, and bookkeeping were done under his general direction by the Bureau of Educational Research and Service and the Extension Division, which had the necessary facilities and experienced personnel for those tasks.

Automation of sorts made its first appearance on the Iowa campus in the early thirties to meet the need for greater speed in reporting program results. A keypunch, a sorter/card counter, and a numeric tabulator were installed in the barny, pipe-festooned west wing basement of East Hall, and were operated by part-time student workers. The tabulator jogged along at about 150 cards per minute, while the sorter raced at 400. Computation of averages and many other statistical operations were still accomplished mainly by hand, with the aid of desk calculators, some manually operated. Equipment was scarce and expensive; clerks were plentiful at 35 cents an hour. The two sources of labor were combined in whatever manner happened to be the most expedient for the particular time and need. Gainful work was thus afforded many clerks who would otherwise have remained unemployed in a stagnant economic period.

Procedure, while not an objective of the testing program, was its underpinning. In this and all later phases of the Iowa Testing Programs, precisely formulated and executed procedures have been fundamental to the success of the undertaking.

Focus on Educational Values

THE EXTENT to which, early on, the professional substance of the project far exceeded that of a mere contest may be illustrated by the section headings in the third announcement bulletin (1931). Under "The Measurement of Achievement," for example, the topics considered are: "Equality of Opportunity," "Local Adaptation of Content," "Reliability of Norms," "Local Significance of Norms," "Adequacy of Norms," "Separate Norms for Each Enrollment Group," "Comparability of Norms for Different Tests," "Norms for Composite Achievement," "Summary of the Significant Characteristics of the Every-Pupil Tests," and "Importance of the Measurement Function."[12] In such manner a tradition was established of examining with participants the complexities of educational measurement and at the same time instilling confidence in the quality of the program.

In the third and each succeeding program, much creative effort was centered on the preparation of brochures for distribution to the participating schools. The announcements, administrative manuals, and interpretative follow-up materials together constituted a mini-course in measurement practice. The following excerpts from the announcement bulletin for the fifth (1933) annual contest suggest their scope.[13]

On the general characteristics of a good testing program:

> The needs of the high school call for a comprehensive battery of test materials involving all the fundamental subjects. These materials must be consistent in quality and form from subject to subject, must be revised annually in order to keep pace with changing curriculum demands and improvements in testing techniques, and must be provided with highly

reliable and meaningful norms that are comparable from subject to subject. Most of the agencies upon which we rely at present for the production of standardized test materials are dependent upon scattered and individual initiative in separate fields of subject matter, and have inadequate facilities for tryout and standardization. The characteristics essential to an adequate testing program can never be achieved through agencies of this type.

On the practical uses of test results:

To the school administrator or supervisor, therefore, the Academic Contest provides a unique source of important information about his own school. It furnishes him with a reliable means for evaluating the quality of instruction in his own school, as well as for checking the validity of the content taught; it helps him to discover those teachers on his staff most in need of supervisory aid, those subjects most in need of curriculum revision, and those pupils most in need of individual attention; it increases the reliability of the marks used for the promotion and demotion of pupils; it makes possible better educational guidance, and it gives him an indirect measure of the effectiveness of his own organization and administrative policies.

On the value of test results in motivation:

The better pupils, through the State Scholarship Contest, are given a real incentive to make the most of their abilities, while the average and below average pupils recognize that they are equally responsible for the showing of their school in the every-pupil comparisons. The best teachers welcome the opportunity to have the success of their efforts measured; they are pleased to know that competency and efficiency will be definitely recognized.

On improving the content and methods of instruction:

A wide gap has always existed between accepted theory and practice in high school teaching. . . . The carefully prepared research reports and curriculum materials [available to schools] . . . in many cases have only gathered dust on neglected book shelves. What is needed is an immediate and concrete incentive . . . to make use of these materials for the improvement of teaching.

. . . [In the Every-Pupil tests] an effort is made to avoid the use of textbook language, to call for applications rather than statements of laws and principles, to require the interpretation of diagrams and illustrations . . . and [recognition of] the implications of facts.

It is the hope of the sponsors . . . that one of the most valuable outcomes of the Every-Pupil testing program will be the encouragement of renewed emphasis on teaching for meanings rather than for the mere recall and repetition of uniquely phrased facts and principles.

The pamphlets called Subject Matter Circulars introduced in 1931 for teacher use were a novel means to several ends.

The purposes of these circulars are to describe the nature of the tests to be used in each subject and to demonstrate, in terms of specific illustrations and on the basis of facts acquired from previous testing programs, that these tests do require a reasoned understanding of the subject matter on the part of the pupils and that rote learning and mechanical drill procedures in the contest subjects are likely to defeat their own purposes. These circulars, furthermore, contain specific suggestions for the improvement of instruction in this respect, and give a brief description of the subject matter content upon which the tests are to be based. By thus acquainting the schools beforehand with the testing techniques to be employed and the subject matter to be covered, they remove to a large degree the surprise element which might otherwise account for differences between schools, and thereby improve the testing program itself as a valid basis for comparison of achievement from school to school.[14]

A more subtle intent and effect of the Subject Matter Circulars undoubtedly was to foster the enrichment of curricula. The outlines of possible test content presented in the circulars embodied the best (in the consensus of faculty advisers) of instructional and curricular materials in current use. At times, these pamphlets may have pushed the borders of actual practice toward ideals of more comprehensive, more *life relevant*, and more interesting course content. They spurred the review and expansion of local curricula. Thus the warnings, so to speak, implicit in the circulars protected the interests of pupils who might otherwise have been disadvantaged by facing unfamiliar content in the test items.

The research possibilities of the program results were also pointed out to the schools.

Very few research organizations have the facilities to handle problems of the type in which the teacher or the school is the basic unit rather than the pupil, and in which achievement test data must be collected on a very large scale, not only from one hundred or so pupils, but from the pupils under one hundred or more teachers or in one hundred or more school systems. Many of our most pressing and crucial educational problems call for this latter and extensive type of attack. The relationship between class size and academic achievement, between size and type of school organization and results achieved, or between such factors as the training and experience of teachers and the achievement of their pupils, for example, are all problems that require the collection of data on such a wide scale as to render their treatment highly inexpedient, if not impossible, for the usual research agency.[15]

These observations from the thirties are still cogent.

Continuing Evolution of the First Test Battery

IMPROVEMENTS IN the tests—qualitative, administrative, cosmetic—occurred in all editions from the third to the last, most markedly in certain areas and years. The gradual formation of a stable, experienced corps of test builders enabled expansion of the battery as well. In 1931 the use of the English Correctness Test was extended to all four grades. In 1932 new examinations were added in biology and in Latin. That same year all tests were increased in length to sixty minutes, after a favorable preliminary poll of the 411 schools which had expressed intention to participate. (They also voted on the date of the Every-Pupil Contest.) In proposing the increase in length, Dr. Lindquist maintained that it would "result in greater reliability and validity in the measures obtained, . . . allow the pupils more ample time to complete the tests, and . . . in some instances permit the building of tests that are diagnostic in nature."[16]

In 1935 the Test of Understanding of Contemporary Affairs for grades 9-12 was introduced, and the Test of Reading Comprehension of Literature replaced the separate tests previously offered for classes in English and in American literature. In 1936 the Latin Test was drastically revised to measure directly only reading comprehension of the language. The only *reduction* in the battery was the discontinuance of the Economics Test in 1938, presumably because of the declining participation in this subject.

A trend toward the use of more complex multiple-choice items in preference to true/false or matching is evident in successive editions. Conspicuous also is the increasing employment, wherever appropriate, of figures, charts, and maps to be interpreted by the pupils. As early as 1931, for instance, most of the items in the Physics Test were based on diagrams, with the pupil called upon to recognize a principle illustrated or to supply missing information or to solve a problem delineated in the figure. Such approaches to the application of knowledge enhanced the practicality, depth, and interest of the test content, and were not a common characteristic of most tests then available, either commercial or teacher made. The Iowa test builders were certainly helped in their task by the detailed analyses made of marked papers. At the close of each annual program, a representative sample of participating schools was asked to return its test papers: in some years, all papers; in other years, every seventh paper or in some subjects every fifth. On these samplings were calculated test reliabilities, estimates of item difficulty (percent of pupils responding correctly) and indices of item discrimination (difference between the proportions of correct responses by pupils in roughly the upper and lower scoring thirds of the group analyzed).

Throughout the period 1929-42, the Every-Pupil Program received test construction services from members of the University Experimental Schools and the College of Liberal Arts. Fortunately, the highly controlled Scholarship Tests could be reused to some extent, but annual editions of all the Every-Pupil Tests were required. This was a formidable task. The test construction assignments were made without any specific reduction in normal loads and with no professional compensation other than the ever-widening visibility as test authors. In time, when funds permitted, the testing program alleviated the overload in some instances by financing graduate assistants for the professors involved. The numerous persons responsible for the high quality of the *Iowa Every-Pupil Tests* from 1931 through 1942 are listed in Appendix Table B. As general editor, Dr. Lindquist advised on and monitored all the test construction and reviewed the final manuscripts.

The three tests that Dr. Lindquist considered to be most truly originals were the tests in English Correctness, Reading Comprehension of Literature, and Understanding of Contemporary Affairs. They were precursors of the *Iowa Tests of Educational Development* and the *Iowa Tests of Basic Skills*. They shared several characteristics: They directly measured understanding through the *application* of acquired knowledge. They were not bound to the confines of specific courses and therefore could yield measures of certain desired outcomes of secondary education not hitherto obtainable. They measured the pupil's grasp of elements related to everyday life.

English Correctness

The English Correctness Test underwent more changes in form than any other in the battery in the quest for reliable measurement of those writing skills which the director and the test author considered necessary in practical affairs. The most radical change occurred in 1931 when a new type of test was devised. The pupil now had a double task: to *discover* errors implanted in stories or essays comparable to high school themes, and to *correct* each error by writing in a marginal blank the proper spelling, capitalization, punctuation or usage required. The following illustration is adapted from the 1931 test.

A peculiar thing has happened to me this term. Ancient History, which I had considered boring has become my favorite study.

Dr. Lindquist has averred that the 1931 Every-Pupil English Test was the first of its kind in the field. It was considerably more complex and more difficult to construct than the two preceding forms. The usages tested had to command general acceptance, the context had to be free from misinterpretations, and all reasonable means of correcting the included errors had to be anticipated.

Five years later, in the continuing pursuit of efficiency, a quite different approach was tried. Likely error situations in spelling or usage were underlined, and the skill category of each was indicated by the letter *s* or *u* below it. In a rectangle above it, the pupil was to write either the correction or a zero to indicate no mistake. Punctuation errors were to be corrected on the page; capitalization errors were to be indicated by a vertical line through the offending letter. The following lines from the corrected sample exercise in the 1936 test will illustrate.

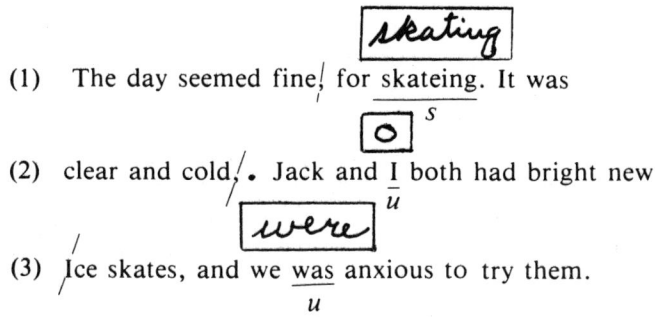

The test was scored by means of stencil overlays on which the appropriate corrections were printed.

Dr. Lindquist described the main advantages of the new form as being that: it more closely approached the actual writing situation; it was simpler to administer, to "take," and to score; it reduced irrelevant writing by the pupil and comprised a larger number of error situations per page and per unit of testing time.[17]

These high expectations must not have been fully realized, for the integrated form was abandoned the following year in favor of testing the four major skills in four separate sections. This allowed a greater saturation of items in each category and a wider range of difficulty to cover the four-grade span. Multiple-choice items were presented in spelling and usage, write-in paragraphs or sentences in punctuation and capitalization.

In 1938 further change was necessitated by the decision to adopt tear-off answer sheets with all of the tests. In capitalization the words to be considered were numbered, and response boxes labeled *C* or *s* were placed on the answer sheet, along with boxes for the spelling and usage sections. Multiple responses to the punctuation items appeared on the test pages, and the pupil's choices were marked there. The title page, the punctuation section and the answer sheet formed a four-page folder separable from the rest of the test for ease of scoring. This pattern remained unchanged through the subsequent editions.

The technical experience gained through these design advances and related experimentation underlay the development of the later English tests in the *Iowa Tests of Educational Development* and the *Iowa Tests of Basic Skills*.

Comprehension of Literature

The Test of Reading Comprehension in Literature concentrated upon the one measurable outcome of literature courses fundamental to all others: development of the ability to read literary materials with understanding. Unlike its predecessors, it contained no section on literary information and history. Like its predecessors, it presented a variety of passages from literature accompanied by multiple-choice items that approached the central goal from many angles. Some were direct questions about meanings, general as well as detailed. Others probed grasp of the author's intent or attitude. There were items touching upon a host of elements contributing to understanding of the passage: meanings of unusual words, figures of speech, allusions, mood, structure where form was important to sense, and so on. Occasional items measured more subjective appreciations of style or quality but only when these were distinct, not disputable, and perception of them was intimately related to comprehension of the passage. The preoccupation with reading comprehension was not meant to denigrate other less tangible and more personal outcomes of the study of literature. Rather, it was another expression of the director's uncompromising standard: to measure what the test purported to measure and could measure reliably.

The same test was administered in all literature classes in grades 11 and 12. Separate norms were established for American and for English literature (regardless of grade) in 1935 and 1936. From 1937 on, separate norms were supplied for the two grades (11 and 12) rather than the two subjects. Individual schools could thus directly compare performance from course to course or from grade to grade and draw more meaningful conclusions concerning pupil progress in reading comprehension in the last two years of high school.

Contemporary Affairs

The Test of Understanding of Contemporary Affairs was a far cry from the conventional "current events" quiz that had become a popular feature in magazines, newspapers, and radio programs. The announced concern in this test was with the development of three important outcomes of high school instruction: (1) a background of information about the evolution of social, economic, and political institutions and practices, (2) the ability and inclination to apply that information to contemporary problems, and (3) the disposition to grow in rational understanding of current affairs through wide and thoughtful reading. The multiple-choice items covered a wide range of domestic and international affairs. Samples from the first (1935) edition raise such diverse questions as:

4. What was the most important change made in United States currency between March, 1933, and January, 1935?
40. Which of the following objectives has the present German government *most* successfully achieved to date?
60. Which is *not* a present trend in law enforcement?
82. Which change in education has been taking place in public education in the last five years?
94. What is the topic discussed in the book, *Merchants of Death*, published in 1934?

The response choices were searching. For example:

39. Which has been a recent result of the mechanization of industry in this country?
   1) Lengthening of the working day of employees
   2) Doing away with the need for labor unions
   3) Production of more goods than the public can buy at current prices
   4) Increased cost per unit of output
99. What is the purpose of the proposed Eastern Locarno Pact?
   1) To prevent aggression across Germany's eastern frontier.
   2) To check Russian expansion in China.
   3) To prevent Turkish aggression in the Balkan Peninsula.
   4) To establish mutual non-aggression between Japan, Russia and China.

The Contemporary Affairs Test was offered for administration to all pupils in all grades—a recognition of the cumulative influence upon performance of instruction in all subjects. However, selection of grades (but not of pupils) to be tested was permitted. Norms were computed for each grade. Because the test was not tailored to a particular academic subject and because its use was entirely optional, it was kept independent of the competitive aspect of the program. The scores were not included in the pupil and school composites. The procedure for the Contemporary Affairs Test differed further in that the scores were corrected for guessing by subtracting from the number of right answers one-third of the number wrong ($S = R - \frac{1}{3}W$).

The new test was well received. In the first year of issue, the number of schools represented in the norms ranged from 129 in grade 9 to 161 in grade 12. Comparative figures for English Correctness were 274 in grade 9 and 255 in grade 12. This level of acceptance remained quite stable through succeeding programs. Performance on the test, however, was lower than anticipated by the test builders.* On the 105 items, the median scores in the four grades were, respectively, 12.0, 16.5, 23.3, 28.6. There was little real improvement in performance on subsequent, comparable editions of the test. An apparent rise in the median scores from 1938 on is attributable mainly to a change in the scoring formula in 1938, when $S = R + \frac{1}{4}$ *Omits* was adopted for the entire battery. No concessions were made by building "easier" items. Quite the contrary. The tests of the forties, for instance, probe deeply into complex aspects of World War II.

The Summary Report of Results for the 1935 program contains a characteristically penetrating and thorough exposition by Professor Lindquist of factors affecting the content of the test, its apparent versus real difficulty, and the effect of correction for guessing in lowering the scores.[18] He also pointed out the criticism of secondary education implied in what he considered disappointingly low achievement on the initial test. He concluded with the hope that the challenge would be met and that the testing program would be instrumental in bringing about improvement in the curricula of Iowa high schools. The continued participation in this test suggests that the schools did face up to the challenge, but with only moderate success. In the final year of the program, the director was still lamenting that "high school pupils in general are very seriously uninformed about contemporary affairs, and . . . a very large proportion of them know practically nothing about what is going on in the world today."[19]

Correction for Guessing

Two important and related developments in procedure date from 1938. One was the separate answer sheet; the other, adoption of correction for guessing in the scoring of all the tests. Hitherto, only a few sections of two-response items (true/false, right/wrong, sense/nonsense) in the Latin and Economics Tests had been scored by subtracting the number wrong from the number right ($S = R - W$). The one notable exception to a simple count of right answers was the formula scoring

---

*H. R. Anderson and E. F. Lindquist, with the collaboration of six other professors in as many departments of the university. See Appendix, Table B.

of the Contemporary Affairs Test (see p. 19). A lengthy explanation of the shift to correction for guessing on all tests is given in the 1938 Summary Report of Results (pages 17 – 18). The reason given for not correcting scores in the past was that it would have compounded the opportunities for errors in teacher scoring. The use of the separate answer sheet so greatly simplified the scoring, according to Lindquist, that correction for guessing could now be undertaken as a standard procedure. In order to make the scoring even more convenient and foolproof, he directed the scorers to employ a formula of $S = R + \frac{1}{4}$ *Omits* rather than the more commonly used $S = R - \frac{1}{3} W$. The exposition in the Summary Report demonstrates the equivalence of the two formulas and explains how they would *rank* pupils in exactly the same order.

The Separate Answer Sheet

Dr. Lindquist's idea of devising a separate answer sheet for the hand-scored Every-Pupil Tests was fundamental to the eventual development of the Iowa scoring services. The sheet he created was used without change in the last five annual programs. Its basic design was a set of numbered boxes, plus blanks for essential identifying information, printed on the reverse of the title page of the test booklet. In taking a test the pupil was directed to tear off the answer sheet along the spine of the booklet, to keep it always as close as possible to the questions being answered, and to make heavy crosses in the boxes corresponding to the correct answers. The 8½-by-11-inch scoring key was punched to reveal only the crosses that were correct. The answer sheets thus could be collected separately for scoring at the end of the test period, and the rest of the booklets could be disposed of as the school administrator saw fit.*

This basic design served all but a few of the tests. In the Algebra and Plane Geometry Tests and Physics Part II, which used a free-response format, blanks for the pupil's responses were printed on the answer sheet instead of boxes. The correct answers were printed along the margins of the one-page scoring key. Special ingenuity was required to accommodate the English Correctness Test by means of a four-page answer folder, in the manner described on pages 17 – 18.

Through this new feature in test format, accuracy of scoring was improved, while clerical work and paper handling were reduced. Lindquist has said, "We . . . were, I believe, the first to use separate

---

*In 1941 and 1942, to reduce further the costs of test administration, multiple use of the Literature and Contemporary Affairs tests with additional separate answer sheets was permitted. This idea surfaced again some years later.

answer sheets and various improved manual scoring procedures in a wide-scale program."[20] This first Every-Pupil Test answer sheet became the ancestor of hundreds. Its demonstrated practicality over the next several years certainly must have crystallized the director's decision to work out a scoring service for the new battery of tests already taking shape in his plans for the future.

The Intelligence Testing Program

A SHORT-LIVED graft on the main stem of this first Iowa program was the Every-Pupil Intelligence Testing Program conducted experimentally in January of 1934. Created in response to requests from school people, it was designed with the same precision as the parent achievement program and along similar lines.

The test employed was the *Psychological Examination for Grades 9–12* by L. L. Thurstone and Thelma Gwinn Thurstone, published by the American Council on Education. Dr. Lindquist considered it the most suitable and reliable group test of general intelligence or scholastic aptitude then available for high school use. The 60-minute test could be conveniently administered to pupils in large groups. Because of its own interest in this experiment, the American Council provided a special edition of the test at cost for use in the Iowa program.

The values inherent in the program were two-fold: those independent of the subsequent achievement testing program and those stemming from the combined programs. Besides the customary values of a good intelligence test, this program offered the further and unique benefit of *Iowa* norms for both pupil scores and grade averages. After the achievement testing in May, on the basis of results for schools that had participated in both programs, special "ability standards" were computed for each achievement test for various levels of performance on the intelligence test.[21] Again, these specialized norms were calculated for individuals and for classes. Of the 218 schools that administered the intelligence test, 130 participated also in the achievement testing program.

In the preliminary bulletin, Dr. Lindquist pointed out the important uses to which both sets of norms might legitimately be put, cautioned against extravagant interpretations, and briefly cited other factors to be considered in applications of the results.

> Achievement test averages could . . . be taken as highly valid measures of teaching effectiveness only if all . . . other factors were controlled. . . .
> . . . Of all the factors which influence achievement, in addition to

the quality of teaching, the *pupils' ability to learn*—as determined by native intelligence and past training—is certainly among the most important. This factor . . . can be measured with a reasonable degree of accuracy, and . . . can . . . at least be partially controlled in comparisons of achievement test scores.[22]

An analysis of the results of this intelligence testing program is contained in the M.A. thesis of Albert E. Nimtz, which was completed in 1934 under Dr. Lindquist's direction.

Why the intelligence testing program was not repeated is not entirely clear, but there are clues. It had proved expensive, even with the initial subsidy of cheap test materials. It had put heavy demands on processing facilities and on school personnel. A new testing program for the elementary level was being readied for January 1935 which would require the full attention of the director and his staff for some time.

Branching Out

THE IOWA PROGRAM and the Iowa Tests rapidly gained national attention. Out-of-state demand led to the decision in the mid-thirties to allow schools in states adjoining Iowa to participate in the program on the noncompetitive basis. In addition, arrangements were made with the Bureau of Educational Research and Service to sell the Every-Pupil Tests nationwide for independent administration at any time of the year. Thus, quality tests at a reasonable price were made widely available, and a small profit accrued to the program and the bureau. During those early years, when the revenue from the state program could barely meet its on-going direct expenses, the out-of-state sales helped balance the budget. By small accretions, a modest surplus was built up in the program accounts for use in test development and research.

A stepchild of the Iowa program was the Missouri Achievement Testing Program sponsored annually from 1937 to 1942 by the Missouri State Department of Education.[23] It was administered by C. W. Martin, director of the Testing Bureau at Northeast Missouri State Teachers College. The test materials used were identical to the Iowa editions but with the Missouri name dubbed into the titles. Complete data processing services were provided from Iowa City, including the preparation and publication of Missouri norms. Materials and services were furnished to Kirksville at virtual cost.

Research

STRIDES WERE made in pursuing research possibilities forecast in the early announcements. Many and varied studies based on the program results were carried out. Most of these were conducted by M.A. and Ph.D. candidates under Professor Lindquist's direction and became the bases of their dissertations. Others were by students in other departments. Some studies were partially subsidized by the testing program.

The range of topics investigated included:

— analyses of performance on specific Iowa tests
— statistical evaluation and comparison of types of test items for a given subject-matter area
— experimentation with new types of test items
— measurement of various elements in achievement, such as retention
— relationship of various factors to teaching effectiveness
— relationship of scholastic ability to other variables
— prediction of test scores
— effects on test performance of class size, ability grouping, cramming, and so on
— test validity, reliability, and difficulty
— the influence of the testing program itself upon teaching in Iowa high schools.

Fruition

UNDER SUCH careful cultivation, the original high school program had grown from a disadvantaged sprout to a hardy perennial. The name was changed in 1935 from Iowa Academic Contest to Iowa Every-Pupil Achievement Testing Program, and again in 1936 to Iowa Every-Pupil High School Testing Program to distinguish it from the new elementary program. There were no important structural changes.

During the late thirties, while public interest peaked, Dr. Lindquist's waned. The program had served well its purpose of stimulating scholastic effort, generating local interest in academic improvement, and priming professional awareness of the possibilities and proper use of standardized tests. Stereotypes had been shattered in exciting discoveries of individual talent where none had been recognized before the Every-Pupil testing.[24] But all this no longer satisfied the director, who was already at work on the ITED battery.

Furthermore, the spirit of competition among participants had remained inordinately high despite his efforts to dilute it. Administrators who elected to test on a noncompetitive basis sometimes felt pressured to defend or change that decision. There was mounting evidence that certain schools were in the program primarily to win public honor. Rivalries developed. A few participants were suspected of coaching their brightest pupils in particular subjects at the expense of other pupils and other subjects. Only because of the high intensity of interest had the Scholarship Contest been retained so long.

With the onset of World War II, circumstances seemed propitious for a radical change in the program. Under wartime pressures, school administrators appeared less reluctant to give up the very demanding Scholarship Contest. They accepted with expressed regret—some possibly with concealed relief—the news that the 1941 contest would be the finale. The Every-Pupil series of tests ended in the spring of 1942, to be supplanted by a quite different high-school-level battery and testing program.

2 The Early Elementary School Program

Germination

As soon as the high school program was well rooted, the director began spading ground for a second project. His ideas for this were prompted by demand as well as by the evident need for good, coordinated measurement facilities at the lower levels. First efforts were limited to the junior high grades. Two years were spent in organizing the program and developing test materials comparable in quality to the Every-Pupil high school tests. The extension to grades 6, 7, and 8 was accomplished in January 1935.

The Iowa Every-Pupil Elementary School Testing Program became, as had the secondary school project, a model and a laboratory for comprehensive measurement at the level served. It afforded the general advantages of "cooperative" vs. "independent" testing already demonstrated in the high school program and reiterated in the first announcement bulletin. The rationale for this second venture was then presented thus:

> The need for an adequate testing service at this level is indeed as great as, if not greater than, in the senior high school. The basic skills and habits acquired in the elementary school—particularly in reading, in methods of study and in the mechanics of correct writing—are, of course, crucial to the whole educational development of the pupil, and largely determine the extent to which he can profit from high school instruction. Periodic, reliable measurement of the degree of development of these basic skills is therefore essential, not only for effective supervision of instruction and individualization of teaching in the grades, but also for adequate educational guidance of the pupil before, at, and after entrance into the senior high school.[25]

The Shape of the Program

THE CONFIGURATION of the program was sketched in the same announcement.

In its administrative organization, this new program, except for the absence of any competitive features, will be very much like the present high school program. The tests used will be constructed especially for the purposes of this project in the College of Education and the Experimental Schools of the State University of Iowa. The tests will be administered on the same day and under the same carefully controlled conditions in all participating schools. They will then be scored in the local school systems, and the reports of individual schools will be mailed promptly to the director of the program. Norms will immediately be established in Iowa City on the basis of these reports, and a printed summary report of these norms and the statistical facts of the program will be sent to each school system within the shortest possible time after the day of testing. No publicity will be given at any time to the test results or relative performance of any school system. No school except the one addressed will be identified in the confidential report.[26]

The 1935–39 Basic Skills Batteries

THE ELEMENTARY education faculty in the College of Education and the University Experimental Schools at The University of Iowa played important roles in the design and construction of the new battery—particularly Professors Ernest Horn in reading, Harry Greene in language, Maude McBroom in study skills, and F. B. Knight in arithmetic. Professor Lindquist, of course, was initiator and general editor.* This highly reputable team set out to provide Iowa schools with tests concerned exclusively with skills considered basic to the whole educational development of the pupil, and so they did. The excellence of their planning and execution seems confirmed by the fact that in subsequent decades usage throughout Iowa and beyond revealed no substantial faults necessitating any major changes.

The battery as a whole was diagnostic in character. The tests reflected Iowa curricula but were not confined to specific instructional programs or practices. A complete preliminary edition of each test was tried out in a few selected schools and revised as needed in advance of general administration in the January program. Both preprogram and postprogram analyses were studied intensively. The years of experience with the high school program further contributed to the production of high quality materials and services in the elementary project.

At the outset, the undertaking was limited to three tests and three grades because, according to the director, "the sponsors have preferred to make a smaller beginning and to add to the initial program only after

---

*A more comprehensive listing of those involved in test construction is presented in the Appendix, Table C.

their first experiences have assured them that they can procure the personnel and the facilities necessary to maintain a uniformly high standard of quality throughout the entire project."[27] This they were able to do the following year.

The first (1935) battery comprised fourteen subtests, organized in three separate test booklets:

Test A: Silent Reading Comprehension (Paragraph Comprehension, Organization of Ideas, Understanding of Details, Grasp of Total Meaning).

Test B: Basic Study Skills (General Vocabulary, Comprehension of Maps, Reading Graphs and Charts, Alphabetizing, Use of Index, Use of Basic References).

Test C: Basic Language Skills (Spelling, Capitalization, Punctuation, Usage.)

In 1936 a fourth test was added:

Test D: Basic Arithmetic Skills (Fundamental Processes, Verbal Problems, Verbalization, and Correcting Errors in Computations).

Administration times for the tests ranged from 50 to 80 minutes. The testing could be scheduled in either four or eight periods, as the school administrator saw fit.

In the first edition several new approaches to old problems were tried. For example, in an effort to ease the taking and scoring of Test A, the reading selections were printed in large type in a four-page folder separate from the multiple-choice items in the test booklet. Spelling was tested in two ways—by dictation and by proofreading. In the former, printed sentences supplied the context of the missing test words, which the teacher pronounced and repeated, one per sentence. In Capitalization, clues were excluded by numbering *every* word in each printed sentence and asking the pupil to record by number each error found. In Alphabetizing, each test word was to be properly inserted into an alphabetical list of words separated by numbered spaces, and the appropriate space number recorded by the pupil.

Some of these approaches did not survive. In the second edition of Test B, Alphabetizing gave way to Use of the Dictionary. In Test C, the proofreading section in Spelling was dropped, and the Test of Sentence Sense was added, in which the pupil judged whether the words in each exercise did not make a sentence, made one good sentence, or should properly be split into two or more sentences. The test makers thus boosted the notion that the structure of language was important to be known and taught, even if measurement in an objective test was necessarily somewhat superficial.

The Early Elementary School Program 29

In the third edition, the reading selections were incorporated into the Test A booklet with the test items. Introduced that year, also, was a shortcut to obtaining the part scores on the Reading Test, illustrated in Figure 2. Following variously marked paths on a stencil key from item to item, the scorer would obtain and then record *on the test page* the page subscore for each of three parts of the test. By aligning the test pages in the manner shown, the scorer could then add horizontally to arrive at the pupil's score for each part. The Part IV (Grasp of Total Meaning) items were all grouped on page 12; the score for it could be simply counted and entered on the title page to complete the part scores. This system reduced shuffling of keys and test pages, and diminished the likelihood of clerical errors. In the hands of Dr. Lindquist, at least, this was an efficient scoring procedure.

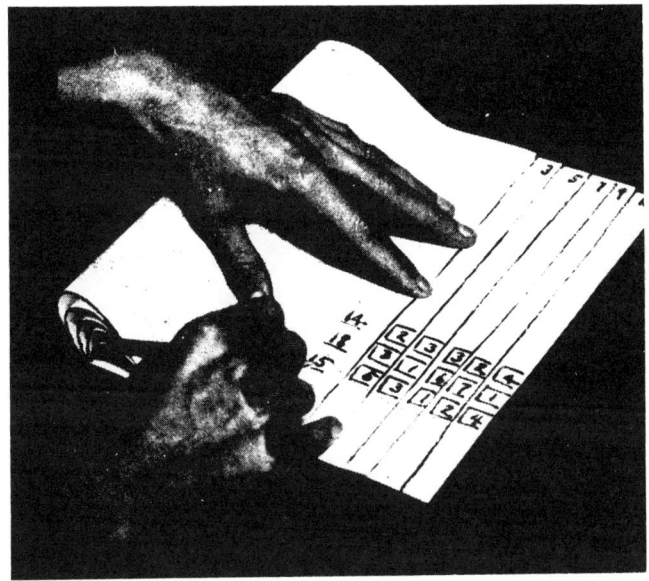

Fig. 2. Procedure in scoring 1937 Reading Test demonstrated by Lindquist. *(Reprinted from 1937 "Directions for Scoring Test A.")*

In 1937 and 1938 a free-response approach was adopted in the Punctuation and Capitalization tests, with the unorthodox twist of using one set of sentences as the context for both. The pupil was penalized one point for each superfluous capitalization or punctuation. As in the high school battery, more variations in technique occurred in the language subtests during the early years than in any others, though the coverage of skills remained stable. Never loath to explore new methods, Professor Lindquist did not hesitate to tackle the thorny problems of language testing with all available measurement tools, including some of his own fashioning.

Test B, Study Skills, contained a great deal of sophisticated artwork: geographical maps, real and fictional, and various types of charts and graphs presenting practical data from actual sources. Test D was replete with everyday problems to be solved.

In 1939, after a year of successful usage in the senior high school program, the same type of tear-off answer sheet was incorporated into Basic Skills Tests A, B, and C. For Test D, Arithmetic, a loose answer sheet was provided, containing rectangular spaces for the pupil's answers.

Expectations for the Tests

THE TEST BUILDERS aimed at producing test materials that would be especially beneficial in remedial and individualized instruction and in educational guidance. The values of the tests for these purposes were particularly stressed in the literature to the schools. It was pointed out further that these diagnostic values required time limits longer than those of most other tests then available. "The test builders have refused to sacrifice quality or adequacy for expediency or in order to conform to 'popular' time limits, but have built each subtest in whatever form and length seemed demanded by its . . . purpose."[28] This unyielding philosophical stance emerges repeatedly in the chronicles of the Iowa Testing Programs.

It was promised that "the results of tests provided in succeeding years will be made *comparable* to those of the tests used this year, and high comparability from test to test will characterize each year's battery. It will thus be possible to keep a cumulative record of the *progressive* development over several years' time of the skills measured for each pupil, and hence to base educational guidance upon a much more meaningful and reliable description of the pupil than could possibly be secured from any single test or battery of tests."[29]

Again, schools were guided in the proper interpretation of test results that might be misapplied. They were cautioned about injudicious actions to correct seeming inadequacies in local programs.

In the discussion of Test A—Reading Comprehension, it was pointed out that because of the high interrelation of the skills separately tested in the several parts, the diagnostic value of the part scores pertained mainly to *group*, rather than to *individual*, performance. But the separation into parts was expected to encourage better instruction in the important skills represented, and eventually to improve what the test authors regarded as unsatisfactory results in the early programs.

It was recognized that the testing of general vocabulary properly belonged in Test A, that its inclusion in B was an expedient of printing and test administration, and that users should consider their vocabulary results in relation to the part scores on Test A. In the 1939 edition, the Vocabulary subtest was in fact moved into Test A, where it remained.

The authors eschewed providing a direct measure of *rate* of reading. They maintained that, even for the same individual, rate was not a constant, but fluctuated with the reader's purpose and with the type of material read.

Test B stressed skills considered essential to effective study in all fields and all grades, upper as well as elementary. The authors entertained, and candidly admitted, the hope that instances of serious neglect of these skills would be revealed and remedied as a result of the testing.

In regard to spelling, the schools were reminded of variations in local grade placement of words commonly taught in junior high and of incidental opportunities for pupils to learn spelling outside the classroom. Nonetheless, the test scores would identify individual poor spellers and would show whether the whole instructional program was developing spelling ability.

Generally, the battery was fashioned upon the principle of measuring development by determining how well the pupil could *use* his skills in practical simulations. Where departures in method occurred, reasons were given. Concerning the Verbalization section in Test D, for instance, the test authors felt that, "while a pupil may be very skillful in computation on a sheer mechanical level without power to state what he is doing or why, he is better fortified for practical work if he also has some power over the meaning of verbal statements of procedures," and further, "the sheer vocabulary burden of arithmetic is sometimes underestimated, and emphasis upon it seems wise."[30] In the final part of Test D (Correcting Errors) the pupil had an opportunity to demonstrate arithmetical accuracy by detecting and correcting computational errors planted in preworked exercises.

An important administrative value anticipated was that of revealing aspects of the *whole* instructional program in need of greater emphasis or supervisory push. But because the skills measured are developed gradually over many school years, the director insisted that the results from such tests "may not safely be used alone to measure the effectiveness of a single teacher's work over a period of only several months."[31]

Originality in Reports and Norms

THE STATISTICAL services to the schools were a unique feature of the Basic Skills Program. Besides shifting the entire computational burden from local school districts to Iowa City, the director conceived new ways of treating and presenting the results, thus expanding their meaning and usefulness for the users.

The Pupil Profile Chart

One of these was the individual profile chart (Fig. 3) on which subtest and total raw scores could be quickly plotted to form a profile of the pupil's percentile standing across the entire battery. The grade profile of the school could be similarly drawn for comparison. The raw score scales printed on the chart corresponded to the state percentiles for the grade, a separate chart form being provided for each grade. *The design of the chart was thus in itself a plotting device*, necessitating no recourse to tables of norms or overlay masks of any kind.

In 1937 the chart form was revised to serve better as a cumulative record of the pupil's performance through the junior high school years —a use stressed in the program literature. A single chart (Fig. 4) was prepared on which the raw scores were fitted to T-scales constructed to yield high comparability in the profiles from year to year.[32] In addition, profiles of selected state percentiles in each of grades 6, 7, and 8 were printed on the chart in blue, black, and red, respectively. The pattern of an individual's scores plotted on this chart served visually a trio of purposes: It disclosed that person's academic strengths and weaknesses, it permitted quick estimations of the pupil's percentile rank on any test, and it enabled direct comparisons with state norms for three grades. Charts for subsequent years were similarly constructed so that a cumulative record could be maintained by simply *tracing* profiles from chart to chart.

This ingenious form of chart was employed until 1940. The third version, modified at that time for the plotting of standard scores, is still in use.

The Building Average Reports

For the graphic portrayal of average results, a percentile chart like that illustrated in Figure 5 was devised for each of grades 6, 7, and 8.

The Early Elementary School Program 33

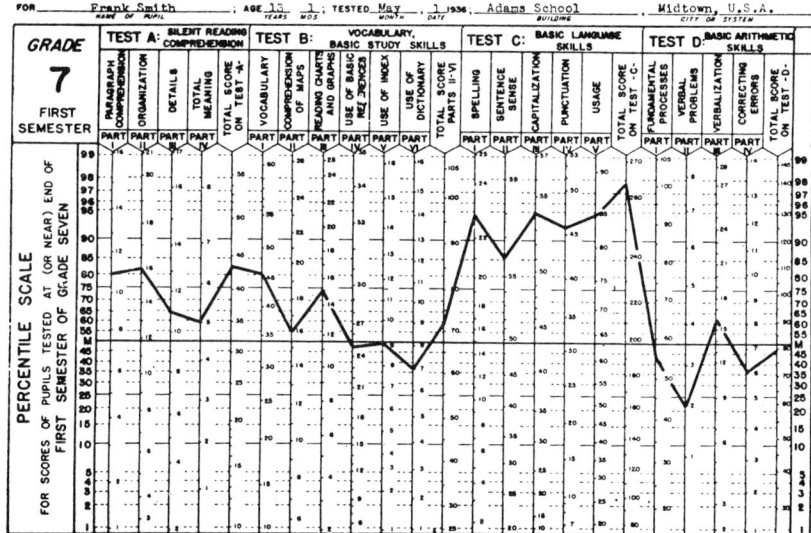

Fig. 3. Early form of individual profile chart, showing hypothetical profile.

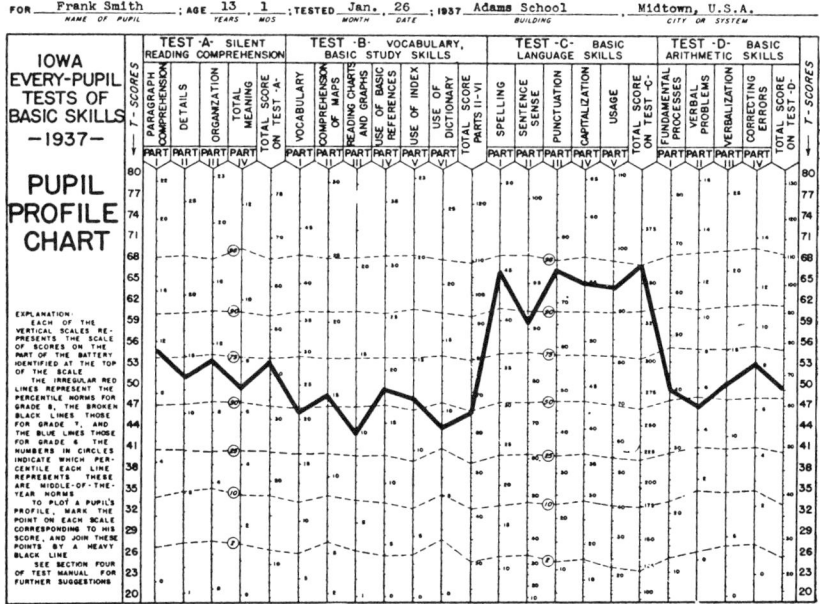

Fig. 4. 1937 revision of pupil profile chart. The actual chart also carried profiles of selected percentiles in red (for grade 8) and blue (grade 6) comparable to the broken black lines (grade 7) shown here.

Each participating school received a set of charts plotted in various colors—as many charts for each grade as were needed to accommodate all of its building and system profiles. Comparisons in several directions within the system and the state could readily be made from these colorful panoramas of group accomplishment. As the director pointed out in the 1936 bulletin, "this single chart . . . tells everything that would otherwise be contained in a large number of frequency distributions and percentile tables, and presents this information in a form in which it can be read with the maximum clarity and convenience."[33] This indestructible design has continued in use to the present and in thousands of schools throughout the country.

Besides the graphic reports, each school received a tabulator listing of its grade and building averages in its Confidential Report of Average Scores.

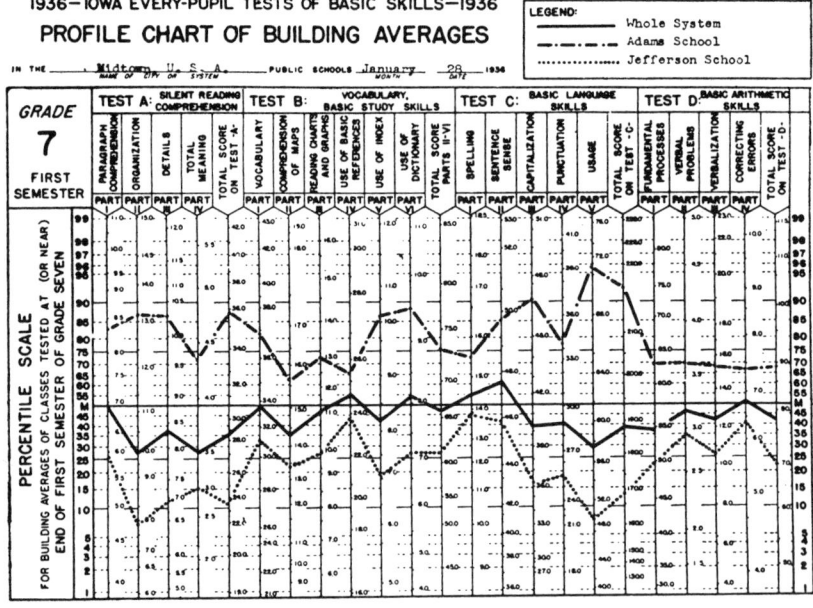

Fig. 5. Plotted profile chart of building averages.

Norms for Many Needs

In the mid-thirties, standardized tests of elementary school achievement were generally accompanied only by grade norms and/or age norms for pupil scores. For the Basic Skills Tests, three types were established: grade norms, age-at-grade norms, and grade-percentile norms. The commonly used age norms were rejected in favor of age-at-grade norms, although the former would have been less difficult and costly to compute. Dr. Lindquist considered the latter more meaningful and specific, since performance at a given age must be interpreted in relation to the pupil's grade placement.

Of the three types of pupil norms provided, he recommended that test users place principal emphasis in interpretation on the grade-percentile norms, which he characterized as easier for the teacher to plot on a profile chart, subject to sounder interpretations, and free from assumptions and interpolations associated with other types of norms. These reasons were elucidated in considerable detail in the user's manual.[34]

Separate norms were established for pupils promoted from grade to grade at midyear. Their scores were not included in the data for the regular norms.

The participating county school districts received also abbreviated tables of percentile norms established separately on the scores of rural school pupils only.

In 1937 and 1938 a very special report was issued of mental-age norms by grade for total test scores and for the vocabulary score. These were calculated in conjunction with results from a program of mental testing conducted by the Bureau of Educational Research and Service in the preceding October, statistical adjustments having been made for the four-month interval between testing dates. The mental-age norms were offered as supplementary to, and supportive of, the information implicit in the regular age-at-grade norms.

Intelligence testing was not a part of the Basic Skills Program. However, it was suggested to participants that, in lieu of the usual measures from a group intelligence test, a composite of the reading comprehension total score and the vocabulary score might be employed for ranking pupils in order of scholastic ability.

The norms of school achievement were the grade-percentile type. Again, in providing its elementary schools with highly representative statewide norms of average performance on a standardized test battery, Iowa continued a unique service begun in its high school program.

Other Follow-up Aids

The *Manual for Administration and Interpretation*, which expanded from a sixteen-page to an eighty-eight-page booklet in the course of five years, was replete with technical information, explanations, suggestions, and cautions relating to the tests, local results, the state norms, and the program as a whole. An earnest, careful user could hardly go astray in understanding and applying the intrinsic values of the testing.

Pages were devoted to such important considerations as the relation of test content to curriculum content, norms vs. standards, and the use of the test results in teaching. Extensive suggestions were offered for remedial procedures, specific to the principal skills measured in each subtest of the battery. In this connection, the exercises in Tests A, B, and C were classified according to skills involved; the most commonly prevailing grade placement was also given, as a rough indication of what skills the pupils might reasonably be expected to have mastered in the grade tested or earlier. The later (1938 and 1939) editions of the manual carried also an interestingly determined attempt by the test authors to eradicate bad language practices. A "Diagnostic and Remedial Chart" listed possible causes of, additional evidences of, and remedial treatment of, low scores on the various parts of Test C. In spelling, for instance, the suggested possible causes range through attitude, inexperience, and certain physical handicaps, to such specifics as tendency to spell all words phonetically. The corrective suggestions are not mere balm, but realistic treatments of the disorders.

Improved Service Systems

CENTRALIZED SCORING service for ITBS users was still twenty years distant, but in this early Elementary Program more was done for the participants than ever before. In line with the notion that the time and talents of trained educators should be put to educational uses—not dissipated in tasks that could be performed by others—the director devised systems which relieved the schools of all statistical work in the analysis and interpretation of their test data.

From the alphabetized lists of raw scores submitted by the schools, personnel in Iowa City computed all averages, compiled frequency distributions, established pupil and school (grade/building/system) norms, and prepared tabular and graphic reports of the results. All this in a mere few weeks. At the University Statistical Service, the keypunching of 800,000 raw scores into tabulating cards alone was a demanding job for a small staff. Innumerable sorts, card counts, and card runs through the tabulators followed, to produce the sums of scores on each test for each grade within each participating building. The tabulators operated at no more than 150 cards per minute. Desk calculating machines were used in computing all desired averages from the sums of scores, as well as the percentile scales from the raw-score distributions. Printouts of the confidential reports to the schools were made on the tabulator. From the normative data compiled by Statistical Service, the director's support staff of two prepared camera copy for inclusion in the final summary manual.

The building averages charts were completely filled out for the schools. The task of hand plotting some 5,000 profiles in about seven days necessitated training a special squad and wangling work space in a large study room (once a hospital lounge-sunroom) on the second floor of East Hall. Equipped only with rulers and pencils in six colors, this zealous crew of women plotted profile after profile in assembly line fashion.

For the pupil charts to be filled out by the classroom teachers, special stencils were provided that made the plotting semiautomatic. Along slits in the stencil, the raw scores corresponding to selected percentiles were printed. These were positioned so that by simply marking and joining a series of points, the teacher created a profile of the pupil's percentile ranks on all tests taken.

The entire Elementary Program results were processed annually in two to three weeks. This feat entailed much overtime but at regular rates of pay. Statistical Service costs were modest. In 1936, for example, its bill to Iowa Testing was only $640 for the compilation of averages and norms and the printout of confidential reports. Charges for subsequent special work, including item analyses on the tests, brought the total bill for the Basic Skills Program that year to just $1,127.

In the late thirties the testing project as a whole was still operating on a shoestring budget, supported solely by income funds, and the expansion into the elementary grades did not improve its treasury. Schools testing all pupils in all grades paid only 12 cents per pupil the first year and 16 cents thereafter for the tests and services. (Charges varied slightly for limited testing.) During the first several years, the deficits of the new elementary program were barely offset by gains in the high school program. In 1938, for example, the former ran about $1,000 in the red, while the latter gained approximately $1,500. So precarious was its financial survival at times, that unusual expenditures for experimental testing could throw the program account into the red. Any such negative balances were reversed eventually by program income; they were not written off by university appropriations or absorbed into other accounts.

Reception by the Schools

IN THE INITIAL Basic Skills Program, 217 school systems and three county systems administered the full battery under uniform conditions to about 26,000 pupils on January 29, 1935. These figures included 1,710 mid-year-promotion pupils in 11 systems and 985 rural pupils. A few additional schools elected to give selected tests from the battery. Of the 217 systems fully enrolled, 214 reported scores on 22,350 pupils within the ten days allotted for inclusion in the norms distributions.

During the next four years, participation ranged up to 265 systems, testing roughly 30,000 pupils.

By 1939 registration in the program had been opened to parochial schools of Iowa and to public schools in neighboring states plus a few in more distant locations. The out-of-state participants received, at a slightly higher price, the same services and reports as did the Iowa schools.

From 1936 on, out-of-state schools could also buy the tests through the Bureau of Educational Research and Service for independent administration at other times than January. Many took advantage of this opportunity. Some—such as the Kansas City Public Schools system—purchased from the Iowa Testing Programs special tabulations of their own scores and the compilation of local norms. For several years the University of South Carolina sponsored a state program directed by Professor W. C. McCall that similarly utilized the *Iowa Tests of Basic Skills* and statistical services.

Beyond Expertise

DR. LINDQUIST'S oft-voiced concern for the deeper values and purposes of testing is the central thought of his remarks at the 1938 Annual Conference on Administration and Supervision sponsored on campus by the College of Education. Along with a summary of current and future developments in the Iowa Testing Programs, he pointed out twin aspects of the programs deserving special and separate consideration.

> One has to do with the technical and administrative features . . . [such as] organization of the programs, . . . quality of the test materials, . . . techniques of measurement employed, . . . and statistical services provided. . . . The other, and clearly the more important, . . . has to do with the actual uses of the test results in the participating schools and with the extent to which these uses have resulted in an improved educational product. . . .
>
> . . . There are no other organized regional testing programs, to my knowledge, that are more comprehensive in scope or that involve a

greater amount of testing per pupil than the Iowa programs, particularly that in the junior high school grades. . . .

All of this improvement in the technique of measurement, however, is of very little consequence unless it is accompanied by a corresponding progress in the application of the test results for the improvement of instruction in the individual schools. The idea has frequently been expressed in other fields of endeavor, notably in science and industry, that it might even be worthwhile to call a halt on further technological improvements until we have learned to use more wisely those which we already have. I am sure that we have not yet reached this state of affairs in educational measurement, but certainly our knowledge of how to construct test materials is far in advance of our ability to use the test results wisely. For the present, then, while further technical improvements and additions are still desirable, our major concern must be with the problem of making more effective and worthwhile use of test results.[35]

In an effort to determine actual uses in Iowa schools, Dr. Lindquist had personally administered a questionnaire to a group of superintendents and principals in Iowa City during the State Scholarship Contest the preceding spring. The October conference address dealt at length with his analysis of the questionnaire results, and pointed out what more might be accomplished or at least be done better. He exhorted his audience to follow up their advantage of having a fund of information from the testing programs "by taking a real leadership in the recent trend toward individualization in public education." That application he ever regarded as the most important of all.

PART TWO:
THE VIGOROUS FORTIES

THE FORTIES:

THE FORTIES were a dynamic decade. In spite of World War II, and partly because of it, activity in the Iowa Testing Programs sphere accelerated even more than in the thirties. The chief new developments were:

— the extension of the Basic Skills Program to grades 3–5
— national publication of the ITBS
— the replacement of the first high school program by the Fall Testing Program, featuring the *Iowa Tests of Educational Development*
— the launching of an independent program measuring knowledge of contemporary affairs.

These are described in the next several chapters, along with important peripheral involvements of this period.

3 The Extended Basic Skills Program

The New Series of ITBS

THE EXPANSION of the Basic Skills Program afforded in grades 3–5 the same type and quality of tests, services, and measurement policies hitherto offered only for grades 6–8. The same values propounded earlier are reemphasized in the announcements and manuals of the forties.

The 1940 edition of the Basic Skills Tests, designated Form L, was the first in a series of annual forms, L through T, published during the next eleven years (see Appendix, Table D). These nine parallel forms met the needs of the statewide programs for fifteen years, with occasional reuse at widely spaced intervals. This rotation of forms made it reasonably certain that the annual norms would be based on scores derived from test content not previously familiar to the pupils.

In each edition, a separate battery, of appropriate difficulty and item content, was developed for the lower grades. The Elementary Battery of Form L yielded 18 measures (15 part scores and 3 totals); the Advanced Battery, 17 measures (14 part scores and 3 totals). The following changes from the format of the earlier tests were made.

In Test A, only two scores were now derived—one in reading comprehension (Part I), the other in vocabulary (Part II). While the four main reading skills previously identified were still addressed in specific items, they no longer were scored separately, because of the interrelationships pointed out in earlier program manuals. However, classifications of the Part I items according to principal skills tested were provided for use in remedial instruction.

In Elementary Test B, Study Skills, Part V was concerned with alphabetizing rather than with interpretation of graphs and charts.

The new Advanced Test C did not include a test of sentence sense.

Verbalization and the correction of arithmetical errors were no longer tested in either level of Test D.

The separate or tear-off answer sheet was continued in the 1940 Advanced Battery but not yet employed in the Elementary. There the answers were recorded on the test pages and were scored with stencil keys.

General improvement in the legibility and appearance of the tests was achieved by lithoprinting from typeset composition rather than from typewritten copy.

Each participating school could choose either battery for grade 5, provided all its fifth graders took the same one. Extent of participation in the program was also optional. The per-battery charge for the tests with services was 16 cents for the Advanced and 12 cents for the Elementary. A 15 percent discount was allowed to schools that registered for full participation (administration of the complete battery to pupils in all six grades). As before, the dates of the program were the last two weeks of January, and scores were to be reported very early in February.

The expansion from three grades to six greatly increased the editorial and administrative responsibilities of preparing materials and conducting the program. To meet this situation, some changes were made in the roster of major test authors. Professor H. F. Spitzer, then principal of the University Experimental School, assumed overall responsibility for the preparation of both batteries, with the continuing collaboration of Professors Horn, McBroom, Greene, and Lindquist, and with the assistance of other faculty and staff members in item writing and editing (see Appendix, Table D).

To guide the authors in subsequent test development, item-by-item analyses of the results were made each year in the early forties, based on the papers of one-fifth of the pupils tested. An automatic designation of the papers to be returned to Iowa City for this purpose was provided by marking with an asterisk every fifth line of the report-of-scores form supplied to the schools. Administrators were asked to return the papers so designated after completing their alphabetized lists. In this way the task was simplified for them, and a large representative sample was assured.

A high degree of comparability was maintained in the tests and the norms with the original ITBS, as well as from the Advanced to the Elementary battery and from one annual edition to the next. The same three types of norms previously provided (grade, grade-percentile, and age-at-grade norms) were established for each battery and published in the "Supplement to Manual for Interpretation."[36] Approximate age norms were made available separately, hedged with reservations and statistical explanations. Candidly skeptical of the dependability and meaningfulness of norms for age levels only (distinct from age within grade), the director regarded these as probably neither better nor worse than those provided with any other current standardized battery.[37]

Amplified manuals continued previous efforts to make the tests and the results meaningful and useful to the users—to help administrators decide "what to do about their test results" in practical ways. Plotted profile charts of building averages were again supplied for each of the six grades in the extended coverage.

The Individual Cumulative Record

One distinctive feature of the ITBS program, the pupil profile chart, was further improved in 1940. The new individual cumulative record (Fig. 6) utilized a "standard" scale based on the grade norms. For example, 55 on this scale corresponded to the median raw score made by fifth-grade pupils tested at the end of the fifth month; 50, to the median at the beginning of the fifth grade; and 59, to that at the end. Masks for easy plotting were supplied, in which the raw scores printed along vertical slits fit the grade-equivalent scales on the profile chart. Thus, the plotting of raw scores through the mask constituted an automatic conversion into grade-equivalents. This method for simultaneously accomplishing score conversion and profiling was entirely original. Separate coordinate masks were provided for the Elementary and Advanced batteries and for each annual edition so that results on successive testings could be added to the pupil's original chart. A properly plotted chart thereby became a graphic record of the pupil's performance and relative growth in the basic skills over a six-year period.

The individual cumulative record introduced in 1940 is still an effective and focal element in the application of Iowa Basic Skills test results. The "innovative" quality of its design has become obscured by its own durability and historical acceptance.

Problems and Progress

MANAGEMENT of the testing programs in the early forties was plagued by inevitable wartime problems: shortages of materials, delayed deliveries, and, especially at Statistical Service, loss of experienced personnel and an increase of work load generated by military programs on campus. But none of these obstacles stopped the action.

Several new procedures were tried in efforts to deliver promised services to the schools with minimum delay. One important experiment that foreshadowed future methods was the introduction of a mark-sense card for score reporting (Fig. 7) that could be punched automatically on an IBM mark-sensing reproducer. In the 1943 program, such cards were supplied to the schools, to be marked locally and returned to Iowa City, where list reports for school use were then prepared from

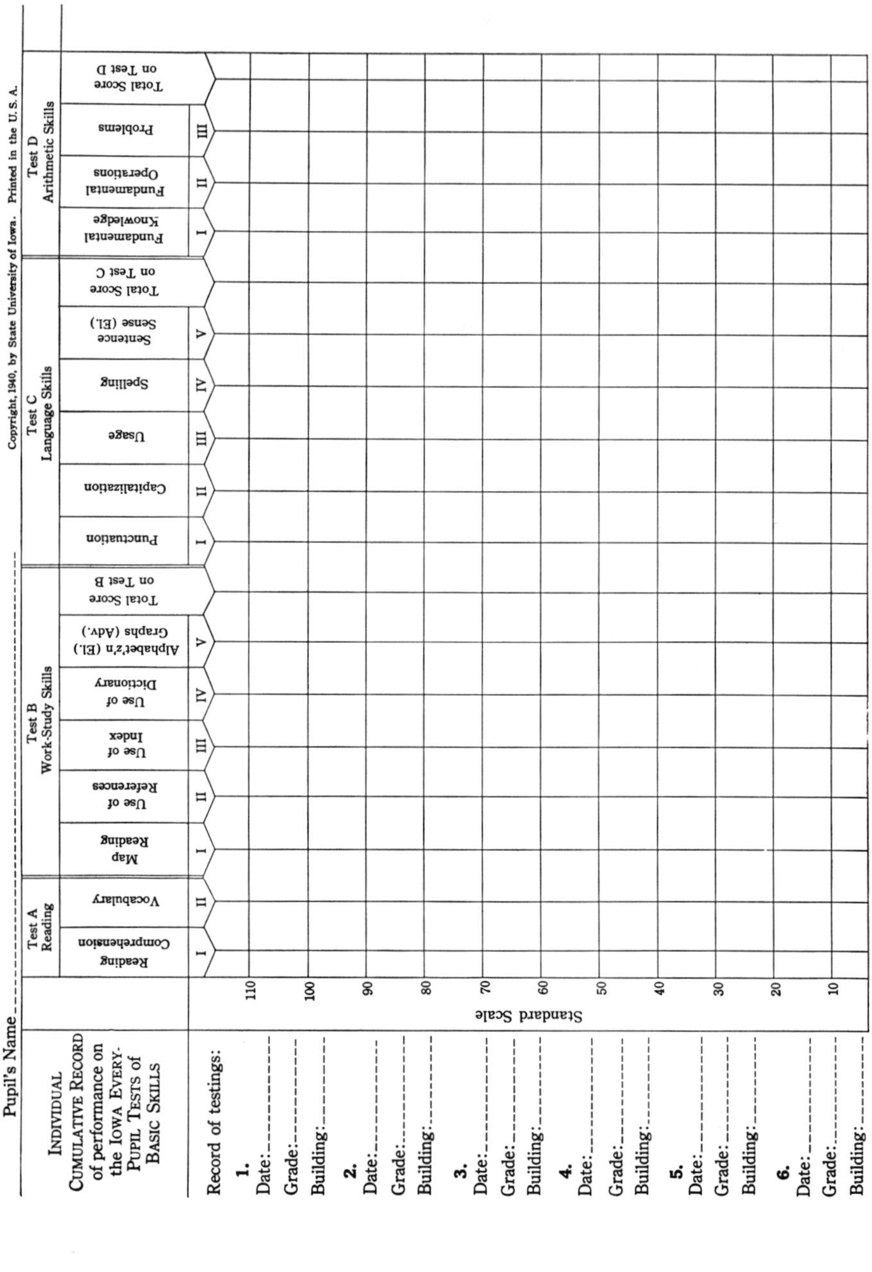

Fig. 6. Individual cumulative record of ITBS scores.

the cards. The marking and assembling of hundreds of these cards by local school personnel proved a task of discouraging proportions. The next year, the pupil cards were marked by clerks in Iowa City from list reports filled out by each school as in the past. A corps of women was recruited and briefed intensively on how to inspect and transcribe the scores, recognize and correct errors, and properly organize the packs

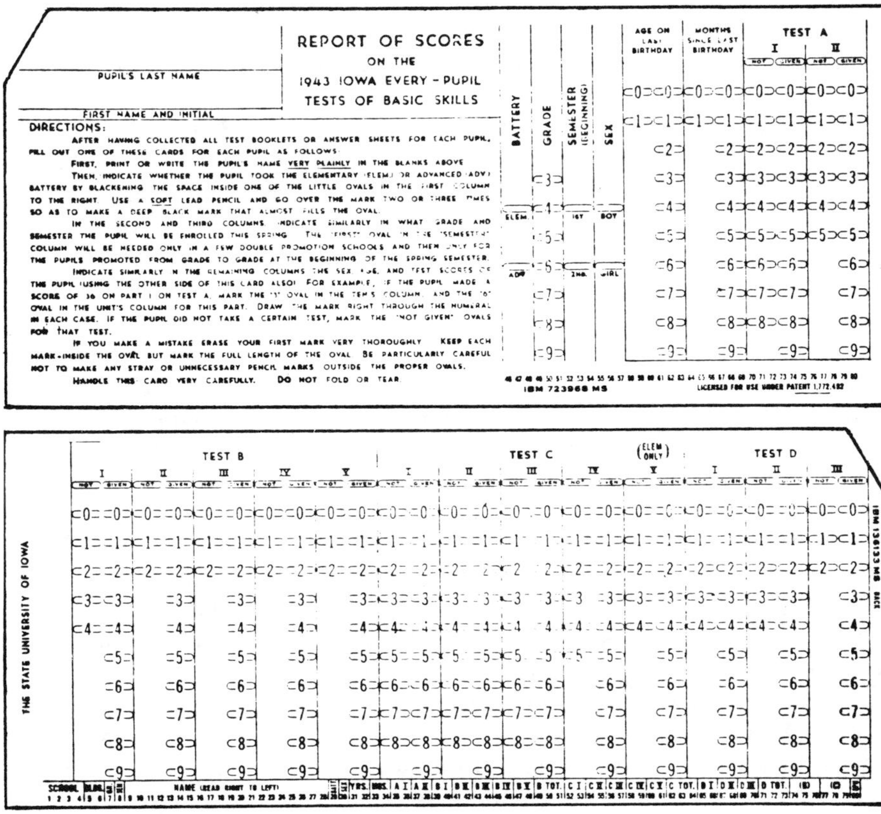

Fig. 7. Mark-sense card for reporting test scores. (Top is front of card, bottom is reverse.)

of cards. The statements of procedures, running to a dozen pages, manifest the astonishing amount of responsibility shouldered by this crew. The card marking required three weeks. This task and the congestion at Statistical Service caused substantial delay in the computation of norms and the reporting of results to the schools—whereupon the director devised another new and corrective procedure for the next annual program.

He announced that henceforth the pupil profile charts and the pupil norms for the new test edition would be supplied to the schools along with the test materials in advance of the January program. Thereby, the results of the January administration could be put to use immediately. The advance establishment of norms was to be accomplished by experimentally equating each new annual form of the tests with the one used in the preceding program; thus, norms based on the latter could be used in interpreting pupil scores on the current edition.[38] The transition necessitated reuse of two previously used batteries, Form N in 1945 and Form O in 1946.

Having eliminated the need to run distributions of all pupil scores, he further organized a system of obtaining the grade averages of each school by hand. Teams of clerks, using comptometers and calculators, summed the scores on the school's list reports, checked these totals, then determined (and checked) its grade average on each part by reading from tables (or by computation for groups of more than ninety-nine pupils). This method eliminated a great deal of processing at Statistical Service and proved remarkably successful. In the first year of its use, records show that an estimated 30 errors occurred in some 2300 *sets* of averages for the 360 systems enrolled. All but one of these errors was caught before the reports were mailed, detected mainly through visual inspection of the plotted profiles.[39] This procedure was used well into the fifties.

Also in 1945, a more efficient and democratic system was formulated for the tryout of items for the annual editions. With massive amounts of new material needed for the two batteries, it was no longer fair or desirable to seek tryout cooperation repeatedly from certain especially cooperative larger school systems. Under the new procedure, the preliminary test items prepared for each skill were organized into "Experimental Units" requiring only twenty minutes of class time. Registrants in the program agreed to administer one such unit to each pupil. A necessary burden in test development was thus borne lightly by all schools rather than heavily by a willing few.

Each year the many units readied for tryout were arranged in rotation for distribution among all pupils and schools in the current annual program. This cyclical distribution provided a very representative basis for the analysis of tryout item characteristics on samples of 300 to 400 pupils. The pupil's total score on the corresponding test in the full battery became the external criterion used in analyzing the experimental unit. This system was later built into the Fall Testing Program as well. Dr. Lindquist considered it greatly superior to the traditional tryout practice of administering an experimental test to all individuals in selected groups and employing the score on that test as an internal criterion of the efficiency of the tryout items.[40] The Iowa system could accommodate annually the tryout of thousands of test items for new forms of ITBS and ITED. By special arrangement, it has served also as the conduit for the tryout of other nationally important test materials, particularly those of the American College Testing Program and the National Merit Scholarship Program.

With the advance equating method of establishing norms, it became possible in 1947 to print on the scoring keys the tables for transforming raw scores into grade-equivalents. A two-pronged gain was thus accomplished: the schools could report their test results to Iowa City in grade-equivalents, and they could plot their individual cumulative records immediately without using masks. The item of masks could now be eliminated from the ITP production schedule.

Such increases in efficiency had also an important bearing upon stable pricing in a period of escalating costs. The 1940 per-battery charges of 12 cents and 16 cents remained effective until uniform pricing of both batteries at 19 cents was adopted in 1949. This rose only to 20 cents in 1950 and to 22 cents in 1952, remaining there until the introduction of scoring service in 1955. In the ITBS Program, as in others, the director was concerned with balancing two important considerations: what the schools could afford to pay for services, and what services they would actually put to good educational use. He wished to give Iowa schools as much as possible for their money, yet not set price levels to cover materials or services that might be technically or educationally desirable but were likely to receive scant attention in the schools.

Appointment of Director Hieronymus

THE 1949 program brought a very important change in the administrative hierarchy. It was announced by Dr. Lindquist in a letter to Iowa school superintendents.

> The Basic Skills Testing Program will henceforth be under the direction of Dr. Albert N. Hieronymus, who this summer joined the staff of the College of Education. The various Iowa testing programs have been growing steadily during recent years, and the work of administering them has greatly increased. However, with Dr. Hieronymus' help, we hope not only to maintain the quality of the services offered in these programs in the past, but to continue to improve and to expand these services.[41]

Dr. Lindquist retained overall direction of the Iowa Testing Programs, the administration of the high school program, and leadership in research and development, particularly of certain exciting ideas he was hatching for the next decade. During completion of his graduate studies, Hieronymus had worked intensively on the preparation of Basic Skills test materials, particularly Form S. His initial role as administrative director of the ITBS program operations expanded steadily during the next thirty years to encompass all the Basic Skills test construction, national standardization, and liaison with the Boston publishers—in short, virtually all ITBS undertakings.

An unusual responsibility in his first year was occasioned by a request from the Iowa State Department of Public Instruction for ITP cooperation in a special study of the possible need to reorganize Iowa school districts. The proposal involved the administration of the Basic Skills Tests to all Iowa sixth-, seventh-, and eighth-grade pupils, for the purpose of comparing achievement in the one-room rural schools with that in graded schools in communities below 10,000 population. The State Department paid the costs of this mandatory testing. The ITP administrators agreed only to direct the testing and to prepare the specified analysis of results within the regular program framework. Later, however, they became caught up in a public furore over media reports of test performance in large versus small school districts, and spent hours in consultation with officials from the Department of Public Instruction.

The study also had a more than temporary effect upon the program enrollment and consequent work load. Participation had held up well during the war years, with an average annual registration of about 60,000 pupils in roughly 350 school systems. The reorganization survey produced a surge to 146,000 pupils in 1,005 systems in 1949. Evidently many involuntary participants that year became converts. The wave effect of the survey testing carried the 1950 program enrollment to 106,300 pupils in 536 systems, a level from which it never receded.

Coast-to-Coast Clientele

FROM THEIR inception, Lindquist had considered the *Iowa Tests of Basic Skills* to be greatly superior to other standardized tests of that period, including the widely used Metropolitan, Stanford, and Progressive achievement tests—a contention he readily defended point by point on numerous occasions. His confidence and the substantial out-of-state acceptance in the early years prompted thoughts of enabling even wider usage through commercial distribution by a well-established and highly respected publisher of educational materials. This he arranged in 1940 with the Houghton Mifflin Company of Boston.

Form L, he maintained at that time, was the *first nationally available* elementary achievement test battery that incorporated *all* of the following features:[42]

(a) was entirely concerned with those basic skills which contribute to achievement in all school subjects, rather than with specific subject-matter content;
(b) yielded separate scores for as many as 14 skills, plus 3 total scores, all from subtests of sufficient length to yield truly dependable measures;
(c) featured complete tests of certain skills (notably work-study) that were measured scantily or not at all in other batteries;
(d) was standardized on a very large and clearly defined population of school systems (335) and pupils (52,561);
(e) was accompanied by norms of *school* achievement, as well as both age-at-grade norms and percentile norms of pupil performance;
(f) would be available in several parallel editions, with up-to-date norms newly established for each;
(g) provided for the systematic maintenance of cumulative individual records of performance and growth, facilitated by the periodic issues of new test forms;
(h) was provided with a comprehensive manual for the use and interpretation of the test results.

The agreement with Houghton Mifflin Company provided that each of Forms L, M, N, and O would be issued nationally following its use in an annual Iowa program. The publisher considered four forms sufficient to satisfy the general demand for some time.

Under the contract with Houghton Mifflin, Iowa schools retained the same privileges as before in the organized state program, which remained a University of Iowa project. Out-of-state schools in general bought the test materials at a higher price directly from Houghton Mifflin and received no reporting or statistical services.* A percentage of the sales revenue accrued to ITP and The University of Iowa as the copyright owner and "author."† This publishing relationship, extended to cover later publications, has endured to the present. Over the en-

---

*For a time, those schools outside of Iowa that had registered in the state program recently were allowed to continue participation and were included in the norms population.

†No individuals received any royalty on ITBS Forms L through O throughout the life of the publishing contract.

suing thirty years, the royalties on the four earliest forms alone added $330,000 to the financial resources of the Iowa Testing Programs and the College of Education, from which many educational departments, graduate students, and research projects have directly benefited.

Not only were the ITBS well entrenched nationally by the late forties, but they were also commanding lively interest beyond the United States. British Columbia authorities were negotiating with Houghton Mifflin Company for a special Canadian edition. In distant Australia possible adoptions in various programs were being considered.

Reviews were generally favorable. Criticisms leveled by a few detractors were not difficult to counter. For instance, certain negative comments expressed in Buros' *Third Mental Measurements Yearbook* were readily dismissed by Dr. Lindquist as based on misinformation, unfamiliarity with the tests, or simple differences of opinion.[43] He repeatedly defended the representativeness of the norms for nationwide use.

> There is no reason to believe that the norms on the *Iowa Tests of Basic Skills* are any less representative of nationwide achievement than are the norms for any of the competing batteries, such as the Stanford and Metropolitan. On the contrary, I feel that the norms on the latter tests are even more to be regarded as norms for the population of users of those tests, which is undoubtedly a selected population, rather than as norms for all United States public schools, than is true of the Iowa tests, since in our Iowa Testing Programs we come very much closer to getting the entire population represented than has any other standardization program at the present time. I should say that at least eighty percent of the schools in Iowa participate in our program. Other evidence, such as that obtained through the standardization program for the USAFI [United States Armed Forces Institute] tests, indicates that Iowa is very typical of the forty-eight states.[44]

In 1948, in response to the growing interest in mechanized test processing, Houghton Mifflin issued a machine-scorable answer sheet for Tests A, B, and C of ITBS Forms L, M, N, and for Test D of Forms O and P. Users could arrange for scoring with IBM equipment, either on their own premises or in service centers such as those already developed at the Universities of Connecticut and Illinois.

As another consequence of this interest, Science Research Associates of Chicago reached an agreement the same year with Houghton Mifflin Company to market ITBS Forms R and S *with scoring service*. The SRA ITBS remained on the market through 1956.

4 The *Iowa Tests of Educational Development*

Rationale

IN AN ADDRESS to the Conference on Administration and Supervision in Iowa City in October 1941, Dr. Lindquist announced a new outgrowth of the dozen years of experience in statewide cooperative testing. While acknowledging that the Every-Pupil High School Testing Program had served well its intended purposes, he voiced concern about certain limitations of the Every-Pupil Tests and similar course-oriented examinations when used in individual guidance and overall school evaluation.

> The selection of content of the tests used [to date] has been based on an analysis of the things now being taught in the school subjects, not on our or anyone else's notion of what *ought* to be taught in these subjects. These tests have indicated to the schools to what extent they are attaining certain of the immediate objectives of instruction in individual school subjects, but have not indicated whether or not these objectives are valid in relation to ultimate objectives. Test scores, for example, might indicate how much a pupil has learned of what is now being taught in ninth grade algebra, but they will not indicate how much the teaching of algebra has contributed to his general ability to do quantitative thinking in situations met in life outside of the school.[45]

Other inadequacies of traditional tests elaborated by Lindquist were that: they measured temporary rather than permanent changes in the pupil resulting from instruction; they did not afford "at any one time a sufficiently comprehensive picture of the individual pupil's educational development" and were "too much concerned with content objectives to be of maximum usefulness in guidance and evaluation"; they did not yield "measures of growth"; and they could not provide "strictly *comparable* measures from subject to subject."[46]

The approach needed now, he believed, was to measure, early on, the level of the pupil's *general* educational development, the culmination of all prior years of schooling, and to assess individual ability to benefit from continuing instruction and study.

> Tests that would fill [these] needs . . . have not yet been generally available at the high school level, but present knowledge and skill in test construction are certainly adequate to provide them. What is needed, quite obviously, is (1) a series of general background tests, (2) a corresponding series of reading tests, (3) a test of familiarity with and ability to use important sources of information—such as books and periodicals, general and special reference works, and libraries, and (4) a general vocabulary test to supplement the others in providing a measure of general scholastic aptitude.[47]

Acting on these ideas, Lindquist and colleagues designed and constructed the *Iowa Tests of Educational Development*, embodying many concepts that subsequently were widely accepted. A wholly new vehicle, the Fall Testing Program, was organized for their administration. The project was "innovative" in the broad sense as well as in many specific aspects. Its principal new features were:

— testing by subject matter *areas*
— the use of specialized reading tests in measuring analytical skills and (indirectly) information in broad areas
— adoption of a uniform standard score scale for all tests in the battery
— administration of the same tests in all high school grades
— centralized scoring service.

The Fall Testing Program and the ITED were launched in September 1942. The early autumn date was chosen purposefully.

> Among the things that a teacher of any subject most needs to know about his pupils at the beginning of the term are (1) how good a foundation each pupil has acquired for that subject, and (2) how capable each pupil is of reading and understanding the materials he will be given to study. This kind of information . . . cannot be readily acquired for a large group of pupils by direct observation alone. The only really satisfactory way to get this information about the pupils quickly and dependably is to test them with examinations specially constructed for the purpose.[48]

At any time of year, schools wishing to continue certain previous uses of the Every-Pupil Tests could obtain recent editions for independent administration without central services.*

---

*The UI Bureau of Educational Research and Service continued for many years to reprint and sell the Every-Pupil Tests, in other states as well as in Iowa.

Guidelines for the Fall Testing Program

THE BASIC standards set up by Director Lindquist for the design and conduct of the Fall Testing Program are outlined in the following statement of criteria from the 1942 announcement.

IMPORTANT CRITERIA OF AN EFFECTIVE WIDE-SCALE PROGRAM OF TESTING FOR EVALUATION, GUIDANCE, AND THE INDIVIDUALIZATION OF INSTRUCTION.

1. The tests used should measure as directly as possible the attainment of the ultimate objectives of the entire school program.

2. All of the tests should be administered, under standard conditions, to the entire student body. . . .

3. The program must provide for the measurement of growth. . . .

4. The tests used should measure the more permanent of the changes produced in the pupils. . . .

5. The test results should not be usable in the rating of individual teachers. . . .

6. The description of the pupils' educational development provided by the tests must be expressed in readily interpretable form. . . .

7. The test profile for each individual pupil must be readily available at all times to each of his teachers and counsellors. . . .

8. The measures derived must be highly comparable from test to test. . . .

9. Each of the tests used must yield highly reliable measures of the abilities of the individual pupil. . . .

10. The testing program ideally should impose no clerical or statistical burdens whatever upon teachers and administrators, and in all other respects should involve the minimum of administrative inconvenience. . . .

11. The total cost of the services of the program must be within the reach of the majority of the public schools.[49]

Now well into its fourth decade, the Fall Testing Program has consistently adhered to these standards.

Salient Characteristics of the ITED

Subject Area Testing

The ITED were unique in providing differentiated measures for each of several *fields*. These "core tests" focused upon four main areas: social studies, natural science, English, and mathematics. The nine tests in the battery were titled:
1. Understanding of Basic Social Concepts
2. General background in the Natural Sciences
3. Correctness in Writing
4. Quantitative Thinking
5. Ability to Interpret Reading Materials in the Social Studies
6. Ability to Interpret Reading Materials in the Natural Sciences
7. Ability to Interpret Literary Materials
8. General Vocabulary
9. Use of Sources of Information.

Lindquist maintained that "in consideration . . . of the necessity of restricting a program of this kind to the evaluation of only those outcomes of instruction that are *measurable*, objectively, comparably, and dependably, this list is about as inclusive as one can reasonably expect any such list to be."[50]

In addition to the nine test scores, a composite score on Tests 1 – 8 was computed.

The results on the first four comprehensive tests indicated primarily the pupil's level of general background and growth in each *area* but were applicable as well to subjects within the area. Tests 5 – 7, measuring ability to comprehend and interpret reading materials in the given skills, supplemented the related background tests. Test 8, Vocabulary, strengthened the composite score as an indicator of general scholastic ability, while Test 9 measured a special awareness and skill obviously important to effective study at any level.

There were no part scores in these tests, no breakdown into government, chemistry, geometry, and so on. The test items rarely demanded specific recall of names and dates or statements of rules and formulas. An important specification of the test design was that the items should, as far as possible, measure aspects of the subject matter highly related to the contemporary scene. The reading tests presented passages from recent books, magazines, and newspapers, dealing with timely social, natural, scientific, and cultural concerns. (To the dismay of the test builders, a few such passages roused unexpected controversy in certain other states in the fifties and sixties, when efforts to measure sensitive social issues or propaganda techniques were themselves misconstrued as intentionally propagandistic or subversive!)

The 780-item battery was long by today's instancy standards, requiring eight and one-half hours of actual testing time. Lindquist considered this length necessary for reliable measurement of the wide range of ability found in grades 9 – 12.

Two equivalent forms, X – 1 and Y – 1, of the ITED were introduced in the first Fall Testing Program. Each form was supplied to about half of the participating schools. Alternation of forms in succeeding programs minimized the likelihood that any pupil would take the same form two years in a row. The second edition, a partial revision of the first, was published in 1948. Subsequent editions were issued in 1952, 1960, 1970, 1972, and 1979. (See also Appendix, Table E.) The two principal changes in the battery thus far were made in the seventies: a reduction in length and the adoption of a two-level format. These are described in chapter 12.

The second edition (Forms X – 2, Y – 2) contained newly constructed tests in natural science background and in English correctness. The new Test 2 emphasized understanding of more recent scientific developments and the role of science in the contemporary world. In the English test, a new format (described below) was employed. In the other seven tests, only a few replacements or revisions were made of items that particularly needed updating or clarification. The new science and English tests were tried out experimentally in 15 selected schools in May 1948. The finished forms, assembled during the summer, were equated in the fall to Forms X – 1, Y – 1 in 12 schools which had scheduled their testing on September 2 and 3—early enough to accommodate the necessary statistical work on equivalence scales without unduly delaying the processing for the entire program. The percentile norms for school averages (by grade and by enrollment class) were established directly on the results of the annual program.

Subsequent editions of the ITED have been equated in the Fall Program the year before general adoption of the new forms in the program.

The Reading Tests

Lindquist considered Tests 3 – 8, and *particularly Tests 5 – 7*, to be the heart of the ITED battery. The latter three, those concerned with reading materials in social studies, science, and literature, were definitely avant-garde in 1942. The use of specialized reading tests as a basis for measuring achievement in subject areas had not occurred before in any published standardized examinations. The test items *indirectly* measured the pupil's knowledge of principles, concepts, and methods through his/her success in comprehending and interpreting passages dealing with scientific, literary, and social studies topics. Certain items tested the pupil's ability to recognize valid or spurious argument, logic or the lack of it, fact vs. propaganda, distinctive treatment, and so on.

The decision to employ separate reading tests in the three areas took into consideration differences in the three types of reading materials, in the problems they presented, and in the difficulties of comprehension—differences that Lindquist believed could not satisfactorily be bridged in a single generalized reading test. He also considered and pointed out the important relationship between reading comprehension and informational background, the latter becoming more important and mechanical reading skills relatively less so during a person's progress through the grades. If a high school pupil scored much higher on the background test than on the specialized reading test in, say, natural science, that person might be seriously deficient in general reading skills. Conversely, one who scored relatively much higher on the reading test was apparently already using acquired information to good advantage and needed most to work on gaining more knowledge.[51] Only for the very poor readers, identifiable by low scores on each of Tests 5, 6, and 7, did he consider it worthwhile to administer a diagnostic reading test as well.

In subsequent manuals for school use Lindquist continued to drive home the rationale of the ITED reading tests. For example:

> While constructed in the external form of a reading comprehension test, these three tests are designed to measure much more than generalized reading skills. Essentially, they are intended to measure the pupil's ability to do *critical thinking* in the broad areas designated. They are concerned not so much with *what* the pupil has learned, in the sense of specific information, but rather with how well he can *use whatever* he has learned in acquiring, interpreting and evaluating new ideas, in relating new ideas to old, and in applying broad concepts and generalizations to new situations or in the solution of problems. These, it is to be hoped, are the lasting and ultimate outcomes—not only of an effective course of formal school instruction, but also any other genuinely educational experience, . . . in-school or out-of-school.[52]

Some critics of the ITED have maintained that the high intercorrelations among the three reading tests indicated that these tests measured essentially the same things. Lindquist's counter-criticism of this reasoning was that their differences could not be judged on the basis of statistical evidence alone. His viewpoint is summarized in a review of thirty years of the Iowa programs.

> To me, by far the most important consideration in achievement testing

is that the test items themselves constitute a meaningful and satisfactory definition (in operational terms) of the objectives being measured. . . .

The answer to the criticisms of the three [ITED reading] tests . . . can be satisfactorily resolved only by making a careful inspection and logical analysis of the tests themselves and by deciding for oneself whether or not the abilities or objectives defined by the items in the different tests are indeed intrinsically different. . . . If these instruments are not *interchangeable* to teachers of the social studies or the natural sciences, either as definition of objectives or as measures of their attainment, then the separate tests are needed, even though the intercorrelations are high.[53]

The English Test

The first edition (Forms X-1, Y-1) of the ITED English Test continued the traditions and the general pattern of the Every-Pupil achievement tests in English correctness. Its four parts were concerned, respectively, with punctuation, usage, capitalization, and spelling, the first three of these skills in sentences of everyday content a high school student might have written.* However, only a *total* score on the test was computed. It was included in the composite score, and, of course, appeared on the pupil profile cards distributed to all teachers. Discussions in the interpretative manuals further served to emphasize the importance of the English skills in general educational development and the need for teachers in all subjects to monitor and improve the quality of student writing.

A greater reach of objectives in the second (1948) edition is implied in the title change from "Correctness in Writing" to "Correctness and Appropriateness of Expression." The intent in X-2, Y-2 was to build a more advanced test for the high school level—"a test that is concerned with such things as word choice, appropriateness of phrasing, paragraph organization, style, sentence structure, etc., as well as with punctuation, capitalization, grammar, and spelling."[54] In this new form, several complete passages—essays, stories, or letters—were presented, in each of which many types of errors might be found. (Only spelling was still tested separately, as before.) The pupil considered the portions underlined in each passage and indicated acceptance or correction of that portion by choosing one of several alternatives printed at the right of the passage. Each passage was first shown as a compact reading exercise, errors and all, to afford the pupil a preliminary notion of the passage and of the task to be performed. The passage was then repeated as a testing exercise, spread out to accommodate the num-

---

*The principal difference in format from the Every-Pupil series was that the alternate choices in punctuation and usage were printed on the separate answer sheet, along with the response boxes for all four parts.

bered underlinings and to align those horizontally with the response choices. This technique, which appears to be original, has continued in use to the present forms of the ITED, with, of course, such refinements in item construction as a succession of experienced and imaginative contributors could devise along the way.

The goal in this more "living" type of test was to parallel as closely as possible the task faced by the high school student in actual writing situations. It permitted, also, approaching some of the subtler facets of composition, such as clarity of expression, continuity of ideas, and sensitivity to language.

Certain technical considerations observed in the construction of all the ITED English tests have been stated repeatedly in the manuals.

> An attempt has been made to avoid testing for usages or practices on which there is not substantial agreement in teaching. The points tested were further limited to those which an extensive experimental tryout indicated would yield the best indication of general mastery of the elements of good writing. Therefore, the test does not cover certain elementary skills that virtually all pupils have mastered before entering high school. . . . This exclusion does not make the test any less valid. On the contrary, it heightens the meaningfulness of the scores obtained, since every item in the test distinguishes between the good and the poor students.[55]

The ITED English test was a product of Lindquist's unrelenting determination to improve the vitality and validity of measurement in English. His natural interest in the subject was fueled by its inherent challenges for the test builder. This fact was evidenced in the many techniques employed in earlier Iowa tests and in other ways as well. His Ph.D. dissertation, "The Laboratory Method in Freshman English," recorded an experimental program of instruction he devised for the university level, its tryout at The University of Iowa, appropriate examinations, and an analysis of the results.* In a 1938 address to high school English teachers[56] and on numerous later occasions, he demonstrated the wide range of individual differences in ability within a grade, and the great overlap in distributions of test scores from grade to grade in English, revealed by his own and other studies of test results. In the thirties and early forties Lindquist served the Cooperative Test Service of the American Council on Education as test author, editor, and consultant, particularly in English and the social studies.

---

*In the program for his doctoral examination Lindquist mentions difficulties tending to thwart the accomplishment of "adequate instruction in the mechanical features of writing and the inspirational element needed to stimulate creative writing"—twin objectives that still today are sometimes regarded as antithetic.

That activity both utilized and enriched the Iowa fund of experience and led to enlistment of some CTS talent in constructing tests for later Iowa programs.

Uniform All-school Testing

A precondition for participation in the Fall Program was that the complete battery would be administered to all students enrolled in the high school. Such uniform testing would yield grade/building averages and norms fully representative of group achievement in the areas concerned. This characteristic of the test results had special significance in a program geared for the measurement of ultimate objectives, rather than course objectives, and for over-all evaluation of the curriculum. *"In general, to evaluate the entire instructional program one must test the entire student body."*[57]

Availability of comparable information for each enrolled student was considered no less important in guidance. Evidence of how well prepared all students were in a certain area would illuminate a counselor's interpretation of a given individual's test performance and other records. It would afford the counselor a stronger basis for advising the student and in some cases might alter the advice given.

Scoring and Reporting Services

The ripple that was to become a wave appeared first in the 1942 Fall Program, when test scoring in Iowa City was offered to program participants. Centralized scoring had not been attempted before in a voluntary public school program of this (or possibly any other) size and scope. It was a landmark in test service, freeing thousands of classroom teachers from the most irksome part of test administration. This first Iowa scoring was a manual operation, a simple counting of Xs marked on an answer sheet and immediate visual conversion of the total to a standard score read from a table (discussed below). All calculations and reporting were in terms of standard scores.

Individual test results were reported on pupil profile cards (Fig. 8). This compact report carried the pupil's standard scores and printed scales on which those scores could be plotted to form a profile. Scores from subsequent testings could be plotted on the same card to form a continuing record. The intent was that each teacher should have such a profile card for every student in that teacher's classes. At first two, and later four, sets of cards for all pupils tested were furnished as part of the standard service. Schools were encouraged to order additional sets as needed for distribution to all teachers.

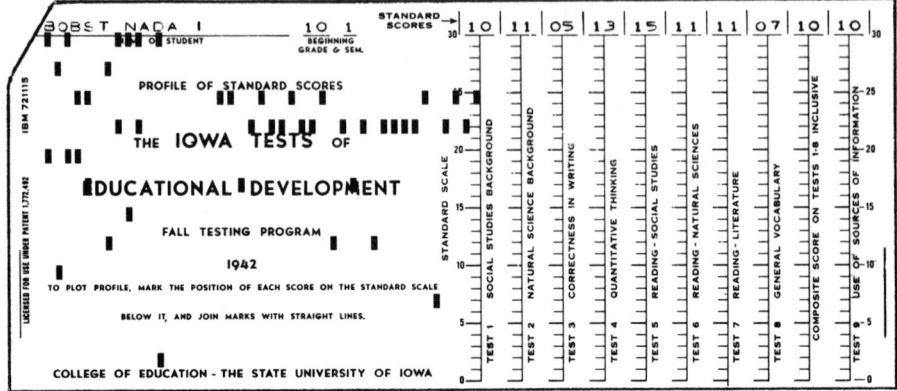

Fig. 8. Punched card pupil profile chart devised in 1942.

Each school's group results were computed and reported to it in a confidential summary report (Fig. 9). This document showed the local grade averages on all tests and composite and the percentile ranks of those averages within the school's enrollment class and among all schools. Profiles of the latter rankings were drawn in grade-coded colors, also. This summary report, in duplicate, was mailed only to the designated school official.

Tables of percentile norms for pupil scores and school averages, and raw-score-to-standard-score conversion tables for Forms X and Y, were also supplied, along with detailed interpretative manuals for teachers and administrators.

The Standard Score Scale

The employment of a uniform standard score scale with equivalent test forms permitted statistically sound and meaningful comparisons from test to test within the battery, from form to form, and from year to year. This was another "first" for this level—and a marked improvement over comparisons made on nonequivalent forms and in terms of percentile ranks based on diverse populations of pupils.

It was decided that a scale of 30 units would be formulated.

> This standard scale will be so adjusted that the distribution of standard scores on each test will be approximately normal and will show a standard deviation of approximately five units for all pupils tested in each grade. The lengths of the various tests in the battery will have been so adjusted that all tests will have about the same reliability. A scale of 30 units will be utilized because it is anticipated that the reliability of the tests will be such that the probable error of measurement for each test will be about one-thirtieth of the full range of scores on the test . . . [that is,] approximately one unit. Accordingly, the chances will be about even

Fig. 9. ITED confidential report of grade averages and ranks. In actual reports, grade profiles were plotted in colors. *(Actual size 8½ x 11 inches.)*

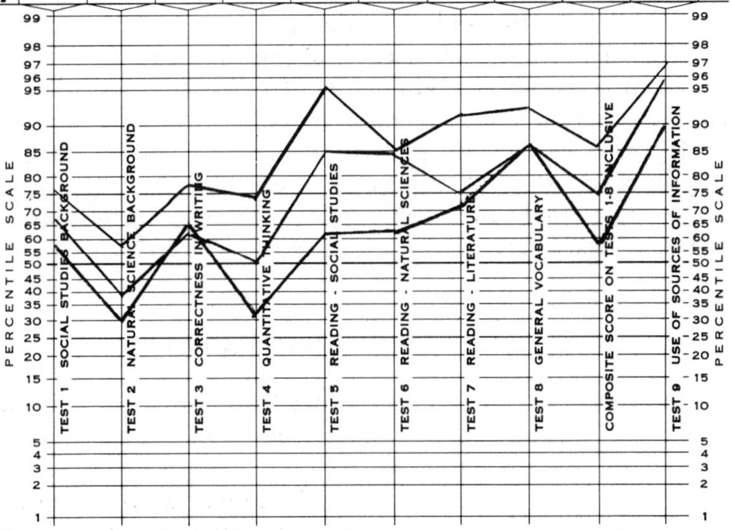

that the pupil's score will not be in error by more than one unit, while one may be very highly confident that an error of two units will not be exceeded, and practically certain that the error will not be larger than three units.[58]

This scale remained in use with all subsequent forms of the ITED, after the equating of new forms to old and establishment of appropriate conversion tables. Eventually the scale was extended to 36 for the subtests and 38 for the composite, the better to distinguish among very gifted high school students and to accommodate use of the tests in grade 13.

In the 1942 program, approximately one-third of the participating schools received Form X-1 only, for administration to all pupils; one-third received Form Y-1 only; and one-third received X and Y alternated. In a round-the-clock effort, score conversion and equivalency tables were established on the results of this administration. The raw-score-to-standard-score conversion tables were based on the raw scores of about 10,000 tenth- and eleventh-graders in the "X only" group; the X-Y equivalence tables, on scores of pupils in the "X and Y alternated" group. Another blitz produced pupil percentile norms by grade, percentile norms for grade averages by enrollment categories and overall, pupil profile cards, and plotted reports of grade rankings. That first fall, distribution of all reports was completed within six weeks after the testing period. In later annual programs, turn-around time from answer sheets to reports of results was reduced to two weeks or less.

Administrative Highlights

THE FORMATION of a new standardized test program is a double train of intellectual effort: the development of the test materials, and the organization of the program itself.[59]

On the editorial track, the ITED activities were quite similar to those of previous Iowa programs. After determination of the content specifications, the work proceeded to item writing and the preparation of tryout units; next, to the administration, scoring, and item analysis of those units; then, to selection, revision, and assembly of tried-out items into final forms of the tests; to the writing of manuals and other accessories; and finally, the publication of all these materials. A new technique in the ITED tryouts was the use of an answer card to be marked with a special electrographic pencil. When these marked cards were run through an IBM mark-sensing reproducer, punched cards were produced, which could then be put through the sorter and tabulator to obtain the count of pupils selecting each response to each item. At about 400 cards per minute, this method seemed briskly efficient.

On the administrative track, the Fall Program ran on new rails. A novel system of marketing and the introduction of scoring service, in particular, necessitated new methods, new equipment, and new help all along the route.

Rental of Test Booklets

Until now, all the Iowa tests had been bought outright and retained by program participants and other qualified users. The ITED, however, could not be purchased in the same manner. They were *rented* (in effect, *lent*) to program participants and were returned to the central ITP office after *each* annual administration. They were not available to anyone else. Each fall about half of the testees took one form and half the other, the balance and alternation of forms being determined in Iowa City. Generally, enough tests were supplied so that all students in the high school could be tested simultaneously, with a few exceptions in some large high schools that preferred to make do with half the customary number. A minimal levy, calculated on the anticipated average "life" of a test booklet, was included in the package charge (initially 25 cents) per student for the entire standard service, including manuals and other accessories, scoring, basic reports (two sets of pupil profile cards and two reports of averages), and handling (exclusive of actual transportation cost).

This lending arrangement afforded maximum security for the test content between programs, relieved the schools of storage worries, and held down printing expense. The nine tests in the battery were bound into a single reusable booklet, to facilitate repeated distribution. On the other hand, the shipping, receiving, and storage of test booklets in Iowa City was a demanding and quite expensive operation, involving many handlers. Reuse also necessitated inspection of booklets after each program by crews of clerks who leafed through the thousands of tests, erasing smudges and graffiti and discarding damaged copies.

Test Security

To protect against coaching and other unwise or unauthorized uses, strict accountability for all copies was considered a must. The serial numbers of the booklets supplied to each school were logged before shipment and checked on return. A $1.00 fee assessed for every missing booklet helped stimulate complete and prompt returns. Only the school superintendent was issued a test copy for keeps. For many years, even libraries could not obtain copies. But the information blackout was not total. To equip test users with an adequate understanding of what they were administering, actual examples of the *kinds* of items in the tests, illustrating range and difficulty of content, were presented in the manual, "Use and Interpretation of the Test Results by the Classroom Teacher," along with verbal descriptions, practical suggestions, and cautions.

Security was further heightened by the practice of substituting new forms, as they were developed, for earlier editions within the Iowa program.

Other Innovations

The brave new look of the Fall Testing Program posed many other administrative requirements. The principal ones, and their solutions, were:

(a) *Reusable shipping containers* for the test booklets. A sturdy hardboard case with telescoping cover and buckled strap was fabricated to specifications by an Illinois manufacturer of laundry cases. The samples underwent a laboratory test of durability by being bounced repeatedly against the walls and floor of his office by the director himself. Many of the original cases are still in use after surviving a hundred or more round trips over long distances. A buffer reminiscent of a foot-operated grindstone was fabricated by the director for cleaning labels and canceled stamps off the boxes after each return.

(b) A *single answer sheet* that would accommodate all responses to the test battery, yet would be convenient to mark and to score. The final product was a king-sized fanfold (Fig. 10) that could be laid close to each test page during marking (Plate 4), yet could easily be flipped open to lie flat for scoring (Plate 6). By 1943 it was found practicable to reduce the size of the answer sheet from 21-by-11 inches to 15-by-8½, fanfolded to a slender 3-by-8½ inches.

(c) A *comprehensive scoring key* that would minimize counting time and maximize counting accuracy. An oversized "sandwich board" key of stiff cardboard, punched to reveal correct response positions only, permitted rapid counting of visible Xs on both sides of the answer folder spread flat between its hinged leaves. Standard score conversion tables were pasted to the key.

(d) *Economically reproducible report forms.* The tabulating card format was chosen for the pupil profile card (Fig. 8) because of advantages in production and use. The 3¼-by-7³/₈-inch card could be prepared and duplicated automatically on electrical equipment already on campus. Multiple copies could be reproduced at low cost to meet school demands. In usage, the card was convenient to handle and file. The pupil percentile

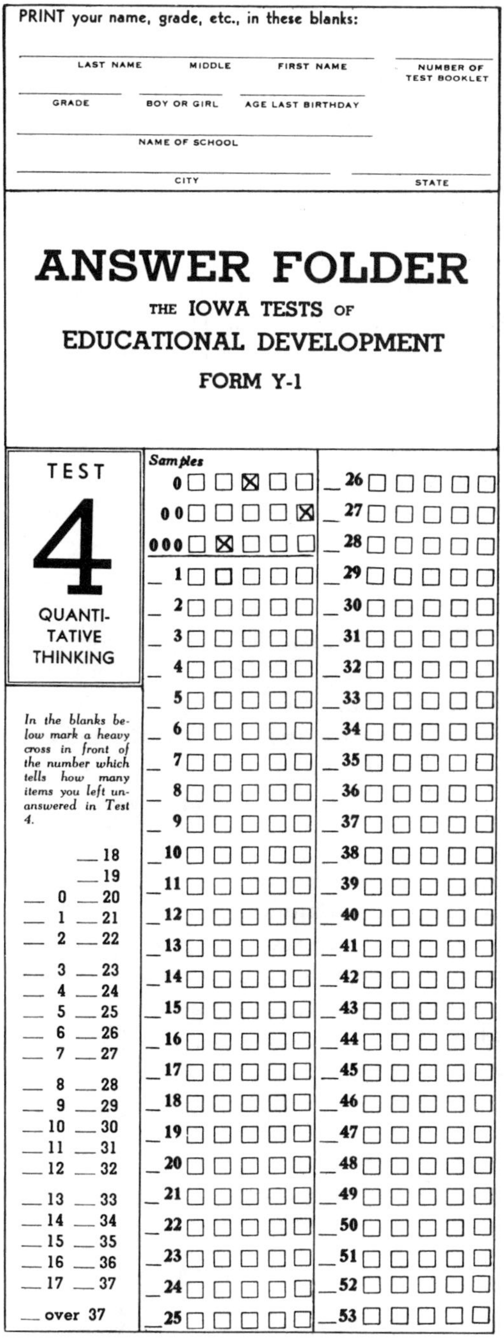

Fig. 10. Answer folder for ITED-Y-1. *(Actual size 21 x 11 inches, fanfolded to 4 x 11 inches.)*

norms and the score conversion tables were printed on companion cards, which could be filed with the profile cards for ready reference. The 8½-by-11-inch confidential summary report (Fig. 9) was designed for tabulating machine printout of grade averages and ranks, with a grid below for the school profiles. Duplicate printouts of the data and tracings of the profiles could be made inexpensively.

(e) *Scoring staff and space.* Clerks were recruited by advertising (Fig. 11) and every available means, including personal appeals to academic friends. An exact system was organized for selecting and training scorers, who numbered 164 in September and 109 in October of 1942, including full-time, part-time, dropouts, and failures. The scoring payroll in those first two months was $2,255 and $1,677, respectively, approximately $.05 per answer folder.

The scoring, shipping, and storage operations caused very heavy space demands on old East Hall. A messy attic on the third floor (W309) was renovated and slightly repaired for a receiving room—dispossessing a flock of pigeons and other wildlife—and three smaller rooms nearby (W410, W414, and W415) were vacated for the booklet checking and storage.* On the second floor the large south seminar room (once a hospital ward room) and the adjacent east study room were assigned to ITP for the scoring function. The director's office and management staff remained on first floor; the Statistical Service Department was located in University Hall (now Jessup Hall). Heavy foot traffic was engendered up and down the stairs and across the campus, the ancient elevator being highly unreliable and interbuilding delivery service nonexistent.

Pre-electronic Scoring

The ITED comprehensive service with manual scoring prefigured fully automated test processing. Its early success stimulated demands that could be met only by the faster electronic methods. Many elements of the 1942 procedure became incorporated into or adapted to the latter. Hence, this midpoint model merits review for historical reasons, as well as for its own neatness of form and purpose.

---

*The Bureau of Educational Research and Service did not assist in the ITED program, except to bill the schools for services from information supplied by ITP. This, too, ceased about 1960.

HELP WANTED

100 Women to Score Tests
during September and October

Easy and pleasant work; no training or experience needed; housewives and students eligible. Work part or full time, day or evening, at your convenience. Do not apply unless you can work at least 20 hours per week for two weeks or more. Call 2111-385 or apply in person at Room W-314 East Hall (third floor, west wing). Apply immediately.

Fig. 11. One of many ads run in local papers during peak scoring periods.

Plate 4. Students at Iowa City High School taking the Iowa Tests of Educational Development in the 1943 Fall Program.

The clerical scheme comes alive even now in the sheaf of illustrated instructions in the 1942 archives.[60] Actions are anticipated in detail down to the turn of a wrist; for example:

f. Grasp key by putting thumbs beneath that part which was left protruding over the edge of the desk. . . .
k. Place fingers of left hand on "mark-sense" card and slide this card so that it is above and to the left end of the key. Place the heel of the right hand on the key to hold it in position. . . .
x. With the right hand pick up the "mark-sense" card. As you lift this card, turn it over clockwise. . . .
y. Lay down answer folder to the upper right of the desk with Test 5 up. . . . As you are laying the folder down with the right hand, reach for a new folder with the left.

"Props" were arranged with equal care, as in the mockup of a scorer's desk shown in Figure 12.

Approximately 50,000 answer folders were marked by pupils in 291 high schools in the first Fall Program. A corps of women clerks, in highly disciplined all-day counting of Xs, scored and rescored these folders at rates of 10–12 per hour, recording nine standard scores per pupil on the mark-sense cards (Plates 5 and 6). A daily performance record was kept for each scorer, showing hours worked, number of folders scored, time used in minutes, errors of one standard unit, and errors exceeding one standard unit. Most scorers worked at the prevailing clerical rate of 40 cents per hour. An incentive bonus of another 5 cents per hour was offered for scoring at least 45 folders every four hours, with fewer than eight errors, not more than one of which might exceed one standard unit. Twenty clerks gained this superstar status the first year. Several maintained such phenomenal accuracy that rescoring of their work could be dispensed with.

The procedure used through 1945 is roughly diagramed in Figure 13.

Benchmarks of the proficiency attained in such methods abound in the records: for example, the notation that in 1944, scoring for the first 13 schools to submit answer sheets was begun September 6, and the finished pupil profile cards were sent to these schools on September 13.

An unusual adaptation of nontesting equipment was the installation in 1946 of commercial bookkeeping machines for use in the preparation of pupil profile cards (Plate 7). This change in method of production reduced ITP's dependence upon the Statistical Service Bureau, which served many other departments and organizations in the university, and which had been under severe strains during the war years. A four-copy snap-apart individual report form, of similar design, was substituted for the tabulating machine profile cards used previously. These

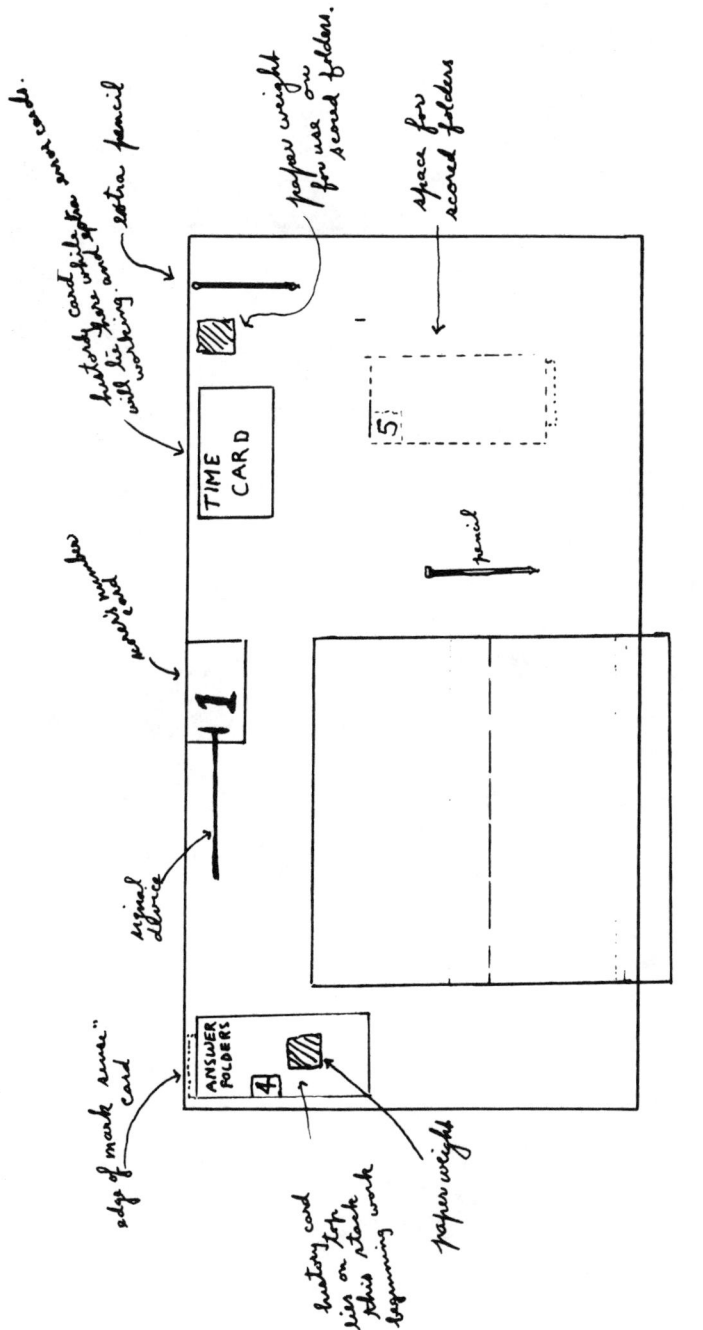

Fig. 12. Layout of scorer's desk.

Plate 5. Scoring crew at work, 1943 Fall Program.

Plate 6. Counting right answers, close-up view.

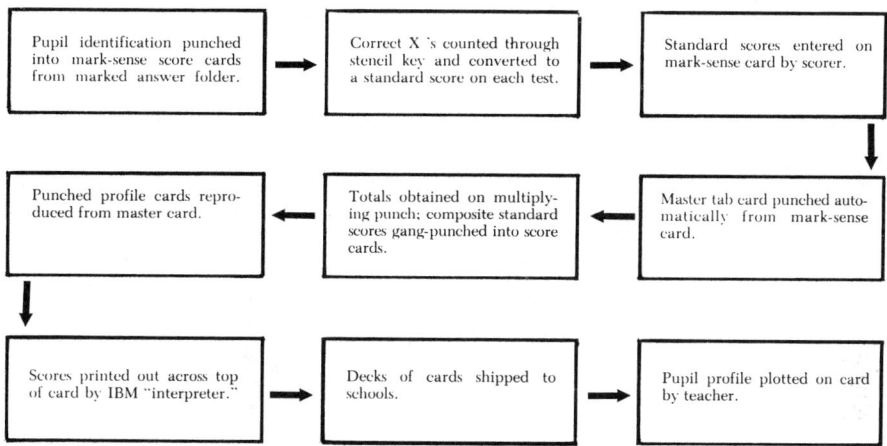

Fig. 13. Steps in production of an ITED pupil profile.

paper forms were typed on the bookkeeping machines from the scored answer sheets on which the standard scores were written. During this typing, a work list in which the pupils were identified by number was produced simultaneously on a continuous blank form carried in the machine. Sums of scores on each test for conversion to school averages were obtained automatically in the bookkeeping machines, as well as a total of all standard scores in a grade in a school. The latter, when compared to a similar total obtained manually by skilled comptometrists, provided a verification of the typing accuracy. The distributions of school averages were tallied by hand in the computation of norms.

In 1946, 90,430 sets of pupil profile cards were typed in this manner at a rate of 85 per hour and a total wage cost of only $613.15.

The bookkeeping machines were used in the ITED and ITBS programs (with modifications in method) for about eight years. In conjunction with them, special answer sheet racks (Fig. 14) and supply cabinets were built to the director's specifications. Other equipment also designed by him and constructed locally included individual scoring tables (Plate 8) utilizing discarded birch doors found in the attic, special comptometer/calculator tables, and later, with the adoption of continuous-form profile cards, a device for mechanically separating the copies — all to make tasks less arduous and effort more productive.

During this expansive decade, the ITP program operations and the management offices became centralized on the third floor of East Hall, occupying the entire floor of the west wing by 1948. Even the multilithing of the redesigned flat answer sheets on a small offset press was undertaken there.

74 The Iowa Testing Programs

Plate 7. Bookkeeping machine being operated in production of ITED pupil profile cards.

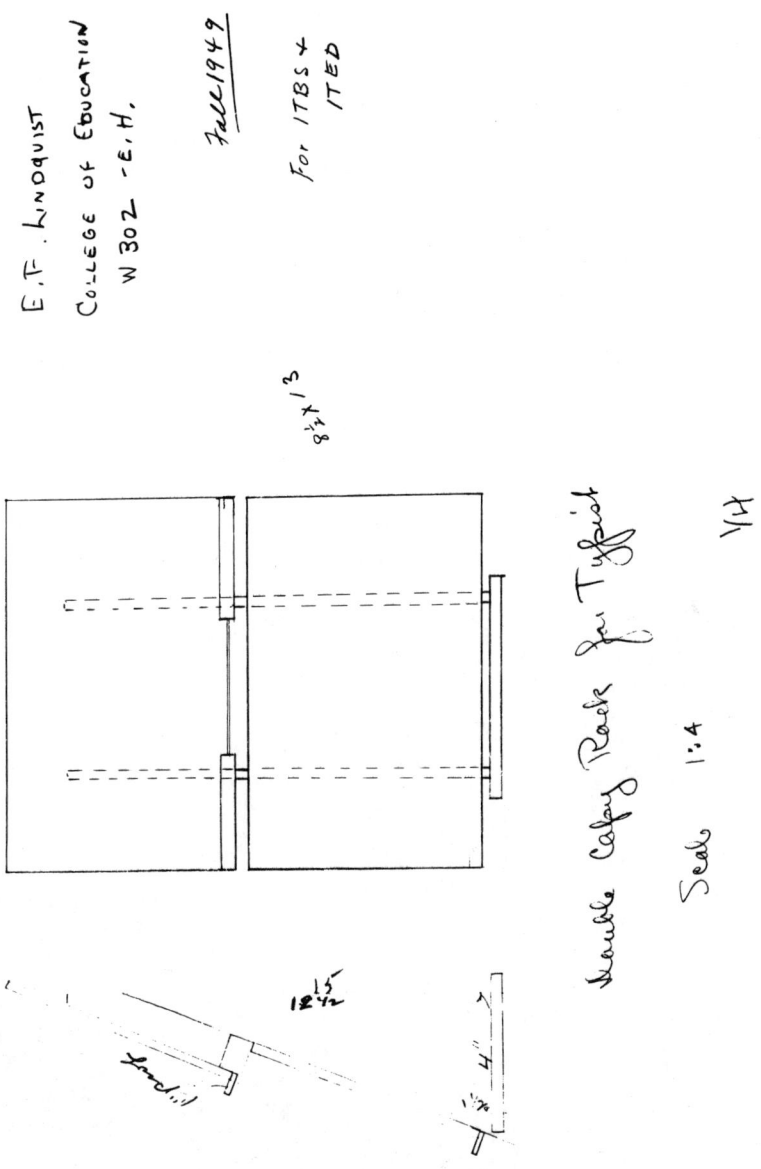

Fig. 14. Original drawing by E. F. Lindquist for construction of answer sheet racks as shown in Plate 7. (1949 ITED and ITBS.)

The Take-Home Profile Leaflet

A SPECIAL self-help item originated for the Fall Testing Program and still supplied to all users of the ITED was introduced in 1948. This is the four-page folder entitled "Your Scores on the ITED . . . and What They Mean." It was created as a vehicle for informing pupils and their parents of the individual's own test results, for promoting improved educational guidance practices in the schools, for encouraging scholarship, and generally for clarifying to students and parents the purposes of the *Iowa Tests of Educational Development* and the proper interpretation of the test results. The pamphlet included charts on which the pupil could plot his/her test results and thereby make comparisons with state norms. This do-it-yourself plotting was intended to foster self-analysis and a facing up to the realities of the individual's test performance, per se and in relation to future plans. With the explanatory text, the folder has constituted a virtually self-interpreting carry-out profile chart, which schools have been urged to distribute and use in the suggested manner.

In that first year of issue, the director particularly sought reactions to the new interpretative pamphlet and asked whether school patrons

Plate 8. Scorers using special easels and tables (about 1950). *University Photo Service.*

found it sufficiently useful to be continued as a service. The following year he reported back to school administrators that the leaflet had proved very much worthwhile, "not only in achieving its announced purposes, but also as a good public relations device."[61]

The thrust of this pamphlet has remained the same for three decades, with occasional updating to conform to improvements in related materials. For example, the charts in the first edition were designed for the plotting of standard scores only but showed selected state norms for rough comparisons. Later, 1961, when both standard scores and percentile ranks of individuals could be reported on pupil profile cards and adhesive labels, chart forms appropriate for plotting either score or rank (or both) were presented in the "Your Scores . . ." leaflet.

Also in 1948, an adjunct booklet entitled *What good is high school?* was made available to Iowa program participants at about one-third the publisher's list price.[62] The special intent in that publication was to examine with the student the values of fundamental instruction in high school for success in later vocations or in continuing education, and to stimulate student/parent involvement in the educational program. Though the style of presentation may seem outmoded, the text is still timely.

These materials were part of a continuing effort to identify gifted young persons and to encourage extended development of their talents. A wave of national concern about utilizing the intellectual resources of the country had prompted studies which revealed that only about 50 percent of the outstanding high school graduates in the United States went on to college. However, a study made at The University of Iowa under the direction of Professor J. B. Stroud showed that in this state, in a representative sample of 2,616 high school seniors tested in the 1947 Fall Program, 92 percent of those who scored in the upper two percent on the ITED were attending college the following year. Early identification of talent through the ITED results, and the effect of this upon the attitudes of students, teachers, and parents, were cited by Dr. Lindquist as probably major reasons for this remarkable record in Iowa.[63]

Acceptance of the New Program

Participation

Approximately one-fourth (289) of the high schools in Iowa enrolled in the first Fall Testing Program, testing some 48,360 pupils. In the second year, 41,380 were tested in 247 high schools (239 systems, including 15 in Illinois, Minnesota, Missouri, Nebraska, North and South Dakota, and Wisconsin). Registration remained quite stable through the forties. In the last year of the decade, program enrollment stood at 330 Iowa plus 9 out-of-state schools and about 50,000 students, exclusive of testing administered through Science Research Associates (see next section).

Support of the program was as strong in the Class A and B schools as in the smaller C and D districts. A summary on file for the years 1944-48 shows that 37 of the Class A senior high schools in Iowa participated during this period.[64] Eight of these tested annually; four tested four times; seven, three times; ten, twice; and eight, once in the period. Use of the ITED within the state program rose steadily during the next twenty years, topping at 184,000 in 1968. This acceptance demonstrates that the program and the test battery served the schools well, not only in the early years of their development, but also in more recent years against increasing numbers of so-called competitors.

Comment

Opinion of the program expressed in early archival correspondence is generally highly favorable, with just enough variety to spice the reading. A superintendent of a larger school reported that his faculty considered the Fall Program the most helpful of any they had experienced and that they enjoyed working with the results. Another said that his school board was sold 100 percent on the merits of the program.

On the other hand, another complained that use of the results was at a standstill because the local board had usurped all authority for running the schools, adding that perhaps this would allow him more time to think!

The superintendent of a Class B school termed the service "invaluable" and said his school would "participate in the program 100%."

One administrator lauded the rationale of the program but found his teachers too busy to put its "beautiful theory" into practice. He complained also of money woes, as did several others, though only one protested the 25 cent cost as too high. Officials of several large high schools said they could afford to test only in alternate years. A number wished to test only in one or two grades each year, but this request was refused in order to protect the all-school character of the state norms. One smaller district was spending its available funds upon "re-medial [sic] materials" for elementary school improvement.

An enthusiastic out-of-state participant in 1942 anticipated even greater values from the growth measures in the second year of testing.

And one disappointed superintendent, who took the testing seriously himself, lamented that many of his pupils did not. Even so, he considered the scores revealing of abilities.

Letters in the 1942 archives addressed to Dr. Lindquist by colleagues in measurement convey consensus regarding the quality of the new program. A few excerpts from these:

> I am very favorably impressed by your plans and think your program should be one of the finest contributions yet made in the field of testing. (Dean H. Leigh Baker, Drake University)

> This seems to me to be miles ahead, in general concept at least, of any other testing program designed . . . for purposes of guidance. (Edward E. Cureton, U. S. Office of Education)

> I have been greatly impressed. . . . You are certainly doing a great piece of work in making such tests available at such a low cost to the schools of Iowa. (Frederick B. Davis, Cooperative Test Service)

> I think your idea of separate tests of ability to read literary materials and materials in the social studies and the natural sciences is excellent. Most tests of reading comprehension include these types of materials, but they do not provide separate scores on each type and they do not have enough material of each kind to yield reliable scores even if it were possible to separate the types. . . . I should like to see the tests become generally available, but I hope especially that you will allow the reading tests to be used outside your own program. (Arthur E. Traxler, Educational Records Bureau)

One surprising compliment has some wry implications:

> One of the reasons I like the [announcement] bulletin is that I can understand it. (Robert N. Hilkert, Educational Records Bureau)

The critiques by other measurement authorities in the *Third, Fourth,* and *Fifth Mental Measurements Yearbook* (Oscar Buros, editor) further attest professional acceptance of the battery for its announced purposes, mildly tempered here and there by a few statistical uncertainties due mainly to insufficient information.

The SRA Connection

ABOUT THREE years after the "nationalization" of the *Iowa Tests of Basic Skills*, the *Iowa Tests of Educational Development* also shifted status from a semiprovincial to a national product. This was accomplished through arrangements with Science Research Associates of Chicago. The contract negotiated in March 1943 called for republication of the first two forms and unrestricted distribution by SRA outside of Iowa. (About fifteen non-Iowa schools that had participated in the earlier Iowa high school programs were permitted to continue in the Fall Program.) The agreement specified that the tests were to be available as a battery only, not as separate tests, and on a rental basis as part of a test service for which users would pay a per-pupil charge—as in the Iowa program but at about three times the Iowa fee. On SRA's net income from such sales an "author's" royalty would be paid to the Iowa Testing Programs, with the further stipulation that these funds were to be spent for research in the College of Education. Any test booklets or other materials acquired by ITP from SRA for its own programs would be furnished at cost.

These basic principles were perpetuated in subsequent agreements or renegotiations occasioned by the issuance of new ITED forms and/or by changes in the processing routines. An amendment made in 1951 granted permission to SRA to issue a separate booklet edition of Form Y-2, following the completion of the new Forms X-3, Y-3 for the Iowa Fall Testing Program. The nine Y-2 tests, separately bound, with keys and instructions for local scoring and analysis, were sold outright in any quantity to qualified purchasers. While not warmly supported by Lindquist, this concession to out-of-state patrons who desired only selected tests for specific local needs somewhat broadened the usage and usefulness of the ITED.

As with ITBS earlier, threefold good flowed from commercial marketing of ITED: It brought a unique type of quality measurement to high schools everywhere, furthered educational research and development at The University of Iowa, and enabled ITP to improve services to *all* customers while maintaining low cost to Iowa schools. In particular, the year-round demand for scoring spread training and equipment expense and bettered the efficiency of operation.

In 1943-44 approximately 20,000 pupils were serviced through SRA; during 1944-45, over 41,000 in 200 schools. By the end of the decade, the annual SRA testing had risen to 117,500 students. The ITP account gained $1,450 from ITED royalties for the first year of the SRA connection. Ten years later, the figure was up to $18,000 a year; it peaked in the mid-sixties at more than $100,000 annually.

Besides extensive independent administration throughout the country (especially in California, Illinois, Michigan, New York State, and Pennsylvania), the ITED became the basis of wide-scale testing programs in a number of states (including Connecticut, Minnesota, Montana, Oklahoma, and Wisconsin) and of organized testing in metropolitan districts. Modeled in varying degrees after the Iowa program, these projects utilized SRA-edition Iowa materials and Iowa services. State or local norms were developed where requested, and in certain instances (notably Los Angeles) highly detailed and comprehensive reports were prepared to meet local requirements.* Regional norms for school averages were compiled when participation in a region warranted them.

One of SRA's tangential services in the late forties and fifties was the offering of a special "scholarship edition" of the ITED adapted from Y-2. This was available to business organizations or other concerned groups interested in identifying young persons of superior ability, particularly among the underprivileged, and supplying needed scholarships for their continued education. One example was the newsboys' testing program sponsored by the Chicago Newspaper Distributors' Association.

From such special projects, as well as from regular administration of the ITED in schools across the country, there emerged records of many discoveries of gifted students not hitherto recognized as such. And of likely dropouts, for economic or other reasons, who, encouraged by high performance on the ITED, went on to college and successful professional careers. A number of these dramatic episodes are recounted in articles published in *National Parent-Teacher* and in *The Reader's Digest*.[65]

In the bustling forties and fifties, as Science Research Associates under the leadership of Lyle M. Spencer grew to prominence in educational publishing, the repute of the ITED spread also. SRA's energetic sales staff and methods, steadied by Dr. Lindquist's professional counsel, must be largely credited with the phenomenally rapid rise of the ITED in the standardized test market. SRA not only sold tests; it offered services, technical information and advice, research reports, film strips, and other forms of educational assistance to its test users. It took the ITED to Hawaii and elsewhere abroad. It became a co-partner with ITP in the early stages of the National Merit Qualifying Test Program and the American College Testing Program. Many of the successes of this period developed from their combined effort and enterprise.

---

*As professional overseer of the Iowa scoring activity and the SRA account, Dr. Rolland Ray closely supervised for many years the preparation of these reports, some of which ran to several hundred bound pages of tables, charts, profiles, and interpretive text.

Military Service by the ITED

DURING and after World War II the *Iowa Tests of Educational Development* served the Armed Forces and the nation in several ways. The ITED or tests patterned after them were used by the military in special programs at The University of Iowa and other colleges—such as the Army Specialized Training Program, the V-12 Program, and the Navy Preflight Training Program. On the strength of acceptable performance on the ITED, many high schools awarded diplomas to returning service personnel who had been inducted before graduation. Perhaps the most substantial of ITP's contributions in military matters were those related to activities of the United States Armed Forces Institute (USAFI).

The USAFI and the ITED

The policies adopted by the United States Armed Forces Institute were formulated in cooperation with the American Council on Education to systematize uniformly across the country the granting of academic credit for general educational growth during military service. Dr. Lindquist, a member of advisory committees to both these agencies, played a strong role in the decisions reached, serving with Ralph W. Tyler and E. G. Williamson on a special subcommittee appointed to propose specific procedures. Subsequently he was in direct charge of the preparation and standardization of the tests employed.[66]

The USAFI *Tests of General Educational Development* (GED) were patterned after the ITED. In fact, in order to implement the accrediting system as quickly as possible, five tests from the Iowa battery were employed in the initial GED form, and the Iowa ITED norms were applied. New GED forms for the high school level were then produced and standardized on a broad national sample under Lindquist's supervision. Local facilities and labor, wherever appropriate and available, were also utilized in other phases of the USAFI program, in cooperation with Dr. Tyler's office in Chicago. ITP's resources were thus deployed on a second front while its own state programs were being maintained without interruption under wartime and postwar stresses.

Periodically in the fifties and sixties, USAFI again contracted with the Iowa Testing Programs for various kinds of assistance in its test production activities.

The *Cooperative Test on Recent Social and Scientific Developments*

THE FIRST attempt to measure understanding of contemporary affairs on a nationwide scale was undertaken in 1946. It was an echo and an extension of a service offered to Iowa schools in the Every-Pupil Achievement Testing Program during 1935–42. The idea of conducting such a program nationwide under the aegis of the Cooperative Test Service, and a practical structure for it, were proposed by E. F. Lindquist to other members of the Committee on Measurement and Guidance of the American Council on Education in the fall of 1945.* Within six months the test was developed and all arrangements were made for administration the following spring.

In pattern and coverage the *Cooperative Test on Recent Social and Scientific Developments* (RSSD) was reminiscent of its Every-Pupil predecessor. Familiar also was the central purpose of stimulating perception of contemporary issues and concern about the importance of such awareness to all members of our society.[67] Published by CTS (later a division of the Educational Testing Service), the test was constructed by E. F. Lindquist and Robert L. Ebel with the collaboration of other University of Iowa scholars in various disciplines and with editorial review by still other authorities elsewhere. The first, two-part, 80-minute test contained 116 items, a third of which dealt with scientific and medical matters separately from social and military developments.

Enrollment in the project was wholly voluntary and open to all high schools in the United States. Participating schools were required to test all pupils in grades 10–12, with the option of testing grade 9. The registrations for all states except Iowa were handled by CTS/ETS in New York. Iowa orders were processed independently by ITP at a substantially lower per-test charge. The RSSD test was administered in Iowa high schools early in April and in schools throughout the country two weeks later. The advance testing in Iowa made possible the provision of estimated national norms for immediate use by the schools in the later program. All scoring, norming, and preparation

---

*At the outset, Lindquist had envisioned the Nationwide RSSD Program as a potential vehicle for collecting by questionnaire a remarkably representative pool of data for research studies that would have many applications and benefits. Never implemented in this program, this "data bank" idea lay dormant for about twenty years. After the development of electronic scanning and processing equipment, it was revived with significant variations in the ITP spin-off, the Iowa Educational Information Center.

of reports were done in Iowa City by the ITP staff. School officials were cautioned not to discuss, or even announce, the testing prior to administration day, in order to preclude cramming that would cloud the results without any lasting benefits to the crammers.

Highly representative norms were established for pupil scores and school averages for the nation as a whole and for six separate geographical regions*—unique features for a test of this kind. In addition, Iowa schools received state norms of pupil and school achievement, the latter by four size categories based on numbers tested in grades 10–12. Percents of correct responses to individual items were also supplied for each grade. An original method of reporting individual results was devised: The scored answer sheets were returned to the schools, each carrying the pupil's part and total scores and percentile ranks; in addition, the correct answers to the items and the tables of percentile norms were overprinted on the answer sheets. By studying these along with the test, the pupils could discover their own faulty or inadequate understandings. Class discussions of the topics tested were also thus facilitated.

The RSSD, and any other good comprehensive test in its field, necessarily addressed controversial issues. Despite the meticulous editing during preparation, some specialists later on might object to certain answers as being simplistic, biased, or otherwise disputable. To argumentative critics, Dr. Lindquist replied that in a contemporary affairs test for high school use it frequently was not possible to provide a single answer that would satisfy all experts—not, at least, without substantial qualification or documentation.

> However, if it were so qualified and documented, [the keyed answer] would become altogether too bulky and technical to serve the test purposes. Our concern is not to provide the best possible answer to each question, in this sense, but to provide an answer that is consistent with the level of development characteristic of the pupils that we are trying to measure, and that will best serve to differentiate the superior from the inferior pupils at this level. . . . [By loading the responses with specific references or statistics] we would only frighten the student away from the question and penalize the student who had acquired sound generalizations, even though he had not become acquainted with the specific authorities quoted.[68]

The initial program enrolled 16,000 pupils in 119 Iowa high schools and a total of over 143,000 in 664 high schools in 43 states. During the next five years, the Iowa participation remained strong, while that in

---

*New England, Middle Atlantic, North Central, Southern, Rocky Mountain, and Pacific regions.

other states declined gradually but substantially. In 1950, because of other commitments, Dr. Lindquist wished to withdraw from the directorship but was persuaded by ETS to remain while the feasibility of continuing the project was analyzed. The test was shortened by half, and an option of unrestricted independent administration with local scoring was introduced. Such efforts could not overcome the competition of free contemporary affairs study aids and examinations offered to schools by publishers of commercial periodicals. Nor could they stem the reported slackening of interest in the schools for providing quality instruction on current events.[69] In the face of decreasing participation and increasing costs, ETS officials reluctantly terminated the Nationwide Program following the 1951 administration. The Iowa Program lived on two more years, though less robustly. Then it, too, gave way to more vigorous and pressing developments in the ITP organization. But the message from a page of that time has not lost its urgency.

> These are tense days. They may stretch into years—years in which democracy will be tried to its very foundations. Many high school graduates will be going directly into the military services. All will assume vital roles as voting citizens. They must know and understand the meaning of world events in order to fulfill their responsibilities in our national life.[70]

PART THREE:
THE ELECTRONIC FIFTIES

5   The First Iowa Scoring Machine

. . . memory drum . . . transformation circuits . . . counters . . . converters . . . photocells . . . vacuum tubes . . . diodes . . . amplifiers . . . light source . . . reflectors . . . pulses . . . channels . . . synchronous drive . . . magnets and relays . . . registration . . .

DURING THE FIFTIES, on such technical elements was focused much of the thought, discussion, correspondence, travel, day work, and night work at Iowa Testing Programs and associated laboratories. Other ongoing activities of the department were eclipsed by the director's overriding obsession: to design and build, for ITP, the first electronic scoring machine.

The mission became harrowing at times. But it was accomplished. Not in a sophisticated industrial plant by high-powered corporation engineers, but in modestly equipped small shops by a pair of determined professors, fortuitously recruited local engineers, and technicians, pooling their ingenuity and expertise and using whatever materials and products could be tracked down, purchased, bent, adapted, rebuilt, or created to suit the need.

The work was begun in September 1952, with a target date of September 1953. The first model went into production scoring in the Iowa program in March 1955.

The original Iowa machine (it never acquired a name, either classical or cute) was initially estimated to cost $50,000 – $75,000. It cost nearer $200,000.

It made possible, within a matter of months, large-volume test processing service to schools across the nation, on a variety of test batteries and at a reasonable charge.

It made feasible the establishment of new nationwide testing programs that have served timely and important educational purposes.

It brought employment to hundreds in the Iowa City area alone.

It earned millions for the benefit of The University of Iowa, channeled principally into subsidies for research, support of student training, experimental educational projects, and a new, fully furnished building.

The Beginning

PROFESSOR LINDQUIST'S interest in scoring machines dated from the early thirties. His academic background in science and mathematics equipped him to understand early efforts in the field and to anticipate future possibilities. The International Business Machines Corporation pioneered with the introduction of its first model in 1936. Although a major advance by the standards of the time, it was a slow, manually operated device, unsuited for large-volume scoring. IBM also was at work then on the prototype of a photoelectric machine, the potential of which excited Lindquist's inventiveness. In midnight spare time he began dreaming up and sketching designs of his own involving various principles of mark reading and recording. In the forties he designed an analog computer. Early in the summer of 1952 he designed three monotone scale converters and initiated construction of one of them. Two of these were similar in principle to the converter later incorporated into the Iowa model, except that the latter employed magnetic marks on a memory drum instead of holes on an endless belt. The change was a Lindquist refinement of his original design.

In May of 1952 his interest in electronic (vs. mechanical) scoring was temporarily dashed by the negative reaction of a University of Iowa engineering professor. It was revived again in late summer following discussions with Professor Phillip J. Rulon of Harvard University, who was also president of the nonprofit Educational Research Corporation in Cambridge. Rulon and Lindquist were at this time consultants to a committee of the Air Training Command, meeting at Chanute Air Force Base in Rantoul, Illinois. Their common interest in educational and psychological measurement, in electronics, and in surmounting challenges, fused in a decision to tackle jointly Lindquist's brash proposal to construct a scoring machine from scratch, on a shoestring budget, and—as usual in Lindquist's undertakings—for immediate delivery. Perhaps the derring-do of that decision and the dogged refusal to abandon it against heavy odds bore as decisively upon the ultimate outcome as any single one of the brilliant ideas and solutions hatched along the way.

Lindquist had by now thought out the fundamental design for his scoring machine. In brief, *a specially designed answer sheet would pass under a row of phototubes in such a manner that each phototube would sense a mark in one of the boxes on the answer sheet when illuminated by a light source, and the pulses from this sensing would trigger a counter cumulating a total raw score for each test on the answer sheet; the raw score would be converted to a standard score in a converter unit; the standard score would be recorded by an output printer geared to the scoring device.*

He proposed using Multilith offset presses in both the answer sheet printing and the scoring, in order to assure identical registration in both functions. Furthermore, the conveyor belt feeding mechanism and the time cycle as the sheet of paper passed under the rotating drum seemed suitable to the scoring purposes. He hoped to procure technical engineering assistance from The University of Iowa College of Engineering and to have production work done in the university shops or by area contractors.

Dr. Rulon, who was himself knowledgeable in electronics, already had work contacts with a small company in Cambridge that had produced special devices for use in research projects undertaken by the Educational Research Corporation. He considered the Krohn-Hite Instrument Company well qualified to meet the new challenges posed.

At a subsequent meeting in Chicago, Lindquist and Rulon arrived at a tentative division of labor, subject to appropriate official approval. The plan was that the Educational Research Corporation (on a subcontract with Krohn-Hite) would be responsible for constructing the electronic components, power supply, and computer panel, while Iowa Testing Programs would concentrate on mechanics, the printing aspects, space arrangements, and final installation in Iowa City. Rulon would supervise all work done in Cambridge, and Lindquist all work done in Iowa, working closely with one another and exchanging ideas as work progressed.

In glowing and forceful terms, Dr. Lindquist had already informed University of Iowa President Virgil M. Hancher, Dean Elmer T. Peterson, and other colleagues about the feasibility and the possibilities of the projected invention, winning their enthusiastic support from the outset. President Hancher agreed to present the matter to the Iowa State Board of Education, which gave its blessing at a meeting on December 5, 1952. This formal approval, recorded in the minutes of the meeting (Fig. 15), authorized the president to execute contracts and any other instruments deemed necessary to realization of the project and to encumber a free balance in the Iowa Testing Programs fund for its achievement.

Accordingly, a formal basic agreement between The University of Iowa and the inventors was drawn up, enunciating the rights and

STATE UNIVERSITY OF IOWA
IOWA CITY
OFFICE OF THE PRESIDENT

A proposed record for the minutes of a meeting
of the
IOWA STATE BOARD OF EDUCATION
indicating action taken by the Board on

DEC 5 - 1952

SCORING MACHINE

COLLEGE OF EDUCATION. Upon the recommendation of President Hancher authorization was granted to construct an electro-mechanical computer of advanced design to accomplish savings in processing state-wide testing in primary, secondary, and higher education, promising opportunities to enlarge areas of fact research as well as mathematical research at the State University, involving:

a. Authority to the President of the State University to execute the contract proposed by Messers. Lindquist and Rulon providing for the above as well as the possibility of revenue to the University from commercial exploitation of the ideas involved.

b. Authority to the President of the State University to execute such ancillary instruments as will be found proper by him to carry out the above contract, such as, but not necessarily limited to
  (1) The retention of a business advisor or consultant to assist in the development program until such time as the non-Iowa, commercial aspects of the program can be independently established
  (2) To request the Attorney General for permission to retain such specialized legal counsel as may be necessary in the performance of the Lindquist-Rulon contract.

c. The encumbrance of free balance in the Iowa Testing Program fund for the achievement of the above objectives.

Copies to Provost Davis, Dean E. T. Peterson, Dr. Lindquist, Business Office (2)

AWD:hw

Fig. 15. Authorization for construction of first electronic scoring machine. *(From ITP files.) Note:* The present names of the state institutions in Iowa City and Ames had not yet been adopted in 1952. The former, now The University of Iowa, was then still called the State University of Iowa, as in Fig. 15.)

obligations of each in the undertaking. This historic document, dated December 8, 1952, was signed by President Hancher for the State and The University of Iowa and by inventors Lindquist and Rulon.

Under this contract, any ideas, plans, and designs for the scoring machine and ancillary equipment were described as the common-law property of the originators, Lindquist and Rulon, eligible for copyright or patent by them. The equipment would be constructed at university expense and become its property, for its use in testing programs or research conducted by the university for the benefit of education in the State of Iowa. No royalty would ever accrue to the inventors from such use. Any remaining rights to the equipment and the use of it rested with the originators. A limited pecuniary return would accrue to the inventors out of any revenues which might be realized from those rights during a period not to exceed ten years. The contract further envisioned the early establishment of a separate nonprofit entity for marketing the services of the machine beyond the uses and needs of the university and for further research and machine development; it pledged the efforts of all three parties toward early accomplishment of this goal. Royalty within the limits delineated would be paid to the originators by that entity. Any net income over the costs of operations and of research and development would be available to The University of Iowa for educational research uses, particularly within the College of Education.

A corollary agreement dated January 2, 1953, between the university and the Educational Research Corporation detailed the performance obligations and financial responsibility of both organizations, the substance of which was that ERC agreed to produce designated electronic components by September 14, 1953, at a cost to the university not to exceed $50,000. These stipulations vividly reflect the euphoria of all participants at that time!

Action mounted rapidly on both fronts in the fall of 1952—with such vigor and promise that the nonexistent prototype was promptly dubbed the "February model."* Messrs. Krohn and Hite "foresaw no technical difficulties" in the proposals, and everyone spoke confidently of scoring "next September" (1953). Pencil-type photocells of the right size readily were located, as well as the small lucite rods needed to guide light to them. This combination, in early trials, seemed to assure equality of light transmission to the photocells. Actually, considerable experimentation with spacing, angling, and so on, became necessary to accommo-

---

*Quotations in this chapter not specifically referenced are from correspondence between E. F. Lindquist and Phillip J. Rulon during the developmental period from September 1952 through July 1955.

date the number of cells and rods needed for the planned number of answer boxes on the answer sheet.

Almost from the outset, "better ways" were being found. For example, Krohn-Hite recommended adopting the Davidson offset press instead of the Multilith, because the larger drum on the former allowed a longer interval between answer sheets for performance of calculations. Lindquist discovered an "add-on" counter that looked promising. He was also having ideas for the design of a "comparator" unit for coping with multiple marks and bad erasures. He resumed earlier discussions with the Mast Development Company (of Davenport) about handling the mechanical modifications necessary to installing sensing heads on the Davidson, and also requested Mr. Gifford Mast to investigate tabulators or other printout equipment suitable for hookup to the scoring machine. It was recognized that the speed of the entire installation would have to be geared to the speed of the printing mechanism, the probable maximum being the 5,400 answer sheets per hour (90 per minute) that was the top speed of both the Davidson and the IBM printing tabulator. Meanwhile Lindquist was thinking out how to adapt the Davidson for experimental runs of a single-column answer sheet on which to test the sensing of graphite pencil marks. He was experimenting also with other types of mark sensing by photoelectric or magnetic process, and investigating the possibility of having special pencils custom-made—a need eliminated by later technical developments. Lindquist and Rulon together determined the specifications for the master answer sheet: its dimensions (8½-by-11 inches), the number and spacing of rows on the sheet, the size and number of rectangles for response marks (5,400 total on both sides), and so on. These specifications affected many aspects of the units being engineered in Cambridge.

Standard products were being investigated for possible incorporation into the scoring machine components—germanium diodes, magnetic amplifiers, static memory drums, and so on. Krohn-Hite began work on designing a unit for converting raw scores to standard scores. Rulon designed a possible mechanism for controlling the printing type bars by vacuum tubes, and a transformation circuit for transforming nine test scores into a total score as well as changing raw scores to standard scores. Many of these designs were but steps along the way. Few of the early ideas did not undergo changes, minor or radical, in subsequent months, and some were abandoned in favor of more efficient methods, but they were all part of the evolution of Model 1.

By mid-October Lindquist had designed in detail an item analysis unit involving mark sensing and 300–500 electrical counters, which, characteristically, he wanted to have ready for use on experimental units of the *Iowa Tests of Basic Skills* in February 1953! The visionary cast of this notion was obvious enough. It was agreed that all effort had to be concentrated on *scoring* first.

Lindquist and Rulon each independently worked out circuits for counting response marks on the answer sheet (Fig. 16). Under the direction of Mr. Mast, in consultation with Professor Elmer Lundquist of the University of Iowa College of Engineering,* work progressed on the mounting of sensing heads in a stripped-down Davidson offset press. In continuing midnight meditation, Lindquist "figured out a way of scoring the *Strong Interest Blank* for any number of vocations in a single run of the answer sheet through the mark sensor," but needed help on "how to feed nine, eight, seven, etc., pulses into a counter from a single pulse from the sensing unit." This subproject also had to be shelved for the time being.

A Davidson purchased for the printing of answer sheets was set up in Iowa City. Trials on accuracy of registration—so critical to subsequent scoring—appeared satisfactory.

During an October visit to the Remington Rand Laboratories in South Norwalk, Massachusetts, Lindquist and Rulon decided to utilize the output printer of a punched card tabulator constructed by the Compagnie des Machines Bull. It was made available to Iowa Testing through the Remington Rand Corporation, although the $11,100 price tag was higher than had been anticipated. Work on separate but related engineering tasks had to be coordinated—such as collecting in counters all the data to be fed into the Bull during a single cycle, and completing promptly the phototube shakedown. The availability of a loan machine from RemRand for development work, pending delivery of new printers to ITP, was an important factor in the selection of the Bull. But a chain of miseries stretched between this decision and the ultimate installation of a new printer from Paris.

In mid-November Robert A. Edberg, a graduate engineer of The University of Iowa, left Collins Radio Company in Cedar Rapids to join the scoring machine project. From December 1952 through June 1953, Edberg worked with the engineering staff in Cambridge on design and production problems; then he returned to work on the Iowa City front, particularly on assembly and installation of components. In Cambridge Edberg worked closely with Dr. Rulon, Earl Krohn, and Andrejs Varenais, a Latvian engineer on loan from the Krohn-Hite

---

*Other members of The University of Iowa College of Engineering associated in varying degrees with early stages of the scoring machine development were Samuel Harding, J. M. Trummel, and Lawrence A. Ware.

EARLY DESIGNS BY E. F. LINQUIST FOR COMPONENTS OF THE FIRST SCORING MACHINE *(FIGS. 16 A-C)*

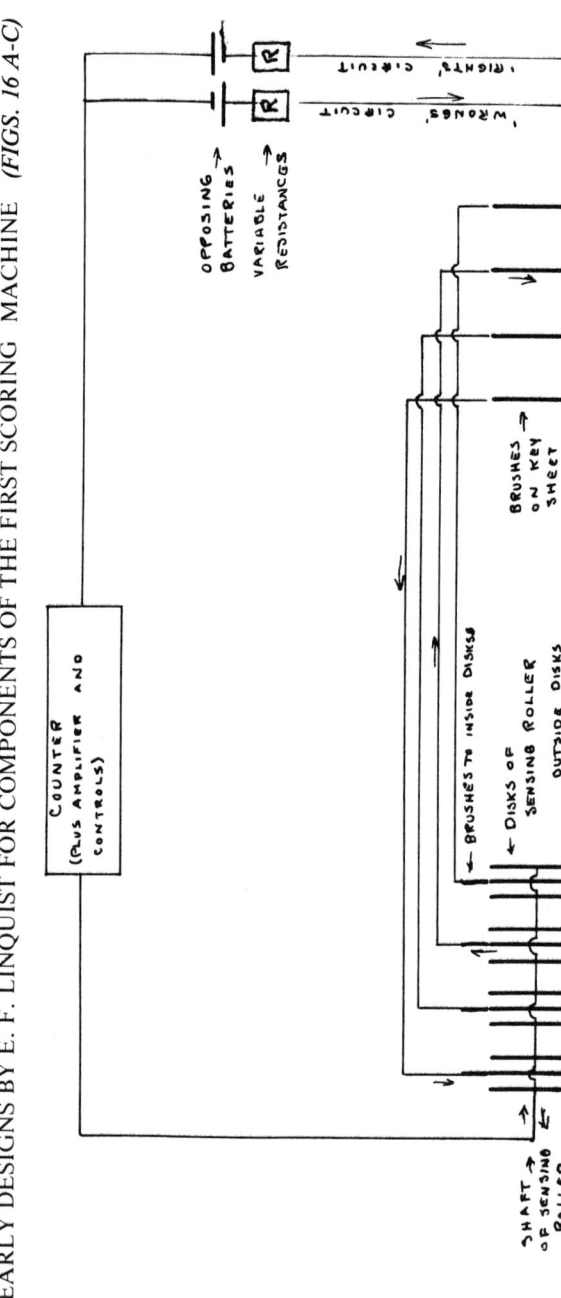

Fig. 16 (A). Counter circuits.

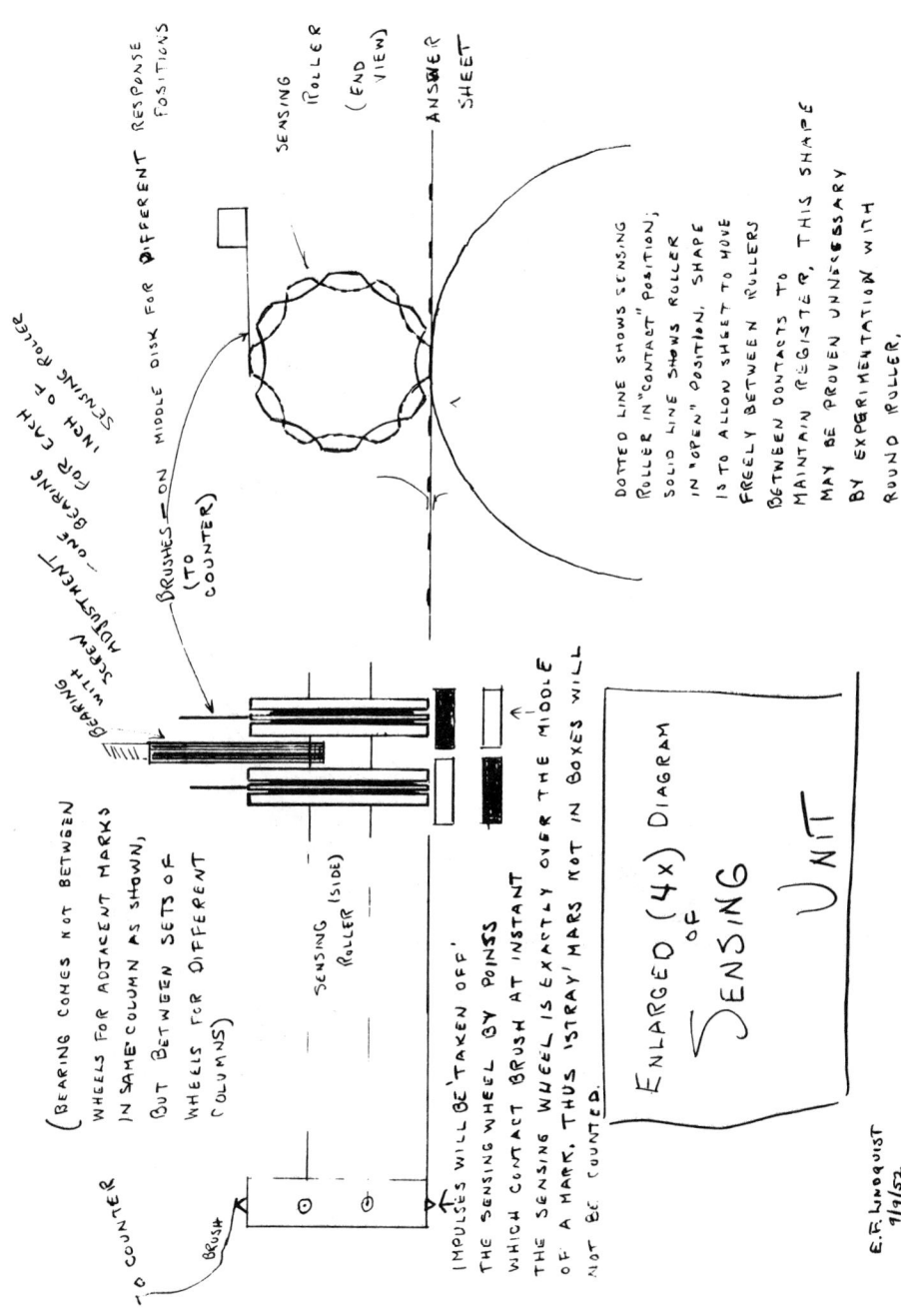

Fig. 16 (B). Mark sensing unit.

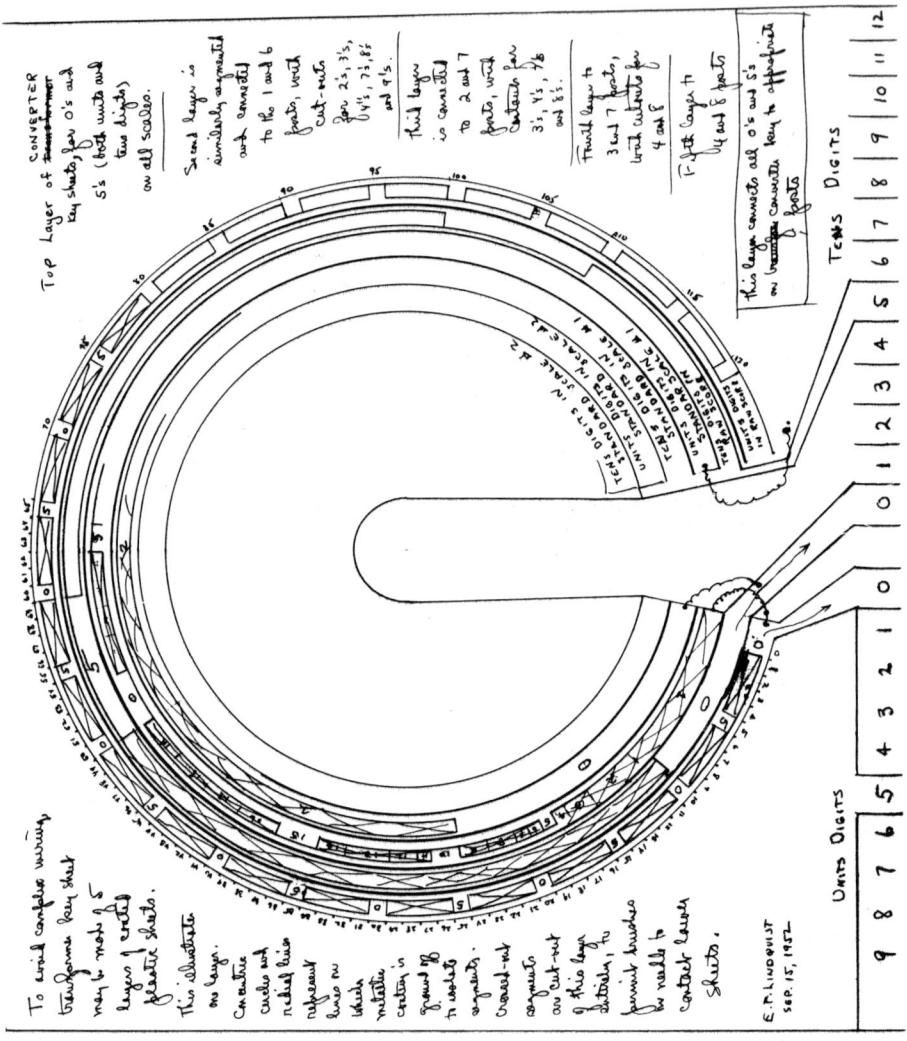

Fig. 16 (C). Device for converting raw scores to standard scores (1952).

staff. Edberg's work through this period has been described by all his co-workers as brilliant and thorough, contributing importantly to the design of various components and the cutting of production knots. Varenais' expertise and persistence through many crises won similar praise.

In late November 1952 Lindquist supplied Cambridge with memos and prints describing his ideas "for coding, storing, and transmitting alphabetic information to the Bull printer" and for other elements, including the basic circuit (Fig. 17), with a plea of urgency in deciding which solution to the whole problem of mark sensing "we are going to place our bets on for the initial Iowa model." By late December he and Rulon were in agreement on the desirability of using a magnetic memory drum for the scoring keys if doing so would not delay the "February model." Original ideas by both inventors for the use of a magnetic memory drum in the converter were combined as the basis for a joint patent obtained later on such a device.

To save time and travel expense, the occasional conferences between the two inventors were usually held in connection with other events at fortuitous times and locations—in Boston, New York, Norwalk, Chicago, Atlantic City, at Lackland Air Force Base (where both served as advisers), in terminals and planes en route to special assignments, in hotel rooms after professional meetings, and other sometimes unlikely places. Gaps between meetings were bridged by telephone or correspondence—long chatty letters from Rulon, short terse notes from Lindquist.

By February 1953 the so-called "February model" became the "July model" of the scoring machine, and a reexamination of priorities in its development seemed in order. The minimum functions to be performable by the July model now were listed as: score the *Iowa Tests of Educational Development* and print out, with the Bull, the serial number, converted scores, and converted sum of converted scores from each answer sheet. Additional functions, such as the reading and printout of pupil names, would have to wait a little longer.

A Davidson press that had been adapted in Iowa City for scoring, arrived (somewhat damaged) in Cambridge for completion of engineering and installation of the sensing head. Now new problems were encountered in sheet feeding and in the interrelationship of light source, reflectors, and photocells. Sometimes seemingly minor difficulties became major headaches. Varied anxieties are voiced in correspondence between the shops, such as:

> There is too much sideways motion of the chain which carries the answer sheet.

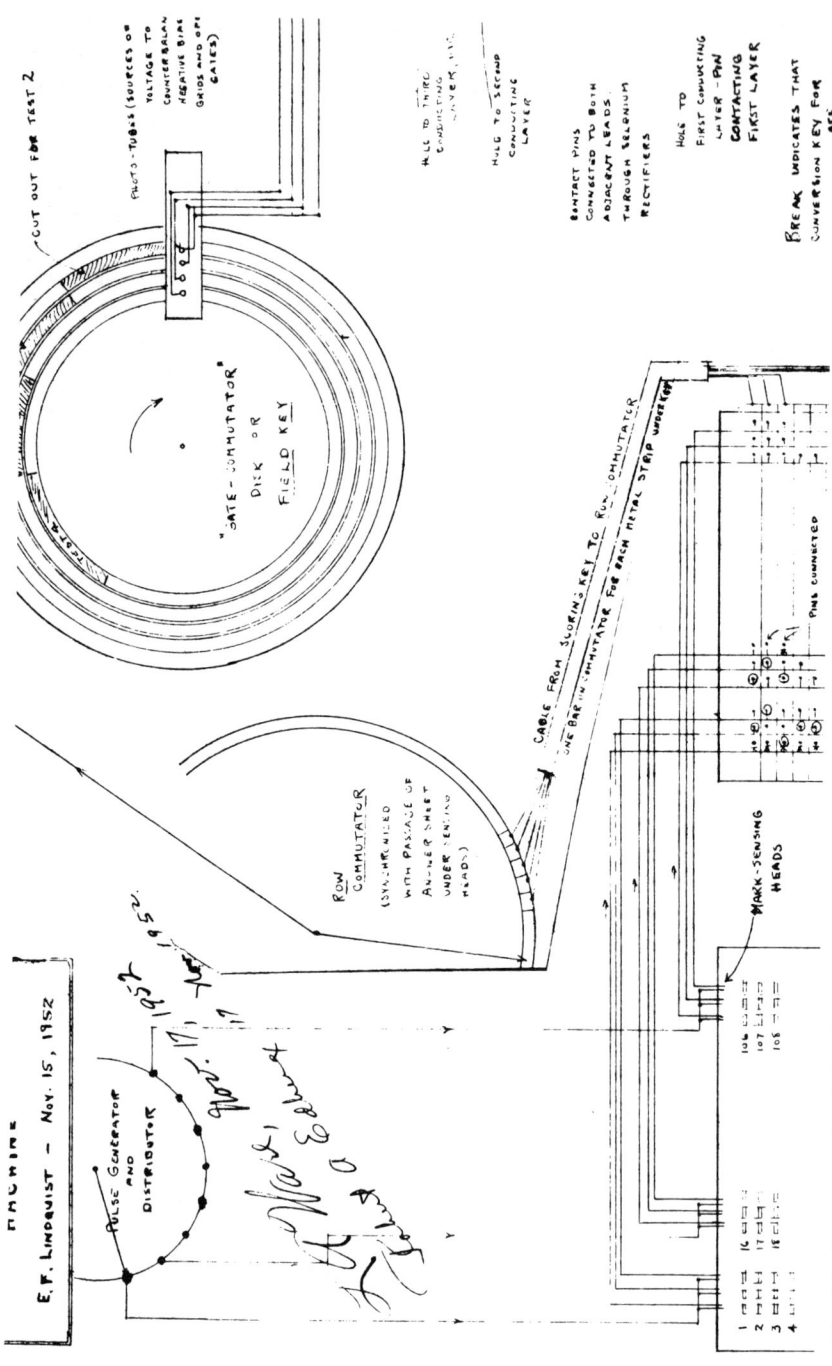

Fig. 17. Design by E. F. Lindquist of basic circuit for the first scoring machine, attested by consultant L.A. Ware and chief engineer Robert A. Edberg (detail).

The business of having a headlamp (automobile) . . . show light on mirrors underneath the photocells is not going to work.

It may be necessary to paint the discs black to keep from having irregularities in the light.

We have found a man to coat the drum for us.

And so on. Photocells bought in quantity from the factory behaved differently and were less sensitive than those purchased locally for experimentation. There was delay in Davenport in the construction of a stand for the Bull printer, and trouble in Iowa City with registration in the printing of answer sheets. Experimentation with various kinds of answer sheet paper proceeded slowly. Urgent discussions were held with The University of Iowa architect toward air conditioning the room in which the July model would be set up. On the plus side, a binary decade counter was operating successfully in the "bread-board stage." The circuitry for this counter had been designed by Varenais and Krohn.

The used Bull printer, promised months earlier as a loan, finally was delivered from Norwalk in April—a rather battered specimen in sticky condition. Meanwhile, concern was mounting about various aspects of this choice of a printer: the engineering necessary to tie the Bull in with the Davidson and to design and construct a paper feed mechanism; the high total cost; the lack of adequate information (despite repeated efforts to obtain it) about delivery of new printers; service and parts availability; and so on.

An opportunity to obtain firsthand information and cooperation from the manufacturers occurred in May 1953, during a European trip that Mr. and Mrs. Lindquist and daughter Louise had been planning for over a year. Considering the state of the scoring machine project, Lindquist might have postponed this vacation jaunt indefinitely except for the possibility of consulting with the appropriate persons at the Bull plant in Paris. In that Gallic camp, this proved a rather formidable assignment for an American professor/tourist, not fluent in French, already worried to a state of ill health, and frustrated by waits, ambiguous replies, and scant rapprochement. Ultimately, he did manage to stir some executive concern for ITP's needs, to learn a great deal more about the Bull equipment, and to exact seeming reassurance about maintenance, delivery, and so forth. All this was relayed to Rulon by transatlantic telephone—in the middle of the night, after repeated connection delays.

Lindquist continued the tour, but not without misgivings. The Iowa

July model was a fourth party on that tour, a constant presence of sufficient dimensions to block the recollection of many memorable scenes from Brittany to Stockholm. Nervousness mounted. Would a new printer really be delivered in time for the ITED fall scoring? Would RemRand demand return of the loan machine prematurely? Was it wise to order *any* equipment from France before *all* engineering hurdles had been jumped?

On learning from Cambridge that a RemRand engineer, L. Y. Chaloux, would be in Paris opportunely, Lindquist arranged a meeting there on the return lap of his vacation. Together, he and Chaloux spent a frantic day of conferences with the Bull people and transatlantic conversations with RemRand, pressuring both offices into a promise of three-month delivery on a new Bull printer. Chaloux's French background helped pry open official doors, elicit information, and ultimately restore a degree of confidence in the original decision.

At the time, that long day in Paris seemed the darkest possible hour. But ten days later a message from Edberg prophesied that "the scoring machine will not be scoring answer sheets in Iowa City before July, 1954, at the earliest." In Lindquist's own words, this pronouncement threw him into "the worst dither . . . [I have] experienced in this project, and I've had some dandies before." He considered abandoning the present design (if not the entire project), stewed about finances, and beseeched Rulon to examine the engineering prospects minutely before Lindquist's return from Paris on July 6 (Figs. 18 and 19).

He went directly to Cambridge and there shed some of his despair. Though the engineering work was still running behind schedule, a number of recent developments were encouraging. Problems relating to the use of lucite rods for conducting light to the photocells were diminishing. The use of selenium diodes in the counter circuits would reduce the amount of power input necessary (and correspondingly the amount of air conditioning). A prototype raw score counter was being built, design work having been completed. It appeared possible to erase scoring keys with the same heads planned for recording and reading. Many problems remained, of course, including sheet feeding on the Davidson, and time was certainly critical.

Finances also had become critical. This problem, too, Dr. Lindquist grappled with while in Cambridge. In view of their involvement in the situation, the Educational Research Corporation and the Krohn-Hite Instrument Company offered loans in the form of payment delays for certain salaries and services. Houghton Mifflin Company, the publishers of the *Iowa Tests of Basic Skills*, offered an advance against future royalties on the tests. With these offers in hand, Lindquist by telephone arranged an impromptu scoring demonstration in Cambridge

Paris, France, June 14, 1953

Dear Phil —

Your letters of June 9 and 10 reached me yesterday. I hope my last letter and enclosures have cleared matters up a bit, but perhaps I had better try to state more explicitly some of the things I have meant to say or imply earlier.

When I sent you my last cable, it looked to me as if we might not be able to get a new printer for six or eight months. I have enough general understanding of our project, I hope, to know that we can get along without a printer for a few weeks at a time, but I knew also that we can't do so for six months continuously. Accordingly, I have been doing my desperate best to keep continuous possession of a printer. I have taken the line that anything else may prove disastrous to our project, and that R-R is morally obligated to see us through. I didn't want to take a chance of having my position weakened again by an admission from you that "a few weeks without a printer would not harm us seriously" — true as that may be. I do not mean to imply any criticism of you for having made the statement, — when you made it you were assuming, of course, as we all were at the time, that six weeks delivery on a new printer was possible.

The situation now looks much more promising than at first. R-R has ordered a new printer from Bull, and as a result of pressures applied here last week, have been promised three months delivery on it. Chaloux and I have hopes that R-R will use the tabulator printer at Newark until the new one arrives, and that we may get to keep the spare printer until our own new printer is delivered. As soon as we are assured of this, I will release the order for our printer, but I hope I won't have to do so otherwise.

As to where the spare printer may best be used in the meantime, that is a matter for us all to agree upon after I return. Certainly it should be used where we all feel it can be used to best advantage. I had hoped that the design and testing of basic circuits in isolation is nearly completed, and that from now on the major "developmental" work would consist of shaking down the different parts in the integration process. I had assumed this could best be done in the permanent location of the machine at Iowa City. Apparently, I was mistaken. If general progress is not as far advanced as I had thought, at any rate, will use the printer — if we are permitted to keep it — wherever you all think is best.

I certainly have no intention of calling K-H off the project until it is completed — completed in the sense in which we have all understood the eventual "Iowa model" will take. Apparently, from present indications, this may mean something like another six months. I do expect the integration and final shake down runs, and the adding of the whistles and bells to take place in Iowa City. When this means that "most of the developmental work" will be shifted to Iowa City remains to be seen.

Fig. 18. Letter from E. F. Lindquist to Phillip Rulon, June 14, 1953. (ITP files)

- 2 -

I'm afraid my letter to Bob, which was written hastily and under considerable stress when things looked worst here, didn't convey my real thoughts very successfully. I have never doubted that our machine can be made to work, given sufficient time and money to spend on it. I have only worried about whether we are going to run out of funds before it does work. The implications of Bob's "next year" cable are that the machine is going to cost considerably more than I had planned it would. The longer the time needed for completion, the less we can afford early investment in expensive printers, especially in duplicate. I had always hoped we wouldn't have to make that investment until we were almost ready to go into production or scoring. What I really wanted from Bob was an assurance that the machine would begin to be income-producing before the end of the year. If it is not, and if we have to pay for two printers in the meantime, I'm going to have to find someway to borrow money. Accordingly, Bob's cable makes it all the more important that we secure continued use of the Spar printer as long as possible, and that we postpone the date of purchase of the new printer, especially the second, as long as possible.

Bob's report about the phototubes troubles me considerably. I wonder if you have sufficiently investigated other available phototubes. I understand that Bull is using a small phototube ($\frac{1}{4}$", I think) very successfully in its mark sensing equipment. I think their tube is manufactured by Phillips — I'm trying to get more dope on it. They are used, I'm told, to sense the presence of a numeral written in pencil on a square this size ☐ and the numeral is sometimes a rather thin "1", e.g. → ☐. They said they had had trouble at first with variable tubes, but that their present tubes are very uniform in their characteristics. Bull, by the way, leads the light to the tubes through lucite rods shaped before thus, ⌐══╕ ⌐══╕, and alternated, so as to crowd in seven tubes to the inch.

Again, please let Bob read this at your earliest convenience.

Best regards,

Lin

Hotel du Quai Voltaire
Paris, France
June 23, 1953

Dear Phil —

Ed Lindquist's last letter, with the statement "the (scoring) machine will not be scoring answer sheets in Iowa City before July 1954 at the earliest" — is so utterly inconsistent with all previous indications and implications — throws me into the worst dither I've experienced with this project, and I've had some dandies before. I guess I was in a weakened condition from the beating I've been getting over the RR-Bell business. If this means that we must spend over $5000 per month with ERC-K-H and also support Bob and his shop in Iowa City for over another year or more, before the machine begins earning — it looks as if we do really, (really?) need (?) the best thing to do is to abandon the present design (if not the project) and see if we can find another which will permit us to begin scoring much sooner, if even with design spirits. If he means that a "complete" machine, which will score a 14 test battery with 3 subtotals and convert both to standard scores and percentiles cannot be promised before that time, — But that a machine which will score the ITED and convert only to standard scores (but not percentiles) and cumulate them, can be ready in January, perhaps we can pull through. Even then, however, it appears that will have a machine which cannot be profitably duplicated, and one that may be quite expensive to maintain and operate.

At any rate, I'm now over the dithers, and am hoping for the best.

You may not hear from me again before you see me in Cambridge on the evening of July 6th. Please make a hotel reservation for me — I'd go directly to the Continental in the hopes you can find a room for me there. I'm depending on you to put your exhibit until 10 work on this problem and to have a hopeful solution ready for me when I return.

I talked to Chalmers this morning and he says he has heard nothing from RRuno since I last wrote you, but he considers that a sign that they may have decided to let us have the position.

Looking forward to seeing you again soon,
Lin

Fig. 19. Letter from Lindquist to Rulon, June 23, 1953. (ITP files)

specially for Mr. Fred Ambrose, the University of Iowa business manager, who was vacationing in the East, and Mr. William Spaulding, vice president of Houghton Mifflin Company. The outcome was heartening.

> The demonstration . . . was very successful and convincing. It consisted in part of printing on the Bull printer a column of letters which had been entered in coded form on a series of answer sheets exactly like those which will be used in our finished machine. These sheets were passed under the phototubes at exactly the same rate as in the finished machine. The demonstration consisted also of printing a three-digit score for each answer sheet, although the "score" came from pulses generated in a standard pulse generator rather than from pulses arising from marks on the answer sheet. However, the score was recorded in a raw score counter identical with that which will be used in our finished machine, and was converted from binary to decimal form and recorded in a conversion counter identical with that designed for the finished machine. Thus we proved that we can accurately sense pencil marks on answer sheets fed at the intended rate of 6000 sheeets per hour, and that we can print on the Bull printer exactly the same kind of information that will be printed in the finished machine. In other words, we demonstrated that we can perform all of the crucial operations that are involved. The problem from now on is therefore primarily one of multiplying and of producing in finished form units or components which have already been designed and tested.[71]

Mr. Ambrose not only approved acceptance of the proffered loans, but also

> assured me [Lindquist] that if still larger amounts are needed there will be no difficulty about securing them as advances from the University General Fund during the coming biennium. . . . This arrangement with ERC and Krohn-Hite will give our engineers a special incentive to complete the machine on scheduled time and will constitute very convincing evidence to others of the confidence of the engineers that the machine can be completed in that time. Again, then, it appears that we have found a solution to what for a time seemed an almost insoluble problem.[72]

Again, priorities had to be reviewed and heavy pressure exerted to accomplish completion and shakedown during the summer of prototypes of the components essential to the basic scoring function.

The Announcement

WIDESPREAD interest in scoring machines had grown rapidly during 1953, as Dr. Lindquist had anticipated. The Educational Testing Service was reputed to be considering construction of an electrical machine that would score marks made by electrographic pencil. A

Minneapolis firm, Engineers Northwest, placed on the market a $50,000 photoelectric machine claimed capable of reading the darkest of multiple response marks and of converting and printing a single score on an answer sheet, but at a speed of only 200 per hour. Armed Forces committees were scouting for high-speed equipment to process a rapidly increasing amount of military testing. Test publishers and metropolitan school administrators expressed interest in negotiating for processing services and or equipment.

Lindquist recognized the importance of gaining a lead in this market. The ability to provide scoring service would permit widening the sale of the ITED and the ITBS outside Iowa. The royalties that would thus accrue to ITP and the university were badly needed to offset the escalating construction cost of the scoring machine. A secondary goal was to supply processing service to the publishers of other test batteries and to commercial or government agencies. Although it now appeared impossible to take on the latter type of business for another eighteen months, early publicity about the equipment and its capabilities would give prospective customers time to reach decisions, make plans, and design materials compatible with the specs of the Iowa equipment. Accordingly, Lindquist elected to gamble with the fates of engineering and unveil the unfinished invention.

He did so at the Invitational Conference on Testing Problems in New York on October 31, 1953. The text of his address to the conference was released to the press at the same time and was subsequently published in the *Proceedings of the Conference*.[73]

The announcement was quite comprehensive. It described the principal features of the equipment, its sensitivities and capabilities (demonstrated or anticipated), the principles of structure governing certain of its functions, its speed, the design of the answer sheet to be employed, the superiority of electronic scoring over hand scoring methods, the target dates for completion of construction and for acceptance of orders for scoring service, and the procedure evolved for offering the service through a nonprofit corporation, the Measurement Research Center.

In a different vein, the talk dwelt at some length on the significance of electronic test processing for educational and psychological measurement and research in general. Salient points made were: It would afford faster return of results in large-scale programs, more comprehensive services, and new types of reports. It would reduce the cost of testing and the administrative inconveniences to the schools. It would facilitate inauguration of new cooperative programs providing specialized benefits to the members. Publishers could offer processing service from a central agency as part of the purchase price of tests sold for independent use by individual school districts. New types of tests requiring formula

108   The Iowa Testing Programs

scoring too complex for manual methods could become practicable with electronic equipment. For educational and psychological research, such a rapid, low-cost means of analyzing results from experimental tests, questionnaires, surveys, and so forth, opened possibilities hitherto unattempted or unattainable.

The announcement sparked lively comment at the conference and widespread interest generally—as clippings in the ITP archives attest. So, in another derring-do, all bridges were burned. This was *the* point of no return.

Struggle

THAT SPEECH would haunt its maker for months to come. The distance between announcement and fulfillment lengthened, cluttered with technical problems and procurement complications.

The Bull printer, promised for October, arrived from France in December—damaged and without ribbons, spare parts, or tools.

"There is cross-talk in the cables" of the converted score counter, one communique' from Cambridge reported.

There was cross-talk in the cables between Iowa City and Cambridge, too, and mounting tension at both ends.

It was evident now that Bob Edberg's gloomy prediction six months earlier was sound. There really could not be a "July model" until the summer of 1954, and no scoring of an ITP program before the following September. Meanwhile, engineering costs in Cambridge already had passed the original estimate by one-third.

By mid-January 1954 it was possible to stage a simple scoring demonstration in Cambridge for UI President Hancher, but only after Professor Rulon and an assistant had worked all night setting it up and tuning the phototubes. From realistically marked answer sheets, a tape list of raw test scores was produced. It was not the demonstration Lindquist had hoped for, nor was the scoring perfect, but it was good enough to convince Dr. Hancher that the idea of scoring electronically was sound and should be supported to fulfillment, even though the ITP accounts might remain temporarily in deep arrears.

The struggle went on. A critical problem of unequal wear in the chains of the feeding mechanism on the Davidson occupied a great deal of engineering time in Cambridge. After several months of frustration, this was finally solved in Iowa City through the use of a special steel tape-chain-gripper-bar assembly invented by Lindquist and fabricated by Edberg. During the spring of 1954 several components of the production model were assembled and delivered to Iowa City, including the converted-score counter rack and the read and write amplifier racks, but others (the timing rack, printer rack, and phototube amplifier rack) did not arrive until summer. Still others were not complete even then.

Meanwhile, the Iowa City staff had wrestled and resolved many technical difficulties associated with the printing of the answer sheets. One major and time-consuming task was the selection of a paper stock possessing the required properties of durability, homogeneity, a satisfactory degree of opacity for the proper amount of light transmission, and true cut. (Maintaining a consistent, dependable source of supply at an acceptable price remained a recurrent problem in succeeding years.) Lindquist's researches into the paper market led to discussions with the president of a Michigan paper company, who became so intrigued by the scoring machine project and the inherent challenge to paper manufacture that he elected to oversee personally the formulation of a paper stock that would meet the need. An important element in the making of this paper was the manner in which the pulp filaments were laid down to assure homogeneity and stability of structure. Blotchiness in the paper would interfere with light transmission; in the extreme, it conceivably could trigger false pulses to the score counter. The thickness or caliper of the paper was also important, as well as exactitude in the final trimming. And the amount of moisture in the finished paper had to be closely controlled.

Maintenance (or restoration) of this moisture level during the stages of printing, shipping, marking, and scoring the answer sheets presented another hurdle. If the paper became significantly drier or wetter at any of these stages, resulting changes in sheet dimensions would distort the position of the trigger marks and response marks under the photocells and could cause misreading. In the early production of answer sheets, humidity in the printing room on the third floor of East Hall was maintained with an ordinary room humidifier. The *de*humidifier for hot summer days was more primitive: bags of calcium chloride crystals slung from racks above pans (pig feeders?), which sopped moisture from the air blown across them by oscillating fans. Eventually, after basement rooms for both printing and scoring were air-conditioned, Lindquist invented another device for controlling paper humidity. This was a homemade, "Rube Goldberg-ish" ferris wheel that carried the answer sheets slowly around its circumference on protruding metal spines (Plate 9). The rate of motion was set so that one trip on the wheel sufficiently exposed the sheet to the conditioned air of the room to bring its moisture content to a satisfactory level. This ingenious thing picked up and released the sheets automatically from and to small stack-

110   The Iowa Testing Programs

Plate 9. (Above) Device for normalizing the moisture content of answer sheet paper, observed by the inventor, E. F. Lindquist.
(At right) The device after enlargement and improvement.

ing trucks that had also been designed and built locally. Moisture was measured by a swordlike hygrometer thrust into the reams of paper. Sometimes whole shipments of *new* paper had to be conditioned before printing because the moisture content varied from specifications. On such occasions operators worked three shifts to maintain a ready supply of conditioned white paper.*

Professor Lindquist devoted full time to the scoring machine project in the summer of 1954, perfecting various design and production procedures. He improved the adaptation of the Bull printer to its new use, and personally designed a new skip mechanism for advancing multicopy forms through the printer.

By August the venture had reached its most exciting phase: installation and shakedown of the finished components arriving from Cambridge. Varenais was dispatched to Iowa City to assist Edberg in this painstaking work. They spent the next several months transforming an empty basement room of East Hall (Plate 10) into a marvel of blinking

Plate 10. East Hall, birthplace of all the episodes in this history; subsequently renamed Seashore Hall. (1958 photo.)

*During long-term service as supervisor of the printing and platemaking functions, Edward ("Ned") Davitt learned firsthand the peculiarities of printing documents for optical scanning and participated in solving problems and meeting requirements as they evolved.

112 *The Iowa Testing Programs*

Plate 11. Views of the first electronic scoring machine: *(A)* Model 1 being studied by engineers Robert Edberg and Andrejs Varenais and originator E. F. Lindquist. *(B)* The scoring room and Mod. 1 tended by John Dolch. *(C)* The other side of the circuit panels, one section opened to reveal interior cabling. *(D)* A scoring run being monitored by Edberg; answer sheet printing area visible in right background.

The First Iowa Scoring Machine 113

panels backed by a forest of cables that could ingest pulsations and emit a record of achievement from the brief encounter of small black marks on paper and the photocells in a reading head (Plate 11).

While this archetype was taking shape, the Fall Program answer sheets had to be hand scored as before. All engineering effort was now trained toward electronic scoring of the ITBS in January. In mid-January Lindquist reported to Rulon that 1,200 pupil-marked ITBS answer sheets had been scored with a degree of accuracy better than that in verified hand scoring. He hoped to be ready to do large-scale scoring for reporting purposes in another three weeks.

Victory

AT LAST success seemed a reality. But it came in limping, and might not have arrived in time (if at all) without what Rulon termed "the intervention of Providence." Some months earlier a new phototube had become available that seemed especially well suited to this project. An advance sample order of tubes obtained had tested out very satisfactorily. However, to the utter dismay of Lindquist and company, the production units delivered later in quantity failed to live up to specifications and to the claims of the manufacturer. Still other brands were hastily tried, but all exhibited the same weakness as earlier ones: They could not be kept properly "tuned" during continuous scoring. A phototube reading the same mark might produce a stronger signal at one time than at another. A consequence of this instability in the phototubes was that a weak (or erased) mark for a given test item might yield a stronger signal than a denser (intentional) mark for the same item, thus causing an error in scoring.

Once more, gloom shrouded the Lindquist camp. One hundred thirty thousand answer sheets awaited scoring. Some 645 school systems awaited their Basic Skills results. The harried inventor conferred constantly with the engineers and with ITBS Director Hieronymus, his consultant, confidant, comforter, and cosufferer throughout these years of electronic crises. Daily and nightly, they considered ways and means of solving this one—even the extreme alternative of returning all those answer sheets to the schools with keys for hand scoring.*

---

*On many occasions, the captains and the crew were sustained at midnight with snacks of sandwiches prepared and delivered personally to East Hall by Mrs. Lindquist and Mrs. Hieronymus. For many ITP families the scoring machine project was one more episode in a long train of sufferances.

An unbelievably timely development averted disaster. A solid-state germanium photodiode was introduced that had the same electrical properties as the phototube devices employed in the original machine design, but was far more consistent in performance. Coincidentally, it had the proper dimensions to fit exactly the holes which had been made for the lucite rods in the reading head. Its compactness was a bonus advantage. On special entreaty, delivery of the quantity needed by ITP was expedited. The wayward phototubes and the lucite rods were yanked out of the scoring machine and hastily replaced. (Model 1 is shown in Plate 11.)

During this changeover, Professor Hieronymus continued his pacification crusade, explaining delays and revising promises to participants in the ITBS program. Iowa educators were quite sympathetic and reasonably patient. Perhaps they were almost as eager for the advent of machine scoring as the inventors themselves. This was fortunate, because some had already waited as long as two months for the results of their January testing.

When the day in March arrived on which Professors Lindquist and Hieronymus, scanning yet another printout (Fig. 20) of ITBS scores, jointly decided to "let her roll," the processing of the answer sheets could scarcely be called automated. Only one scoring key at a time could be recorded on the scoring equipment. Because each grade level answer sheet had to be scanned with a different key, it was necessary to separate all incoming answer sheets by grades for scoring and to reassemble them by school later. Furthermore, with some components still forthcoming from Cambridge and suppliers, the incomplete equipment could not yet read and reproduce pupil names from the marked name grids (alphabet columns) on the answer sheets. The sheets carried no other identification. To have numbered all of them by hand would have added to the delays. Hence, the following procedure was devised: In each stack of answer sheets, on every tenth sheet a machine readable serial number was marked before the scoring. The scoring machine listed horizontally on a two-part form the converted scores from each answer sheet. When the stack had been scored, it was carted *gingerly* from the basement scoring room to the first floor office, where typists using electric typewriters transcribed the pupil names from the answer sheets to the corresponding lines on the list. The numbered tenth sheets served as benchmarks in verification of the name typing. The original sequence of the answer sheets had to be maintained absolutely in all this handling. Had any stack been upset, reorganization and rescoring would have been necessary.

The originals of these lists were mailed to the schools. Dr. Hieronymus still considers it a remarkable feat that in this first nerve-wracking

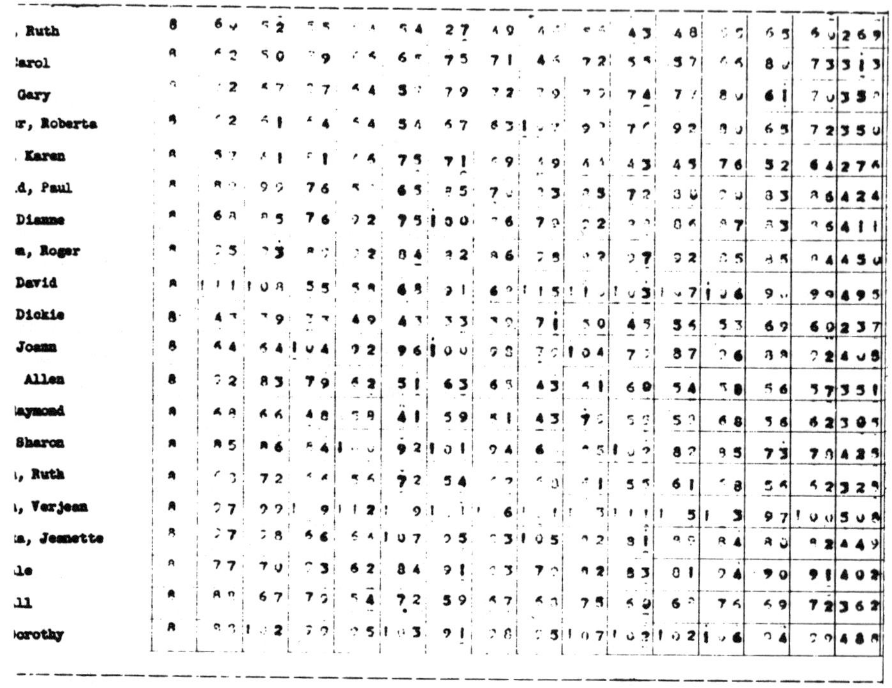

Fig. 20. A printout of ITBS scores from the run that signaled the start of electronic scoring, March 1955. (Typed names purposely obscured in this figure.)

attempt to score a major program, it actually was possible to obtain directly from the scanner-plus-printer a usable list of grade-equivalent scores, including total scores on the three multipart tests and a grand total on the battery. The scoring machine was programmed to arrive at the test total by adding the appropriate fraction of each part score— for example, one-fourth in a four-part test. Somehow, for technical reasons long since forgotten, the machine could not yet simply divide the sum of the part scores by the number of parts in the test.

There were a few deficiencies in these lists. The results shown for the battery were sums, not averages, of the test totals. The recipients were asked to compute each pupil's battery average by doubling the reported sum and pointing off one decimal place—a simple shortcut to dividing the sum by five. The results could be entered in a right-hand blank column. Another shortcoming was that the continuous forms used for these listings had no headroom for identifications and column titles. Therefore, a separate caption sheet that could be positioned to fit the list form during usage was supplied.

The scoring of the 1955 ITBS program was begun on March 16 and finished about March 25. The last of the list reports were mailed to schools about April 8. While ITP relations with the schools may temporarily have suffered somewhat during the delay, Lindquist did not think any very serious damage had been done. He wrote to Rulon on May 23: "It might be more accurate to say that the damage, if any, was not immediately apparent, but will be eventually evidenced in the longevity figures for Edberg, Hieronymus, and myself."

The first reports presented pupil grade-equivalent scores only. Compilation of pupil percentile norms, grade averages, and school norms still had to be done. After a few days of rest, the crew "returned to the fray again" to provide some automatic programming in the work of cumulating scores—so that the sums would be printed out automatically on "command" from a control sheet following each grade group of answer sheets. The anticipated two days' work for making these improvements stretched to almost two weeks of 15-hour days. The rescoring and accumulation of scores was accomplished by May 1, and the mailing of school average reports by May 10. The school norms and reports were prepared from punched cards at the UI Statistical Service.

Hopes had been high that ITP might be able to machine score answer sheets for the Ohio Scholarship Tests that spring. This was not possible, primarily because of a misregister in the printing of the answer sheets. The number of sheets involved being small, the scoring was easily done by hand.

During the summer, further "debugging" and improving of the equipment was accomplished, some parts being redesigned to raise the efficiency of the entire scoring process. Mechanical cumulators were ordered from Remington Rand and a summary punch from the Bull Company. However, differences in the Bull and IBM alphabetic codes posed problems for preparing lists and profile cards. Modifications had to be conceived and incorporated into the alpha rack in order to feed Bull alphabet code to the printer and IBM code alternately to the punch. The alphabet subchassis and the alphabetic registers—the last of the units constructed in Cambridge—did not arrive in Iowa City until late August, too late for installation and shakedown before the 1955 Fall Program. That processing had to be done by a combination of scanning, punching, and IBM tabulator listing.

Approximately 100,000 ITED answer sheets for customers of Science Research Associates were also processed in the same manner, despite several mechanical accidents and more chain trouble, which Lindquist again resolved. This SRA scoring was the first electronic processing done for an out-of-state agency.

In the first phase of the 1955–56 nationwide standardization of the ITBS, pupil names were printed directly from the name grids, but the readings were not wholly satisfactory. This was due mainly to careless marking by the pupils and to the lack of a comparator unit in the scanner to discriminate between multiple marks. Therefore, the directors decided to revert to previous methods of listing pending further experimentation, including a change in the position of the grid. Again the pupil names were typed on the lists in the 1956 Iowa Basic Skills Program.

The steps in this involved process were explained to the schools by Dr. Hieronymus in the letter that accompanied their January 1956 reports of scores.

> Processing this large a program (143,000 pupils) is obviously a huge undertaking. The answer sheets were first checked in, sorted by grades, and numbered. Next they were assembled with control sheets and conditioned to the same atmosphere in which they were originally printed. They were then scored by machine and the scores punched into IBM cards [with Bull punch]. The cards were then checked against a monitor list from the printer, and school heading cards were inserted. The list reports were then printed on an IBM tabulator and totals for averages secured. Finally, the pupils' names were typed on the lists and the reports assembled and checked.[74]

In early 1956 the automatic punch was put into operation, punching the scores into IBM cards as the answer sheets were scored. After the pupil names had been punched by hand into the same cards, the multiform listings could then be printed by IBM tabulator from those cards. This procedure was adopted for the ITED scoring done for SRA. The first reasonably successful use of the modified name-reading components on a limited production basis occurred in April in the scoring of 25,000 answer sheets for the Ohio Eighth Grade Test.[75] Still Lindquist felt that further refinements were needed, and, in fact, this part of the system was not put into operation fully for almost another year.

During the summer of 1956 many improvements and automatic safeguards were built into the equipment locally by a crew that included three full-time engineers, a part-time engineer, and four to five technicians. Construction of a second scoring machine, incorporating all the gains of experience with the first, was also underway in Iowa City at this time.

Not until the autumn of 1957 was Lindquist able to boast that the actual performance of the rejuvenated first model was living up to virtually all expectations.[76] It now could, he said, in a single reading of the answer sheet:

... obtain up to 14 separate raw scores
... convert these into 20 different standard scores, percentile ranks, or converted totals of the converted scores
... obtain simultaneously as many totals and/or subtotals as the desired combinations of counters would permit
... print *and* punch scores simultaneously
... print *or* punch *both* names and scores simultaneously.

In addition, Lindquist and his colleagues had discovered how to make the equipment do a number of "interesting tricks" it was not originally intended to do. For instance, they could use one counter to identify "incomplete" answer sheets (one or more tests not attempted) and exclude these from a composite score. They could manipulate binary and decimal numbers to record several items of information (such as yes-no responses) on a single counter. They could do inverse conversions. And so on—all products of a combination of imagination, mathematical insight, and engineering skill.

Things were going so well at last that a few special projects besides the regular ITP could be handled with Model 1. One of these was the nationwide restandardization of the ITED, conducted in April and May of 1957.

With some hustling, the second scoring machine was completed by the fall of 1958. It was successful from the start, scoring with near perfect accuracy and very little downtime.

Also in the fall of 1958, computerization in a rather primitive form entered into the test processing. The scoring machines then were used only to punch the student's name and *raw* scores into a tab card; the rest of the work was completed on the IBM 650 computer and auxiliary equipment installed that summer in East Hall. This combination speeded up the production of reports to schools and reduced the downtime of the scoring machines.

Gradually over the preceding four years, nearly all the original electronic units in Mod 1 had been replaced or modified, and marked improvements had been made in many of the mechanical components.

"It amazes me now," Lindquist wrote to Rulon, "knowing all that was wrong with it, that we ever got the original machine to work at all!"[77]

The prophecies of 1953 were no longer an inventor's nightmare.

Continuing development from the prototype scoring machine to highly complex scanners and test processing systems became the responsibility of Measurement Research Center upon its formation for that very purpose in 1953. Hence, the story of the Iowa scoring equipment breaks here and is resumed in chapter 8, which details the history of MRC.

Plate 12. ITP/MRC work areas in East Hall (1958 photos): *(A)* Main office. *(B)* Clerks assembling answer sheets for scoring. *(C)* A clerical section examining readouts of scores from the scoring machine. *(D)* Tabulating equipment operations. *(E)* Answer sheet printing. *(F)* Part of shipping and storage area.

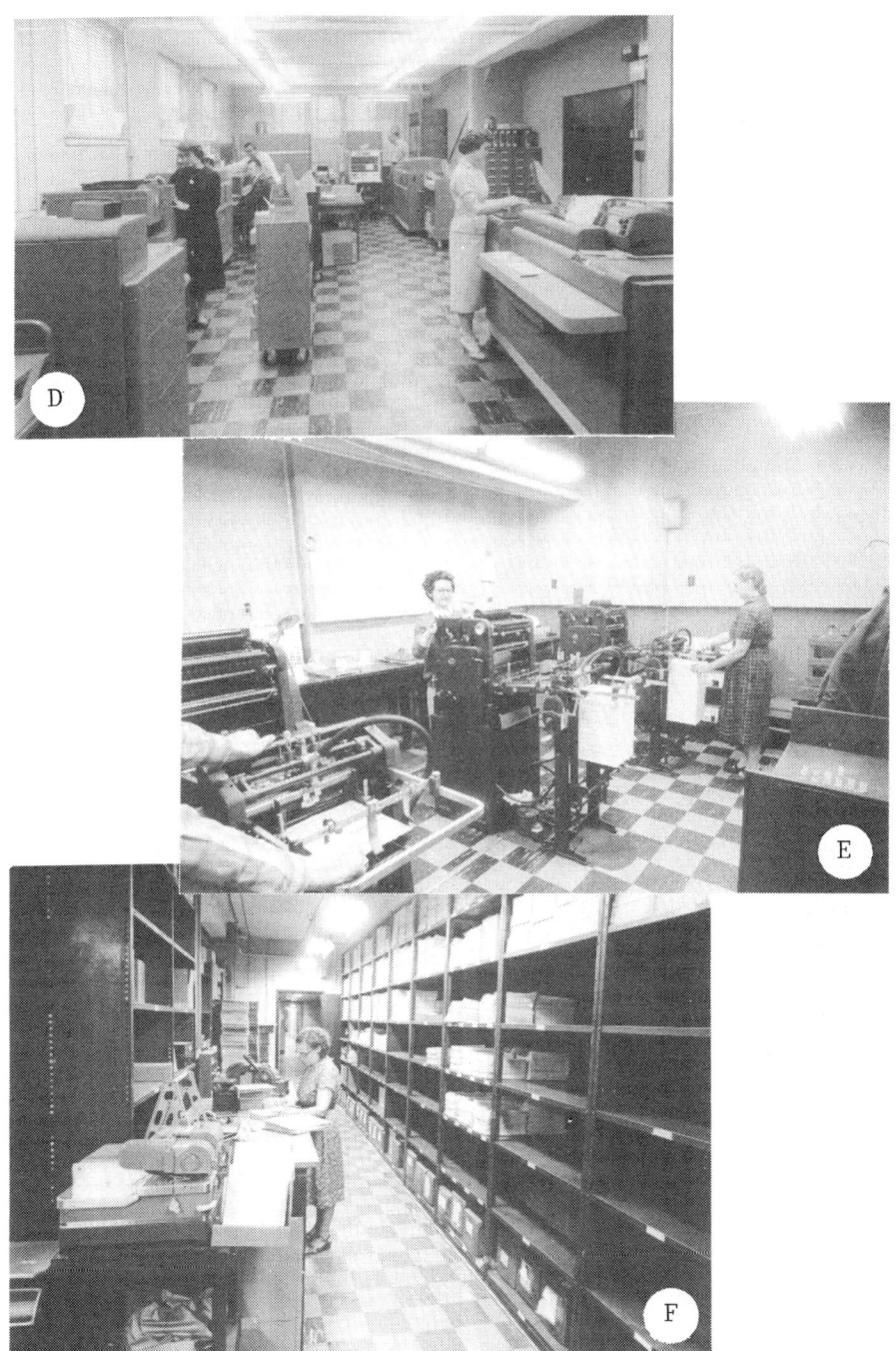

(See "Engineering Developments," pages 153 – 63.) During the fifties and sixties the relationship between Iowa Testing Programs and Measurement Research Center remained close and mutually beneficial. In particular, it was the successful engineering and computerization at MRC that made possible many of the improvements which have unfolded in the Iowa programs.

Summary of the Lindquist Inventions

THE FOLLOWING concepts and creations are what Dr. Lindquist considered the major facets of his role in the development of the original electronic scoring equipment.[78]

(1) He conceived the idea of building such a scoring machine.

(2) He drew up the general specifications for the machine.

(3) He originated most of the basic features of the logical design, including: (a) the idea of scanning the answer sheet row by row with pulses from a generator triggered by a mark on the key sheet itself, (b) the idea of converting scores on a memory drum by counting marks recorded in parallel tracks from a conversion key sheet, and (c) the idea of reading the examinee's name from an alphabetic grid on the answer sheet.

(4) He designed a number of the mechanical components, the most important of which were: (a) the tape-chain device for precise control of the gripper bars, (b) the light source and shutter, (c) the paper skip mechanism on the Bull printer, and (d) the paper conditioner.

(5) He worked out all the details of the controlled precision printing of the answer sheets.

Patents obtained by him on these inventions were turned over to Measurement Research Center.

Later and crucial inventions by Dr. Lindquist during development of subsequent scanner models were:

(6) An automatic slitter for "unbinding" marked test booklets to permit their being scored as intact units.

(7) A high-speed "soft throat" sheet/card feeder (patented by him) capable of feeding documents on computer demand at rates up to 40,000 per hour.

6 ITED Developments 1950–59

Tests and Norms

THE ADAPTATION of materials and procedures to electronic processing was, of course, a pressing activity in all the testing programs during the fifties, but test development was also carried forward at a normal pace.

Forms X–3, Y–3 of the ITED were published for first general use in the 1953 Fall Program. For several years preceding, these new forms had been in preparation by nineteen coauthors and editors, under Dr. Lindquist's direction (see Appendix, Table E). While similar in nature and pattern to the second edition, the test content was new.

The completion of this third edition made it possible to approve SRA's reissue and sale of the nine Y–2 tests in separate booklets without compromising the necessary controls over the battery used in the statewide Iowa program.

About five years later, work was begun on the fourth edition of ITED. The specifications were developed generally along earlier lines, with a few new approaches in individual items. Fifteen item writers assisted E. F. Lindquist and Leonard S. Feldt in the construction of Forms X–4, Y–4 (Appendix, Table E). The new forms were equated in 1960 and introduced for general administration in the 1961 Fall Program.

The necessity of keeping the norms as well as the test content up-to-date received special attention also during this period. In cooperation with SRA, a nationwide standardization was carried out in April 1957, "based on the scores of 148,590 pupils in 254 school systems drawn from every state in the Union and from each of four size-of-community categories in each of nine geographical regions. . . . The distribution of scores for the sample drawn from each category was weighted in accordance with the total enrollment in grades 9–12 in the corresponding subpopulation [in the nation as a whole]. These weighted distributions were then combined for each test to form a representative distribution for the entire country."[79]

These new national norms did not differ substantially from those previously used. However, the standardization program revealed that achievement on the ITED in Iowa was now significantly ahead of that in the country as a whole. This finding prompted the establishment of new Iowa norms for pupil scores and new expanded norms for school averages, calculated from the 1958 Fall Program results representing approximately 75 percent of the students in Iowa public high schools.[80] Differences between the new and the prior Iowa percentile norms for pupil scores were slight in grades 9, 10, and 12, a little more marked in grade 11.[81]

Appointment of Director Feldt

RESPONSIBILITY for the construction of ITED Forms X–4, Y–4 had rested mainly with Professor Leonard Feldt. It was he who recruited most of the item writers, edited their output, and supervised the item tryout and assembly. He also handled many administrative aspects of the Fall Program in the late fifties. This de facto role as program administrator from 1957 was formalized in the summer of 1960. Feldt was then officially named director of the Fall Testing Program, a position paralleling that of Dr. Hieronymus in the Basic Skills Testing Program. Both men also continued their teaching duties, the direction of graduate research programs, and committee and other special assignments in the College of Education. Dr. Lindquist remained general director of the overall ITP complex.

New Services to the Schools

ADVANCEMENTS in electronic technology during the 1950s made possible several improvements in services to Fall Program patrons. Thanks to efficiencies attained in high-volume processing, these were *bonus* services, supplied without any increase in the basic charge of 35 cents per pupil set in 1951.

As early as 1956, a triplicate list of individual scores was furnished to each participating school in addition to the pupil profile cards. Lists and cards met differing local needs, and both were desired by many schools, but costs of production had heretofore necessitated an extra charge for even a single list.

In 1957, following the nationwide standardization of the ITED, the confidential reports of averages to Iowa schools presented the school's percentile rankings in both the national and the current Iowa distributions. The easy plotting of these specific ranks, without the need of masks or tables, was delegated to the local school personnel.

From 1958 on, the list reports and profile cards carried the individual's percentile ranks as well as standard scores.

An entirely different type of report, the adhesive label, was added to the standard service in 1959. This label carried the student's name and his/her standard scores and percentile scores for the nine tests and the composite. The pressure-sensitive labels could readily be affixed to whatever permanent records the school maintained. Their use eliminated the task of hand transcription and the attendant possibility of errors.

With such an abundance of reports and norms information, a rich variety of comparisons and interpretations of local results could be made. Pupil development as evidenced in the ITED scores could be compared, for instance, with that of the individual's own class, grade, and school, with that of pupils in other Iowa schools, and with that in schools throughout the country. Growth in the areas tested could be evaluated in as many ways.

This wealth of comparative information was always accompanied by cautions against misinterpretations or misuse.

> Considered alone, a test score is just a number, as restricted in meaning as is a word read out of context. The context of the score is made up of many parts—the pupil's educational history, abilities, and personality; his environment; the school curriculum, equipment, and instructional procedures. All these factors, and more, contribute to the interpretation that can be made about a score.
>
> The reading of test scores in their proper context requires conscientious effort and some guidance.[82]

The guidance was offered, amply and persistently, in the manuals supplied with the tests.

Extent of Test Usage

DESPITE SOME delays in reporting occasioned by equipment problems, participation in the Fall Testing Program maintained a steady growth. The number of pupils registered for testing nearly doubled in the ten years: from about 62,570 in 1950 to approximately 125,000 in 1959. The rise in number of systems registered was actually greater than the comparative figures (from 345 to 565) imply, because administrative consolidations during the period caused sharp shrinkage in the official number of Iowa school districts. For example, mailing information in the archives indicates that no less than 24 new mergers involving at least 57 hitherto independent high schools occurred in 1957–58, and twice that many in the following year.

Out-of-state administrations of the ITED battery through Science Research Associates increased also to approximately 341,400 per year by the middle of the decade and to 585,000 at the close.

7 ITBS Developments 1950–59

Completion of the L–T Series

NEW FORMS S and T were constructed for the 1950 and 1951 Basic Skills programs, in the pattern of preceding editions. These were the last of the series that began with Form L in 1940. Forms Q, R, and S were reused in the programs of 1952, '53, and '54, respectively, while new test development for the elementary program was taking a quite different direction.

The ITBS Self-Interpreting Profile

A SIGNIFICANT addition to the services at this time was the introduction in 1952 of a pamphlet addressed to elementary level pupils, the counterpart of one designed four years earlier for the high school program. The new pamphlet, initially entitled *Do You Know Your Skills?* (Fig. 21), gave a simplified explanation of what the Basic Skills Tests were intended to accomplish and of what the scores meant. It contained also a chart on which the percentile ranks of a pupil's total scores on the five tests in the battery could be recorded and plotted. Administrators and teachers were urged to distribute completed pamphlets to the pupils to carry home to their parents. So used, the leaflets were a self-sufficient and convenient means of describing the testing program to parents and reporting their children's test performance in the basic skills. This profile form, retitled *How Are Your Skills?* in 1955 and periodically updated, is still supplied without extra charge to all program participants. Director Hieronymus believes that most of the schools have regularly put it to good use.

Do you know your SKILLS?

What are the basic skills?

We know that reading, writing, and arithmetic are important. They are the first things we study in school, and we continue to use them all our lives. Certain other skills are just as important: vocabulary, correct English and spelling, and the use of maps, charts, the dictionary, etc. Without these skills we would learn very little in school.

Think about it a moment. Most of what we know about the social studies we have learned through reading. We need reading and arithmetic to study science. The things we write would be hard for others to understand if we could not spell, punctuate, and use words correctly. These are only a few examples.

These skills are needed throughout all the grades. Good work in high school and college also depends on how well they have been learned in the earlier grades. In all kinds of work beyond school, and even in play, these skills are used daily by everyone. That is why we call them the "basic skills." The tests which measure them are called the *Iowa Tests of Basic Skills*.

Why are these tests given?

To find your weight, you step on a scale. To check your height, you use a yardstick. To find out how well you are doing in school, you take a test. The scale, the yardstick, and the test are all ways of finding out something important about you.

A good test tells two things about you. First, it shows how much you know about whatever the test covers—reading, language, etc. Second, it shows how you stand among other pupils in your grade.

The *Iowa Tests of Basic Skills* give you, your teacher, and your parents this information for the most important parts of your school work. They show how well you have mastered the basic skills generally. They show which skills you have developed most and which least. They also show how your skills compare with those of other Iowa pupils. Every year these tests are taken by thousands of pupils in each grade throughout the

Fig. 21. Title page of the first edition of ITBS interpretive report to pupils and parents.

Old Battery (Forms L-T)	New Battery (Multilevel)
Part Test A: Reading Comprehension I Reading Comprehension II Vocabulary	Test V: Vocabulary (17 minutes) Test R: Reading Comprehension (55 minutes)

Test B: Work-Study Skills
 	
    I Map Reading
  II Use of References
 III Use of Index
 IV Use of Dictionary
  V Alphabetization (in Elementary Form)
      Reading Graphs, Charts and Tables (in Advanced Form)
	Test L: Language Skills (67 minutes)
	
	  L1: Spelling
	  L2: Capitalization
	  L3: Punctuation
	  L4: Usage

Test C: Basic Language Skills
 	
    I Punctuation
  II Capitalization
 III Usage
 IV Spelling
  V Sentence Sense (Elementary Form only)
	Test W: Work-Study Skills (80 minutes)
	
	  W1: Map Reading
	  W2: Reading Graphs and Tables
	  W3: Knowledge and Use of Reference Materials

Test D: Basic Arithmetic Skills
 	
    I Vocabulary and Fundamental Knowledge
  II Fundamental Operations
 III Problems
	Test A: Arithmetic Skills (60 minutes)
	
	  A1: Arithmetic Concepts
	  A2: Arithmetic Problem Solving

Fig. 23. Organization of Content in Old and New Editions, *Iowa Tests of Basic Skills.* (*Source:* Hieronymus, 1955 Conference address, slide 3.)

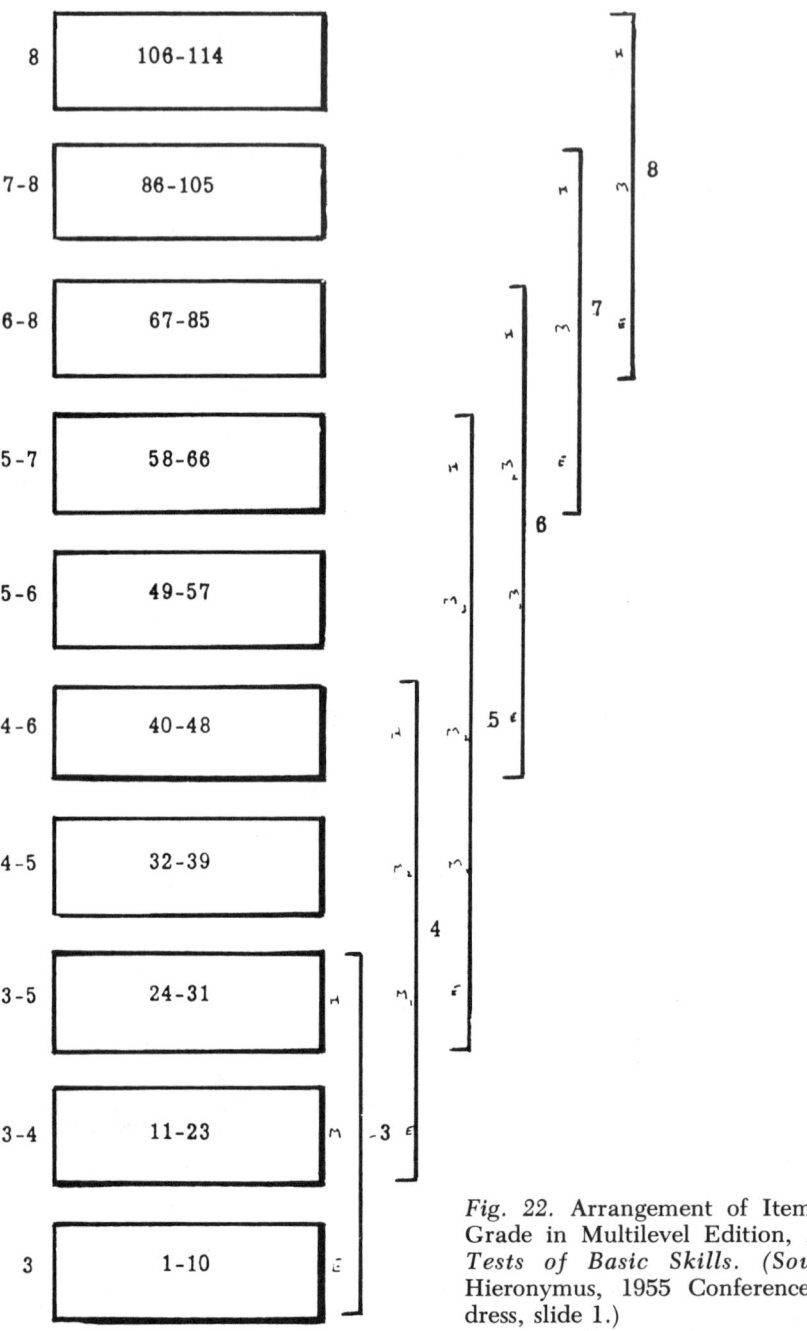

Fig. 22. Arrangement of Items by Grade in Multilevel Edition, *Iowa Tests of Basic Skills.* (Source: Hieronymus, 1955 Conference address, slide 1.)

mus knew. When he broached the possibilities of such a scheme for achievement testing to Dr. Lindquist, the latter "took off" on the idea with typical zeal. Abetted by other colleagues in statistics and measurement during daily think-and-drink coffee breaks in Professor Paul Blommers' office, they thrashed out details of how to adapt the model in a new Iowa Basic Skills battery.

> Back in 1950 we hit on the idea of building for each area a test which would define as completely as possible the objectives for all grades, 3 through 8, in turn. We would start each grade at the point in the test when the items began reflecting the objectives of that grade at an appropriate level of difficulty. The test for a given grade would stop at a point in the test when the items were no longer appropriate in content or difficulty. This would have all of the advantages of a single test per grade, but would take advantage of the overlapping objectives and content for the different grades.
> It was also considered important that the time limits and directions to the pupil be identical for all grades so that the test could be administered simultaneously to two or more grade groups. This was, of course, crucial in rural schools. At the same time it was hoped that the reliability from grade to grade could be made approximately the same.[84]

This stepped design may be illustrated by the Vocabulary Test in the new Form 1. That test contained 114 items and had a working time of 17 minutes for all grades alike. The number of items "taken" by each of grades 3-8 was, respectively, 31, 38, 43, 46, 48, and 48. Grade 3 responded to items 1-31 inclusive; grade 4, to items 11-48; grade 5, to items 24-66; and so on.

In Figure 22 the scheme is portrayed graphically. The average difficulty of each group of items is indicated as easy, medium, or hard (E, M, or H, further qualified as M_1, M_2, M_3). At each grade level, the majority of items were of medium difficulty, flanked by a few easy and a few hard items. A median difficulty close to 60 percent was sought (and attained) for each grade, in order to obtain "maximum spread in the distribution of scores, and therefore, maximum differentiation among pupils."[85]

The organization and content of the new battery are compared with those of the old Basic Skills Tests in Figure 23. Certain differences are evident, apart from changes in sequence. The most important of these occur in the tests concerned with the work-study and arithmetic skills. Test W-3, Knowledge and Use of Reference Materials, gathers under one umbrella the formerly separate sections on general references, the dictionary, indexing, and alphabetization. The principal purpose in this combination was to gain greater reliability. Another aim was better to accommodate in a single test the variations in the treatment of these skills from grade to grade.

The Multilevel Edition

Development of the Battery

THE THIRD generation of the *Iowa Tests of Basic Skills* was the sophisticated product of twenty years' experience in elementary level testing plus very up-to-date research in basic skills measurement. In this edition, the attributes and functions of six separate batteries for as many grade levels were incorporated into a single continuous battery. This characteristic set it apart from all predecessors, in or out of the program. The Multilevel Edition was introduced in 1955.

In a talk on this subject to Iowa educators that year, Dr. Hieronymus pointed out certain superiorities of a test designed for a single grade over one intended for two or more grades.[83] A test for the fourth grade only, for example, can be *limited* to content generally taught in grade four. It can cover that content more thoroughly and need not confront the children with any totally unfamiliar material. All items presented are appropriate in difficulty for fourth graders, ranging from easy to hard, with a preponderance of items of medium difficulty. The length of subtest necessary to obtain reliable measures for fourth grade pupils, especially in narrow skills areas, can be managed best in a test for that grade only, no effort being spent on subject matter more suitable for adjacent grades. Results from a fourth grade test with the characteristics cited could be utilized with optimal confidence in their reliability and suitability for that level.

Hitherto, most builders of multigrade tests had attempted to approach these ideals by constructing one battery for several lower grades and another for the upper grades. In the Iowa program, the Elementary Battery served grades 3–5; the Advanced Battery, grades 6–8. Given the state of the art, these had long represented a peak of efficiency. No sponsor or publisher possessed the resources of funds, facilities, and talent necessary for the construction, tryout, publication, and scaling of periodic editions of separate batteries for individual grades, nor could the schools have afforded to buy them if offered. Moreover, the establishment of comparable norms on such batteries would become extremely complicated. The realities had forced some compromises.

No longer content with compromise, the Iowa test authors sought and found a way around it. According to Dr. Hieronymus, the model for the solution was one long employed in mental measurements (and exemplified in the Stanford-Binet behavior scales) in which the individual took only a suitable part of a long sequential test, the selection based on an independent measure for that person. The design had never been used in a standardized achievement battery, so far as Dr. Hierony-

The new test of arithmetic skills contained no computation test (formerly Test D–II, Fundamental Operations).

> The logic of the computational processes is tested in the concepts test, and actual computation is tested in a meaningful setting in the problems section.
> The main reason [for this change] was that tests of computation do not behave in the same way as the other tests in the battery. Grade-equivalent scores in arithmetic computation are not nearly so variable as scores from any other test. . . . Placement of arithmetic processes is much more rigid than for . . . other skills in the elementary program. . . . Furthermore, with most arithmetic computational processes, learning is fairly complete [at the level taught]. . . . [Hence,] it is virtually impossible to build an efficient computation test for administration in a large number of different schools or at different times of the year.[86]

For some fifteen years, these considerations determined the nature of the ITBS arithmetic test with respect to the measurement of computation skills. In the 1970s, as arithmetic programs and objectives changed, clamor from educators and parents for a separate, visible computation score forced the inclusion of a computation subtest in Form 8 despite the authors' unswerving convictions.

The Multilevel Edition incorporated findings from quite intensive research conducted in the College of Education during the five years spent in developing the new battery. The studies concerned content and placement of skills, behavior of types of test items, and utilization of new technologies in measurement.

One was a study of the practicality of using separate answer sheets in the testing of third grade children. The experimental administrations showed that third graders could handle the separate answer sheet well and with no adverse effects upon test performance, even among the least able pupils. These conclusions were borne out later in practice. According to Dr. Hieronymus, in 1955 approximately 19,000 third-grade answer sheets were machine processed without any need to resort to hand scoring—a better record than that of the eighth graders! For that pleasant outcome, he warmly credited the teachers and supervisors for their watchfulness during the test administration and their careful inspection of the marked answer sheets before shipment to Iowa City.

Other important experimentation dealt with a new type of item originated for the capitalization, punctuation, and usage sections of the language skills test. The old and the new types of item are illustrated by the capitalization examples in Figure 24. In the former type the pupil reacted only to selected situations identified by number. In the latter the pupil was told to find the line that contained a capitalization error. If, as in this second example, the item contained no mistakes in capitalization, the pupil was to mark the fourth response. The punctuation and usage items were similar in nature. Since this kind of item had never before been used in a test, its behavior and merits were investigated thoroughly before its acceptance for the Multilevel Edition. A free-response criterion was employed in capitalization and punctuation, and a right-wrong criterion in usage. The results were favorable to the new items. The very satisfactory reliabilities obtained per unit of time and per item made possible a substantial reduction in the number of items presented in the final tests—as much as half in the capitalization test. In effect, each item actually functioned as a test of several situations, and, the authors felt, more nearly approximated the ordinary "unprimed" exercise of capitalization skills in the pupil's own writing.

Old Type	New Type
"We'll be there on time," he said. 　　　　　　　　　　　　　　7 "my uncle has a new oldsmobile." 　8　　9　　　　　　　10 　　　　C　S 　7　☐　☐ 　　　　C　S 　8　☐　☐ 　　　　C　S 　9　☐　☐ 　　　　C　S 10　☐　☐	1) "I just love the circus, don't 2) you?" asked Marcia. "no, I like 3) the rodeo better," replied Barry. 4) (No mistakes) 1) When we go to the zoo, my sister 2) likes to watch the monkeys, but 3) the lions and snakes frighten her. 4) (No mistakes)

Fig. 24. Capitalization Exercises in Old and New Editions, *Iowa Tests of Basic Skills*. (*Source:* Hieronymus, 1955 Conference address, slide 7.)

The specifications for the content of each test in the battery were, of course, based on analyses of up-to-date curricula, textbooks, articles, and so on. This task was the most difficult for the work-study skills test, since it embraced a conglomerate of skills that could be acquired in any subject and for which no special course of study existed. The search for information from likely authorities proved to be amusingly circular.

> The replies were, for the most part, very similar: "No, we do not have anything that would be of help, but you might try Professor So-and-So." The Professor So-and-So's were also of little help, but two or three called our attention to some "basic research" done by a third party. When contacted, she explained that she *had* published an organizational chart for place-

ment of the work-study skills, but she thought it only fair to explain that it was prepared, for the most part, by analyzing the content of the *Iowa Tests of Basic Skills!*[87]

So it became a do-it-yourself job, involving a meticulous page-by-page trackdown through current textbooks of how, when, and where each work-study skill to be tested occurred in instruction on commonly taught concepts and in common study activities.

> In map reading, for example, we kept a record of the types and complexity of the maps presented in textbooks, the placement of instruction on the geographical concepts involved in map reading, and the placement of instruction in the various map reading skills. . . .
> We concluded that the instructional program in the work-study skills, as represented in the textbooks, leaves much to be desired. . . . [For example,] very little is done in third-grade social studies textbooks to acquaint pupils with the use of maps. . . . Yet some extremely complex maps are introduced to pupils in fourth-grade geography textbooks with very little instruction on their use.[88]

Hieronymus acknowledged indebtedness to the Twenty-Fourth Yearbook of the National Council for the Social Studies, *Skills in the Social Studies*, for the authority underlying the specifications for Test W, especially for the third and fourth grades.[89] As in previous Iowa tests, authentic conditions and data were presented in all maps and tables, including those imagined or contrived. Accomplishing this sometimes meant going to uncommon lengths. One illustration: In order to verify the figures in a table showing the proportions of fat, lean meat, and bone in certain cuts of meat, the test builders enlisted the aid of their friendly neighborhood butcher, who obligingly trimmed and boned similar cuts and weighed separately the fat, the lean, and the bone from each cut.

Especially pertinent to the development of the Multilevel Edition were four doctoral research projects concerned with basic skills development and measurement that were completed in the fifties under the direction of Professors Hieronymus and Lindquist. These are the work of Leonard Feldt in language, Rolland Ray in arithmetic, and Gunnar Sausjord and Betty Humphry in work-study, each of whom also shared editorially in the construction of the battery.[90] Drs. Feldt and Ray carried major responsibility for the construction of the first Multilevel forms in language and arithmetic. (See Appendix, Table F.)

Some of the labor of those five developmental years could be expressed quantitatively:

In preparing for the first form alone, we built 212 twenty-minute tryout units—more than 5,000 rather carefully edited test items. Responses were secured from about 200 pupils per grade, and each of the units was tried out in an average of three grades. The tryout involved an analysis of over three million item responses. We can now build a new form more efficiently, but we still need a tryout of some 2,500 items to get the 1,232 items needed.[91]

The entire battery of tests was contained in one booklet. The first and second forms of the Multilevel Edition were initially printed in an experimental paperback format for administration in the 1955 and 1956 Iowa programs. This was done to confirm that the tests "worked" as anticipated. Then, through contractual arrangements with Houghton Mifflin Company, Forms 1 and 2 were published in stiff covers, spiral bound so that they could be opened and folded flat at any page—a feature of convenience to the pupils. The booklets could be reused many times. These were large-volume printings for countrywide sale as well as for Iowa program use.

A separate answer sheet was designed for each grade, in which numbered response spaces were given only for the items to be answered in that grade. Pupils were thus protected against working on a wrong part of the test or grossly misplacing their responses.

Scales and Norms

Both grade-equivalent scales and percentile norms were established for the Multilevel Edition, in the firm conviction that the two types of scores served equally important but different purposes. The former were recommended for use in assessing growth; the latter, for interpreting an individual's performance from test to test or for comparing a pupil's standings with those of classmates.

In calculating the original grade-equivalent scales for the new ITBS, the overlapping test method was employed. Briefly, "the method . . . is based upon the equi-percentile definition of equivalent performance, and utilized an 'anchor' or 'linking' test as the basis for the scaling."[92] Following completion of additional research on scaling procedures, a revision of the Iowa scales was done in 1959, employing a different growth model. Expansion at the top of these scales (particularly above a GE of 85) gave room for better delineating growth by superior students. Tables for converting former GEs into new GEs were supplied to the schools.

Iowa percentile norms for pupils and schools were established on state program results, in much the same manner as in the past.

National grade-equivalent scales and percentile norms were computed in a standardization program conducted during 1955–56 in 213 schools in 46 states. In this carefully drawn stratified sample, the strata consisted of community size categories within geographical regions, according to classifications by the U.S. Bureau of the Census. Out-of-state patrons who purchased the tests through Houghton Mifflin Company received their reports in terms of these national scales and percentile norms. Although it would have been simpler and less costly to use these in servicing Iowa schools also, the shift was not made. Iowa norms were considered more appropriate and more meaningful for most Iowa users because of the greater homogeneity of Iowa schools and because the state norms could more readily be kept completely up-to-date. In this decision, as in many others, superintendents around the state were given a voice, and a majority concurred. However, Iowa schools have enjoyed access to both sets of norms and to the benefits of the broadened basis for comparing and evaluating their own results.

Additional detailed information about each of the tests in the battery, their statistical properties, the scaling and norms procedures employed, and so on, have been reported in each edition of the *Manual for Administrators, Supervisors, and Counselors*. Until recent years, when costs became prohibitive, separate versions of the manual were prepared for the state program and for out-of-state consumers.

Service Improvements

With the Multilevel Edition, Iowa program participants were given substantially more services than in the past. Besides the provision of test booklets (on loan), answer sheets, and manuals of directions, the elementary schools now received complete scoring and statistical service. This included the computation of 15 grade-equivalent scores for each pupil and of 15 average scores for each grade in each building. These results were conveyed to the school in a printed list report of the pupil GEs and a confidential report of the averages. The latter was accompanied by plotted profile charts for each building and for the system as a whole. Interpretative materials furnished included the pupil profile chart and the take-home leaflet for each pupil, plus extensive information and suggestions to the school staff toward better understanding and application of the test results.

Thus the services of the elementary program were brought level with those of the high school program and at the same basic charge of 35 cents per pupil. This progress could not have been achieved without the new electronic facilities in Iowa City.

Utilization of these services by Iowans rose from about 106,000 testings in 535 school systems in 1950 to 185,000 in 700 systems in 1959.

Swelling school enrollments undoubtedly contributed somewhat to the increase in number of pupils participating.

Expectations

New considerations were already emerging in 1955. Hieronymus brought up a few in his address at the annual fall conference. He believed that it should soon become feasible to permit testing at other than midyear if such a change would have advantages for the schools. He asked the superintendents' opinion on retention of the test rental system versus outright purchase of test booklets, either of which had certain merits. He touched upon the possibility of permitting schools a choice of norms, Iowa or national, in the reporting of their test results.

A very important possibility for improving measurement was inherent in the structure of the Multilevel Edition. Its flexibility permitted at least an approach to the ideal of fitting the choice of test to the particular needs of the person tested.

> This type of battery presents some interesting possibilities for testing remedial or other specially constituted groups. It would be possible, for example, to test a special junior high school class for mentally retarded children with a test at their level of development, i.e., with the third or fourth grade test battery. This same principle could, of course, be extended to [underprivileged] classes or to retarded individuals in an average grade group. . . . At the other end of the ability scale, . . . a superior group of students or a superior individual might be tested with the test intended for a higher grade level, but much of the content [might] not be appropriate.[93]

The continuous nature of the new ITBS battery, with uniform time limits and directions for all tests, would permit such differentiated testing, even within groups, without confusion or disruption of the testing schedule. It could not be practiced to any great extent in the Iowa program at that time because of procedural considerations.

> At the present time we will not be able to exploit these possibilities to any great degree. A junior high school special education class may be tested now with, say, a fourth-grade battery, but the answer sheets must be banded separately, labeled "special class," and sent in with the fourth-grade answer sheets. If this were done on a wide scale, it would, of course, bias the norms. We do intend to study the practicality of other similar adjustments of test content to level of ability, and will try to find ways of making the necessary changes in procedure to accommodate such adjustments.[94]

Some years later, grade designations were omitted altogether from the title pages of certain editions published for Houghton Mifflin Company customers in widely varying educational environments.

Dr. Hieronymus's closing remarks to the fall conference members were warm acknowledgments for the contributions of colleagues in the College of Education and the Iowa Testing Programs. He particularly credited "the standards [set] for the Iowa Tests" in the work of Miss McBroom, Dr. Horn, Dr. Greene, and Dr. Spitzer, "the inspired hard work" of Dr. Leonard Feldt, Dr. Rolland Ray, and others underlying the development of the new battery, and "the fine cooperation from the schools of Iowa." He voiced doubt "that any other publisher in the country could have undertaken a project of this scope. It has been possible only because the schools of Iowa have made it so."[95]

PART FOUR:
SPIN-OFFS FROM
THE IOWA TESTING PROGRAMS

8 The Measurement Research Center (MRC)

Genesis and Corporate Structure

THE MEASUREMENT RESEARCH CENTER was a giant spin-off of the Iowa Testing Programs. Spawned in the ITP orbit, it quickly gained sufficient momentum to achieve an even larger orbit of its own. Within a decade, it developed into the foremost educational test processing agency in the country. Its circle of clients included several nationwide testing programs, many area programs, special purpose projects within and beyond the borders of Iowa, and the major publishers of standardized tests for public use. Concomitantly, it evolved radical improvements in electronic scoring equipment and data processing procedures.

The idea of such an agency developed in tandem with the concept of the scoring machine, but the former could not be fully implemented until the latter was virtually *fait accompli*. Thus MRC was "on the ready" for about two years before its actual launching. From the outset of the scoring machine project, the sponsors anticipated that the capacity of a successful model could exceed the needs of the two statewide testing programs—so far, in fact, that the Iowa scoring might be done in a few weeks of continuous operation. During much of the year, then, the equipment and trained staff would be idle unless put to nonprogram uses. It would be costly and impractical to retrain operators periodically or to rely on an inexperienced staff. Wider and more continuous usage of the facilities by patrons outside the state would benefit Iowa users as well by reducing immediate operational costs and supporting further machine development.

It appeared that the potentials of the new facilities could be fully utilized only as a commercial enterprise, offering varied services nationwide. However, a high-volume test processing business seemed hardly a suitable venture for The University of Iowa. Therefore, Lindquist suggested to his colleagues that an independent, not-for-profit corporation be established to conduct these affairs. This is the entity envisaged in the contract between the inventors and the university.

He proposed that a corporation be chartered expressly for the following purposes: (1) to make the services of the equipment widely available, (2) to conduct intensive research and development toward improving equipment and procedures for electronic data collection and processing, and (3) by these means, to promote improvement in educational practices and to foster educational research, particularly in measurement. The inventors would assign their patent rights to the new corporation, and The University of Iowa, which owned the first scoring machine, would license the corporation to use it when not needed for the Iowa programs. President Hancher and other university officials enthusiastically concurred in the proposal, and the necessary legal documents were drawn up.

Under its charter, no part of the net earnings of the corporation could ever inure to the benefit of any individual, apart from appropriate compensation for work done, goods received, or property acquired for the accomplishment of its purposes. There were no shareholders or stockholders. As announced by Lindquist in 1953,

> The first claim upon the net earnings of the corporation will be for research and development leading to the improvement and extension of the original equipment . . . [and to building up] a general-purpose computer laboratory facilitating many types of educational and psychological research and development. What is left of the net earnings of the corporation . . . will be devoted exclusively to educational research. However, it is by no means our intention to maximize the net earnings of the corporation for these research purposes. On the contrary, our main ultimate objective is to encourage the growth and improvement of measurement in general by reducing its cost to the consumer as much as possible.[96]

The Articles of Incorporation state the same objectives somewhat more sonorously:

> The purposes of this corporation are exclusively benevolent, charitable, scientific, and educational. . . . The general object of this corporation is to benefit the public welfare through research into and the development of devices for testing and measuring the results of such testing to the end that the maximum utilization of human resources can be assisted through the development of increased knowledge concerning the performance of particular tasks by individuals and groups. . . .

And so on. The concluding statement specifically gives the College of Education of The University of Iowa prior claim on any surplus research funds generated by the activities of the corporation.

The Articles of Incorporation of the Measurement Research Center (MRC) were formally executed on June 3, 1953, witnessed by E. T.

Peterson, F. W. Ambrose, and L. K. Tunks. They were recorded in the office of the Iowa secretary of state on June 4 and in the county recorder's office on June 24, 1953.

In accordance with this charter, there were initially seven members of the corporation. The four officers and five trustees were elected by and from this membership. The Board of Trustees was empowered to direct and manage the affairs of the corporation and to formulate appropriate bylaws. No salaries were paid to officers or other board members. Out-of-pocket expenditures for MRC's benefit were reimbursable, of course. The board further could authorize reasonable compensation to individual members when warranted by demands made upon them in behalf of the corporation. Such instances involved mainly the secretary and the treasurer.

The charter members of the corporation are listed below in alphabetical order. Trustees are designated by asterisks. Affiliation with The University of Iowa at that time is indicated parenthetically.

*Fred W. Ambrose, Treasurer (University Business Manager)
*Harvey H. Davis, Vice President (University Provost)
 Albert N. Hieronymus (Associate Professor of Education)
*E. F. Lindquist, President (Professor of Education; Director, Iowa Testing Programs)
*Elmer T. Peterson (Dean of Education)
 Richard H. Plock (Member of the State Board of Regents)
*Lehan K. Tunks, Secretary and Counsel (Professor of Law)
 UI President Virgil M. Hancher was named honorary president of the corporation, *ex officio*.

In October 1953 Charles W. Davidson, professor of law, was elected a member and a trustee of the corporation, and at the same time was appointed its secretary and counsel to succeed Professor Tunks, who had resigned upon leaving the university.

The new corporation had no home of its own. The temporary address given in the bylaws was first the residence of Professor Tunks, and later that of Professor Lindquist. MRC's early and limited activities, being so closely tied to ITP's, necessarily were conducted from East Hall, where the scoring facilities were located. Several years passed before MRC acquired a separate though humble corporate home, a remodeled garage at 108 North Linn Street.

In mid-1956 MRC declared itself "open for business." The announcement was made in a flyer describing the services to be available in September, which was mailed to test publishers, large-scale testing agencies, and the directors of testing in metropolitan school districts. MRC employed no other advertising media, had no public relations

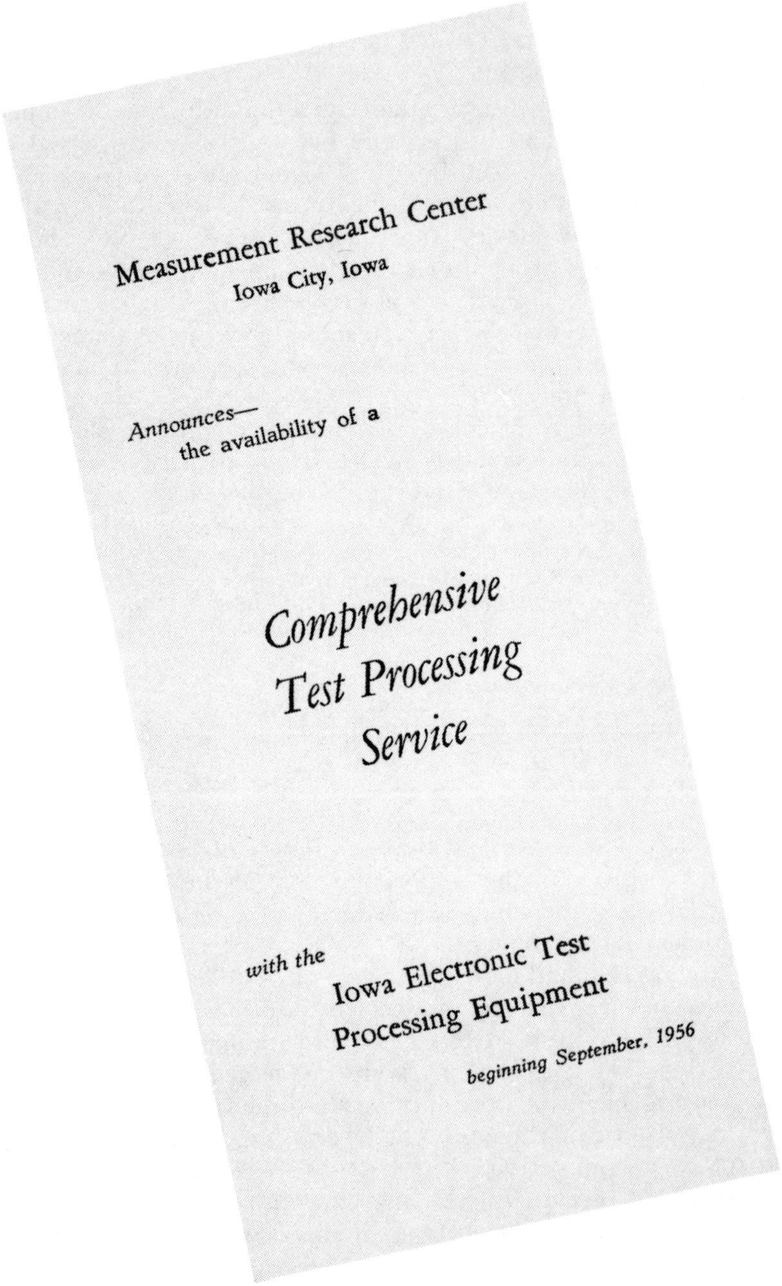

Fig. 25. Flyer announcing the MRC facilities. (Actual size six pages, folded to 4 x 9 inches; original in MRC/ITP files.)

manager, and hired no outside sales consultants. In the ITP tradition, the first flyer (Fig. 25), was the handiwork of the president. Others followed at intervals (Appendix, Table G). These occasional announcements and the nationwide professional grapevine afforded sufficient publicity for the enterprise. The extensive contacts of Lindquist and Rulon in educational, military, and civilian government circles were informal pipelines. The success of such low-key selling confirms that, once again, *the time was right*. The need for MRC already existed— a demand for services no other agency was prepared to meet. And the eminence of the inventors and their colleagues in educational measurement surely fostered confidence in the quality of the offering.

Financial Structure

FROM THE beginning, MRC maintained its own accounting separate from that of the Iowa Testing Programs, which was an income account within The University of Iowa. The Articles of Incorporation and Bylaws shaped a framework of close control by the corporation treasurer and the trustees over receipts and expenditures, annual external audits by a certified public accountant, and complete annual reports to the trustees. Board approval was sought for any significant nonroutine financial transactions. The position of the corporation treasurer as a financial officer of the university gave him a vantage for monitoring ITP/MRC relationships, since ITP affairs were a matter of record in the University Business Office.

MRC's charter provided that, in the event of dissolution of the corporation, "all of the property and assets of the corporation, after the payment of all of its obligations, shall be and become the property of the State of Iowa for use of the State University of Iowa as set forth in Article XV [enumerating the purposes of the corporation]. No dividend or like distribution shall ever be made to any of the members or trustees of this corporation."

There was no immediate need for all this foresight. Financially, MRC began life no more auspiciously than had ITP. Its only asset was the license to use the "free time" of the original scoring equipment, accorded to it by the university and the inventors. For a year MRC possessed not one red cent. Expenses incidental to incorporation (such as legal fees, stationery, postage, and box rentals) were paid for temporarily by the corporation officers, principally the president. In March 1954, the trustees designated the First National Bank of Iowa City the official depository of MRC's mythical funds. It then authorized the president and treasurer to negotiate a loan with which to defray its early obligations and establish a miniscule working balance. A checking account was opened with $1,500 borrowed on the strength of very intangible collateral: MRC's bright prospects and the integrity of its trustees. An operating statement prepared by the treasurer for the ensuing period to September 30, 1955, shows no income, a bank balance of $444.79, and liabilities of $1,781.29 (mainly the renewed $1,500 note). The uphill grade to solvency, let alone affluence, looked mighty steep. However, with the start of scoring operations that fall, the outlook very slowly improved. In November the first MRC invoice for scoring services, issued to Science Research Associates, put $16,500 into the corporation coffers. By the year's end, another $17,625 had been billed: $16,921 to SRA and $704 to the University of Illinois. During the following calendar year, scoring income rose to $135,650; in the second full year, it nudged $165,000. The rise accelerated steadily during the subsequent decade. So also did MRC's expenses.

The financial relationship of MRC to The University of Iowa was a closely considered and explicit one. The principal provisions of the plan of operation formally adopted by the trustees in 1954, prior to the start of scoring, were as follows:

1) MRC would lease from the university any space occupied exclusively by MRC.
2) MRC would reimburse Iowa Testing Programs for the use of ITP equipment (other than the first scoring machine) used in its own operations.
3) MRC would reimburse ITP for the services of personnel on the ITP payroll who would be employed also in MRC operations, at current wage rates plus fringe benefits expense.
4) Additional personnel needed specifically for MRC's operations would be employed directly by MRC.
5) ITP would contract with MRC for the processing of Iowa program tests on a unit cost basis exclusive of scoring machine expense.
6) University facilities, such as printing, mailing, and statistical services, would be available to MRC on a contract basis.

This modus vivendi proved workable, satisfactory, and beneficial to both parties. Its principles were scrupulously observed throughout MRC's corporate life. The provisions were reviewed periodically as changes occurred in technology, inventions and acquisitions, staffing, and space needs. When necessary, revisions were made in details, such as the formulas for rates charged by either side.

The benefits and obligations of the 1952 contract entered into by Lindquist, Rulon, and the State of Iowa were accepted by Measurement Research Center in formal board action. As previsioned in that contract, MRC undertook payment of royalties to the inventors, subject to three important limitations: (1) The agreements pertained only to scoring done *outside* the scope of the Iowa programs; (2) they pertained only to scoring done by means of the first scoring machine, built by ITP; and (3) they were scheduled to expire in ten years, regardless of whether the equipment continued in use for a longer time. On subsequent models and other new inventions, any royalties paid were to be separately negotiated.

MRC did not ever receive any state appropriations or other direct tax support. On the contrary, over the years it contributed significantly to tax revenues, both state and federal. Because it was selling a service via commercial publishers, it was not tax *exempt*, even though its revenues were committed to educational uses. The corporation paid all relevant taxes—income, sales, and employment levies. The sales tax was paid, not only on items MRC purchased directly, but also on those bought through university channels for any procurement advantages that would be beneficial to both parties. Thus, although it was by definition and charter an educational enterprise established for the public good, MRC did not avoid the tax responsibilities faced by private businesses.

In the sixties, when faced with the need to construct a new building, MRC was permitted by university authorities to delay payment of some of its obligations to ITP for materials and services in order to build up a capital expense reserve. Interest was paid on this account at 5 percent. The debt was fully secured by the then appreciable MRC assets. The deferral of payments was thus really an income-producing investment by the university via the ITP account.

MRC paid for and owned all of the electronic equipment designed and constructed beyond the first scoring machine. It leased or built all space occupied by it outside of East Hall. It hired its own accounting and technical staff from the beginning of full-scale operations. In 1965 all of the test processing personnel remaining on the ITP staff were transferred to the MRC payroll.

In addition to the reimbursements and interest payments incurred in its operations, MRC made numerous direct subsidies in support of educational projects on the campus. In another and quite unique sense, MRC was the generator of ITP revenues expended upon College of Education instructional and research activities: Those funds came out of the royalties that ITP earned on the sales of the Iowa tests to users outside the state. With the advent of the scoring machine, which made possible fast and economical processing of answer sheets, the sale of the tests rose steadily, and royalties were collected on services as well as materials. The nationwide mushroom growth in standardized test usage must be attributed partly to the availability of electronic test processing. Without MRC to dispense electronic service, ITP and The University of Iowa would not have benefited as fully as they did from this development in measurement.

By surges and occasional setbacks, the corporation became a multi-million dollar business. The financial harvest from so much effort came in 1968 with the sale to Westinghouse of the MRC assets, name, and goodwill for $5 million in Westinghouse stock, which when marketed two years later had appreciated to over $7 million.

Plant and Personnel

MRC's PHYSICAL development was a haphazard thing of many accretions. It began at East Hall (Plate 10), where the first scoring machine and the clerical staff were housed. From this base, the plant expanded piecemeal into a chain of very elderly buildings strung around the block to the north, anchored eventually by one new MRC structure.

With the decision to start work on the second scorer in 1956, MRC negotiated its first lease: for a former garage at 108 North Linn Street, a convenient half block north of East Hall. This became MRC's first official address. The space and the rental were shared with the Hunter Manufacturing Company for its machine shop and with the Iowa Testing Programs for storage of test materials. In 1958 MRC purchased this building and remodeled the ground floor to accept installation of the second scoring machine. Corporation activities soon usurped all the space, forcing ITP to find other storage in East Hall and in the old Fitzgerald Boat House near the Memorial Union.

When MRC came into being, the block directly north of East Hall was rimmed along its west and north perimeters with low buildings occupied mainly by small businesses. These included garages, a laundry, a barbershop, an icehouse, a store selling religious books and relics, and a pizzeria, flanking a dignified and well-built family home. Gradually, during the subsequent decade, MRC acquired most of these properties by lease or purchase.* For warehouse space it reached out to South Linn and South Madison Streets. In the later years it leased a

---

*By 1968 MRC owned the following properties: 108, 118, and 120 North Linn, formerly auto repair garages; 124 North Linn, a large house; 130 North Linn, a small apartment building; 311–319 East Market, one large building of adjoining shops; 321 East Market, the MRC central headquarters; 319 East Bloomington, a stately two-story brick house used and maintained by The University of Iowa.

In 1968 MRC also was renting: 325–331 East Market, two buildings; 127–129 North Gilbert; a garage at the rear of 318 East Jefferson; and warehouses at 1018 South Linn and 620 South Madison.

large poultry cold storage plant on South Riverside Drive and set up its entire printing department there.

In many instances, to save time and money, the acquired properties were put to use with only minor or crude revisions: a few partitions, lights, phones, a doorway punched out, another plastered up. Desks moved into an apartment created a programmer's office. Garages were easily converted to carpenter shop, machine shop, electronics shop, drafting room, or storage space. Clerks got the best of it, perhaps; for the most part, they remained in East Hall until the new MRC building was erected.

Before that decision was made, serious consideration was given by MRC and University of Iowa officials to the possibility of constructing a building on the Jefferson Street site which Van Allen Hall now occupies. It was to be a joint undertaking, with MRC and the university sharing the costs and the space. However, legal hurdles involved in state financing by bonding, zoning regulations, and other problems occasioned insupportable delays. MRC then forged ahead with independent construction on acquired land.

Plate 13. The Measurement Research Center headquarters building, completed in 1964.

The contemporary three-story structure (Plate 13), designed by the local firm of Hansen and Lind, was completed in 1964 on a cleared site at 321 East Market, in front of a concrete block warehouse constructed a couple of years earlier. The hope of the MRC management was, of course, that the new building would accommodate *all* operations and would permit relinquishment of other occupied properties.

A false hope. MRC's mushrooming activities continued to require more and more supplemental space. By prior agreement, the American College Testing Program occupied some rental space in the new building but only until other arrangements could be made. Even MRC's top echelon was evicted eventually. When the residence at 124 North Linn was purchased, the general manager and his staff moved into it, to ease the overcrowding. They were still "residing" there when Westinghouse took over in 1968.

Plans for a second new MRC building in the same block were initiated in 1966. At the suggestion of University President Howard Bowen, this structure was to be large enough so that the university might lease space in it for several computer-oriented departments—particularly the Iowa Testing Programs, the Computer Center, the Iowa Educational Information Center, and the Iowa Center for Research in School Administration. While still in a formative stage, these plans were shelved when acquisition by Westinghouse loomed as a probability.

Typically, staff expanded faster than physical plant, though not always as fast as MRC's commitments. Paradoxically, perhaps, the automation that made inexpensive processing service possible increased rather than reduced employment in the Iowa City area. The ranks of MRC programmers, technicians, engineers, and draftsmen multiplied, as did the secretarial, accounting, payroll, and print shop positions. Many more clerks and floormen were needed to receive, count, organize, and store mountains of answer sheets; still others, to ship out reports of results and the products from the printing area. Former scorers learned to "edit" (check) computer printouts and perform other new clerical tasks. Classes in keypunching and programming, taught by MRC experts, were offered periodically, sometimes in conjunction with area schools. These courses, being open to the public as well as to MRC employees, also benefited other employers in this section of the state.

Until 1965, primarily for their own benefit, most of the clerks and machine operators remained on the payroll of ITP, which was reimbursed for their services to MRC in accordance with the corporation's charter. The pros and cons of shifting these workers to the MRC payroll had been under consideration for some time. The changeover was not simple. Provisions had to be made for protecting the employees' seniority rights and fringe benefits. Arrangements for group coverage by an outside insurer had to be made. Individual vacation and sick leave accruals had to be computed to the day of transfer. Computerized payroll procedures had to be programmed. When all aspects of the shift had been settled to the satisfaction of the employees, the University Personnel Office, and the MRC administration, the switch was made on July 1, 1965. It was accomplished with dispatch and surprisingly few dissensions.

In employment policies and practices MRC strove to equal, rather than compete with, the university. It conformed generously to area wage standards, but did not seek to outbid the State of Iowa for talent needed by both. The general level of employee satisfaction may be evidenced by the fact that unionization was not adopted by the employees despite some proselytizing by external organizers.

By the end of its first decade, Measurement Research Center had become one of Iowa City's foremost commercial employers. It had a permanent staff of 140, plus from 30 to 70 seasonal hourly employees during peak periods. These figures doubled by 1968.

Regrettably, it is not practicable in a limited history to cite all persons who made important contributions to the development of Measurement Research Center. A few may be named in connection with specific developments, but any more ambitious listing could be faulted for oversights. The success of MRC as well as ITP derived from the labors of a host of workers, each deserving of a generous measure of credit.*

Engineering Developments

THE NEED for a second scoring machine became evident after just one year of operations with Mod 1. For two or three years at least, MRC was likely to have the field of electronic test processing to itself. No other agency, so far as Lindquist knew, had yet formulated plans to build competing equipment, though the Educational Testing Service was toying with the idea. Several major test publishers were ready to offer MRC scoring services to their customers, and would be unlikely to switch to another agency in the foreseeable future because of the heavy set-up costs. MRC thus had a unique opportunity to preempt

---

*Continuity of employment and experience in test processing has been important to the maintenance of quality in operations. Tenures of ten to fifteen years were common among ITP/MRC employees. Records of more than twenty years of service in various capacities, either with ITP or with MRC before its sale to Westinghouse, have been achieved by Helen Black, Emma Rogers, Goldie Sexton, Maria Squier, and Lorraine Tauber. Many others who joined ITP/MRC in the fifties and continued employment with MRC/Westinghouse also eventually achieved exceptional tenures. These would include Ivan Ball, John Cahalan, George Carsner, Edward Davitt, Barnard Dennis, Lena Gritton, John McMillin, Albert Tardiff, Mildred Scott, Dale Schnoebelen, Lois Stoner, and Anna Vandenberg. Apologies are given for any inadvertent omissions!

indefinitely most of the important business in this field, provided it could guarantee uninterrupted service and keep abreast of rapid technological advances in electronics.

In response to Lindquist's perceptive analysis of the market, the MRC trustees in September 1956 approved construction of a second scoring machine. With the assistance of an outside firm, the Hunter Manufacturing Company of Iowa City, a duplicate of the first machine could be completed within a year—or so the engineers predicted. *Two* years later, Mod 2 began its scoring career, installed in a remodeled area of 108 North Linn. It was not an identical twin to Mod 1. Experience with the latter had enabled the engineers to slim down somewhat the bulk of Mod 2 and to increase its efficiency, teamed with the newly acquired IBM 650 computer. It is interesting to note that in the fall of 1960, unscheduled downtime was 11 percent for Mod 1 but only 5 percent for Mod 2 during the peak load months of September through November —a significant gain in efficiency. Mod 3, put into operation that fall, was still being debugged during usage.

The logical design for a scanner capable of reading documents other than 8½-by-11 answer sheets and punching the results into tab cards was being formulated and executed in 1959–60 also. Some eighteen other technical projects at various stages of planning or development are cited in progress reports by the chief engineer to the president. Some were new inventions; others, modifications of existing equipment. A few examples are: A device to detect double or dropped punches in tab cards, for installation on the IBM interpreters before the scheduled NMSQT/NEDT scoring. Additional alpha registers to accommodate an expanded grid for ETS answer sheets. A single gong alarm for low check scores in Mods 1 and 2. Invention and manufacture of an output turnover attachment to a commercial counter in order to maintain the sequence of answer sheets without feeding them through the counter twice. Replacements or modifications of clutch drives, switches, relays, circuitry, amplifiers, and so forth, for the scoring machines. Rewiring and installation of a new Bull punch. Design and construction of a simpler paper conditioner. Development of a character generator on Mod 2. And so on, sometimes repeatedly. For instance, the first version of a gong alarm for low check scores had to go back to R&D because it reacted too well, even to standard control marks on header sheets. Its incessant signaling of fictitious low scores "drove the operators berserk."

Other types of matters requiring simultaneous attention during this period included the planning and furnishing of modernized shops and labs for the electrical and mechanical engineering units in 108 North

Linn and a newly built warehouse nearby (Plate 14). A series of seminars on solid state electronics was organized by the project engineer for the MRC technical people—an informal course on transistors, magnetic cores, and other solid state devices.

Mod 4 (1962) was an improved system specially adapted for the American College Testing Program processing. An even faster Mod 5 was completed soon afterward. Mods 2 and 3 were kept in operation along with these, to provide backup and extra peak-period capacity.

The engineering reports in the mid-1960s continue to reflect the excitement of discovery and experimentation. The range of subjects is wide. One dealing with the testing of a certain silicone diode "for gain and leakage under various combinations of voltage and temperature" poses such concerns as: "Can the head be brought up to the desired temperature within a reasonable period of time?" and "Will diode life be shortened appreciably if they are operated at above ambient conditions?"

Firmly entrenched by now as an electronics resource center, MRC was often approached for electronics assistance by university departments and outside businesses. The medical labs requested advice on various projects, one of which was the design and packaging on printed circuit cards of sixteen differential amplifiers. For the Psychology Department, MRC fabricated a device intriguingly labeled "speech drop-out detector." For the Biochemistry Department, a magnetic contrivance for stirring mixtures. Printed circuits were produced for many customers. And so on.

An extremely important development—arrived at through strenuous combined effort by the joint chiefs of staff and their lieutenants—was the capability of processing marked test booklets received intact from the users. Through ingenuity, experimentation, trial and error, an economical procedure was at last perfected: The specially printed booklets, in stacks, were sliced along the spine without disturbing their position in the stack; the separated sheets were fed through the scorer in their original sequence; and the responses, read simultaneously from both sides of each sheet, were collected into scores—all in one continuous operation. This advance was tremendously important to the Iowa Basic Skills Testing Program, making possible economical scoring of the newly introduced Primary Battery, in which the pupil's answers were marked directly on the test pages.

In 1965 the completion of the "M7" was accomplished. This was the first of a series of greatly improved "document readers." The M7 (Plate 18B) was a completely solid state scanner, equipped with optional reading heads that enabled it to read 8½-by-11 inch sheets by transmitted light or smaller documents by reflected light. It could translate the

Plate 14. Sections of MRC engineering shops and development areas in the mid-sixties. *(A)* Machine shop. *(B)* Electrical shop. *(C)* Design drafting area. *(D)* Printed circuit development area and *(inset)* a printed circuit board. *(E)* Printing plate processing room.

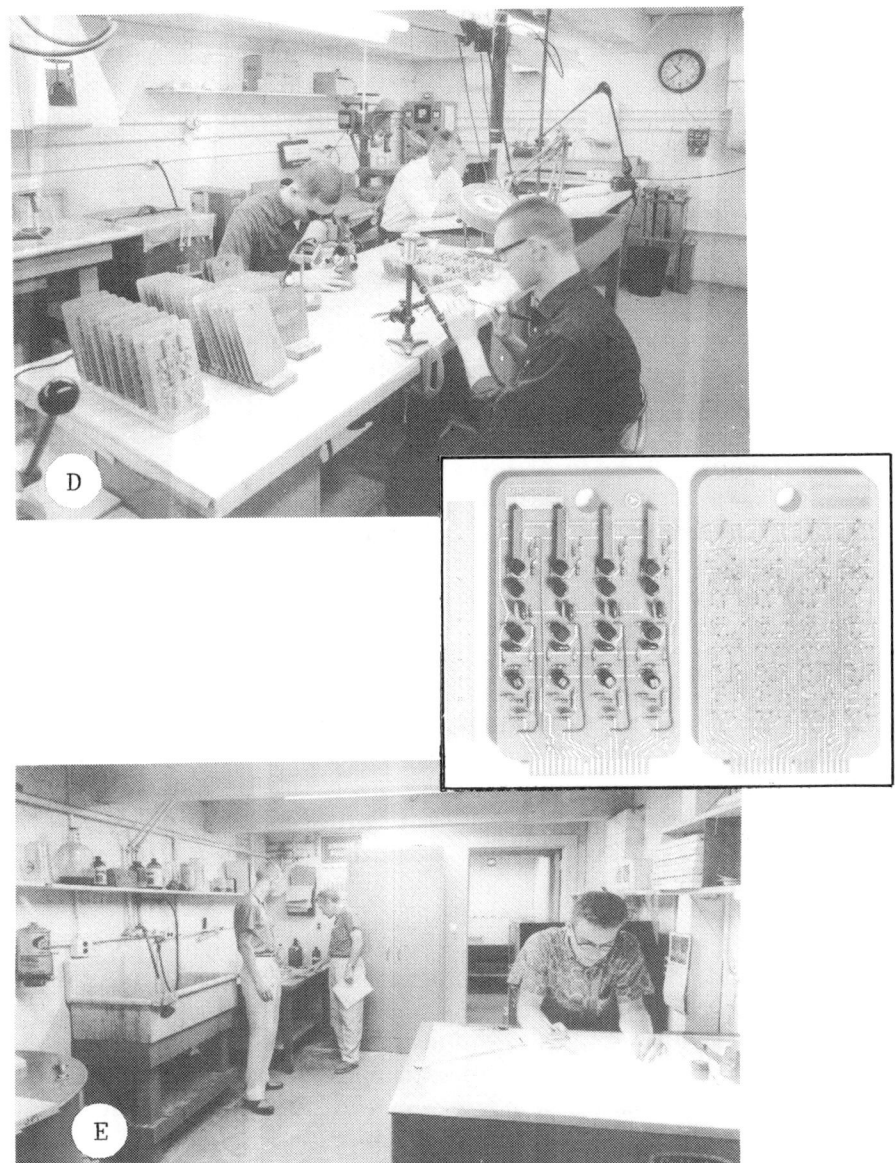

scanned data into appropriate form for "on line" input to a computer, or it could punch the data directly into 80-column tab cards, at the rate of 5,000 records per hour. It incorporated newly perfected controls and error-checking capabilities. These features made it considerably more versatile than the earlier scoring machines.

A great deal of intricate work and experimentation was required to achieve specific improvements in successive models, which were then incorporated into the earlier machines whenever possible. The changes were effected to enlarge their service capacities, to attain a higher degree of automation, improve accuracy, augment portability, and to reduce power requirements and maintenance downtime. Means were continuously being contrived to produce from a single reading, not only more information, but also a greater variety of reports—including eventually a magnetic tape record. A system and a device for automatic selection and application of the correct scoring key to a given group of answer sheets were perfected. Special purpose counters, such as for recording items attempted, and "taken/not-taken" indicators for omitted tests, were devised. Other fabrications permitted scoring and name reading from a combined data sheet in both the scoring machine and the document reader, which did not have identical grid spacings.

Quality control in the printing area also involved the engineering staff. It devised, among other things, an electronic method of checking the exactitude of registration in two-color printing, and a circuit that could measure the color density of control marks and standard check marks on each answer sheet. Paper quality and air humidity problems continued to plague both printing and scoring operations. For a time, the "humidifier" in 108 North Linn was a boiler of water over an open gas flame! Eventually, the criticality of the moisture content in the paper was eliminated by triggering the reading of each row from a mark on the answer sheet itself and through changes in the reading head. These hard-won improvements freed the accuracy of mark sensing from the effects of paper expansion and contraction.

Subsequent MRC scanners were even more sophisticated. The Mod 9 scoring machine was designed to scan booklets that had been printed to less rigid specifications (and thus more cheaply) than those heretofore required. This feature, it was hoped, might enhance eventual salability of this equipment to users elsewhere. The MRC 801 card scanner (Plate 18D) could read punched holes and both sides of marked cards in one pass (at up to 600 cards per minute) and transfer the data directly into the magnetic tape system of a computer. The next card scanner, the 1501 (Plate 18E), could read 1,500 cards per minute, was available with certain equipment options, and incorporated a number of advanced technical refinements.

To complement its scoring equipment, MRC employed a succession of computers: the IBM 650, the Univac, the IBM 7070, the CDC 160, and the IBM 1401, 1460, and 360. Use was shared with the University Computer Center during the earlier years, until MRC's expanding operations necessitated separate computer facilities.

The first scanner constructed for "export" was the so-called Docutran built for Science Research Associates and installed in their plant at McHenry, Illinois, in 1960. MRC's responsibilities included the preparation of operations and maintenance manuals and the training of SRA operators. This equipment was leased to SRA at a fixed rental plus a per-document "royalty" to MRC on the sales of scanning services, and with express strictures on the scope of usage. A second document reader was delivered to SRA about a year later under similar arrangements. Southern Illinois University purchased an M7 in 1965; it was still in use there twelve years later. Several educational institutions ordered the 1501 card scanner. Negotiations with a number of other potential purchasers in the United States, England, and Sweden were underway in the sixties.

For MRC's successful strides in building optical scanners during the sixties Dr. Lindquist has particularly credited the brilliant work of electronics engineer John McMillin, together with the high competence of associates and technicians, especially engineers George Carsner and Richard George.[97] Lindquist's own tireless personal drive continued to spearhead MRC's advance through the technological thicket.

Certainly it was not a rose garden. There were setbacks due to materials shortages, late deliveries, or limited staffing. There were some failures in design. More often the failures occurred in parts production, because of inadequate communication or specifications, haste in machining or assembly, or occasionally careless workmanship. These led to costly remakes, anxiety, perhaps ulcers. Now and then, personalities collided and tempers flared. A few demotions and dismissals for cause occurred. One of the worst and most bizarre delays in production was the loss somewhere in Chicago of an expensive, critical component that had been hand carried (to insure speed and safety!) by an MRC employee to a Chicago firm for finishing.

A particularly dismal fiasco in 1967 almost ruined an ambitious plan to "mass produce" the 1501 card scanner. The time was ripe for a venture into the equipment market. Widespread interest in the ownership of scanners for local use was developing rapidly. The virtues of the 1501 made it particularly fit for sale or lease. Furthermore, MRC could print the response cards for the lessee, thus insuring their scannability as well as reducing the purchaser's investment expense. Unfortunately,

160   The Iowa Testing Programs

MRC did not have sufficient manpower or shop facilities for volume production of machines. A decision was made to farm out the manufacture of the 1501 to a fledgling electronics firm on the west coast known to the MRC general manager. Meanwhile, in response to urgent inquiries, Lindquist had made firm commitments to several educational institutions in the United States, Canada, and Sweden to supply card readers by an early date. But the manufacturer failed to complete a single 1501. It produced only an adaptation (the "1502") for "Ma Bell,"

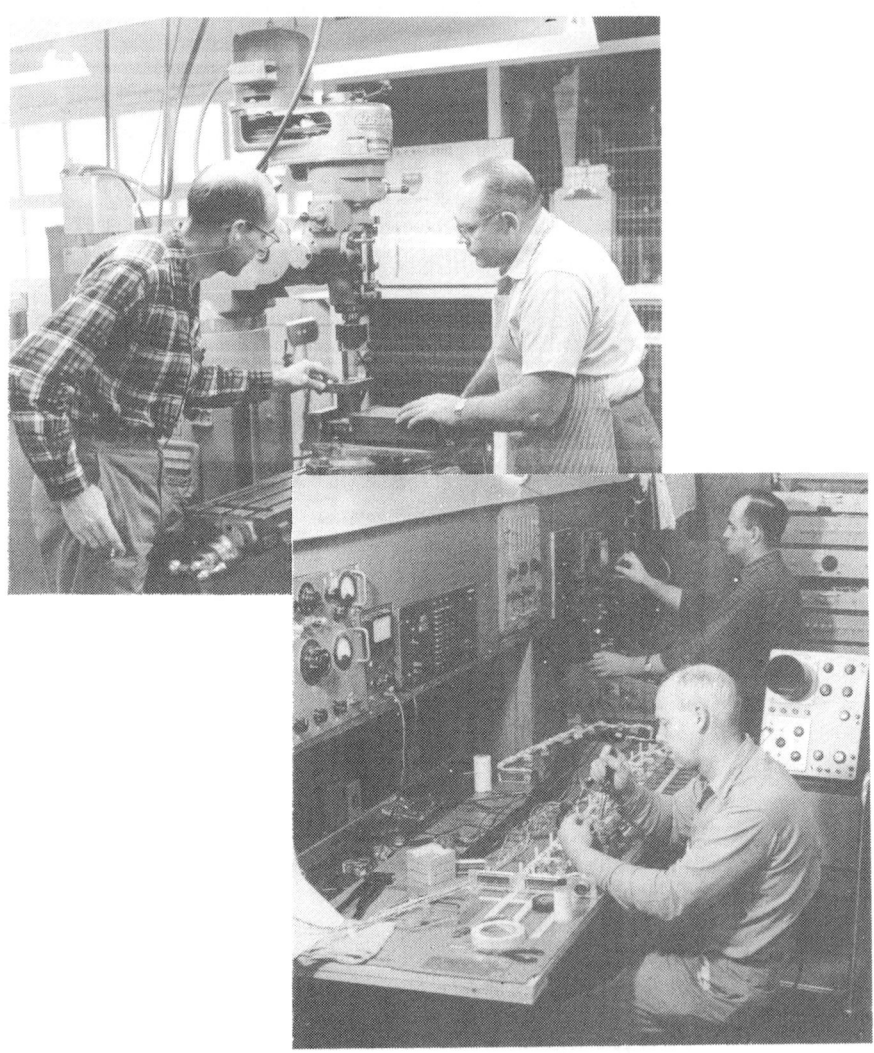

Plate 15. Assembling and testing scanner components.

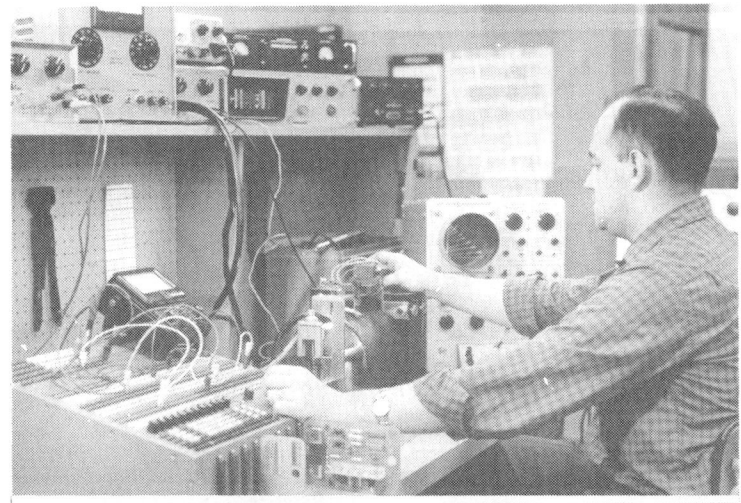

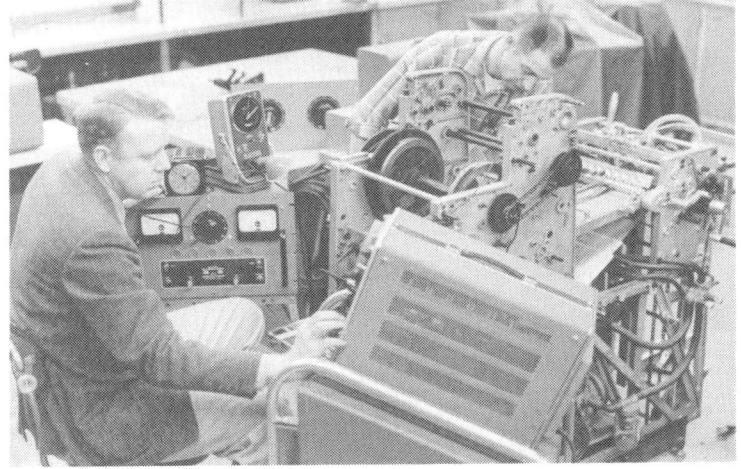

for use in connection with long distance toll cards. This dilemma finally was resolved through the fortuitous merger of the failing contractor with a New York company. Lengthy negotiation ensued for releases and new contracts. The resulting agreement envisioned production and sale or lease of at least 68 scanners in the first three years, with a royalty on each transaction accruing to MRC. The manufacturer would handle distribution to commercial users; MRC, to educational users. Six months later, this contract was assumed by the Westinghouse Learning Corporation in its acquisition of Measurement Research Center.

By that time, MRC in travail and triumph had developed a dozen advanced versions of the prototype scoring machine, several document readers, card readers, and related equipment. Lindquist personally had invented and patented a special ultrarapid "soft throat" sheet/card feeder, and had designed a simplified paper conditioner and other smaller devices. Members of the engineering staff had created other specialized equipment also, one being an implant device for use in medical research.

Plate 16. An MRC engineers' huddle: (from left) Robert Edberg, George Carsner, John McMillin, and Tom Jacob.

Thus, in a mere dozen years, out of the same unlikely stable that produced the first electronic scorer, there emerged a whole family of scanners, each generation smaller but mightier than the preceding. Models were graduated downward from a flashing, buzzing, hot giant of wall-to-wall panels and tubes to a trim, cool, quiet, portable console.

In the winter of 1963–64, having outlived its usefulness and usurping space badly needed for printing operations, Mod 1 was unceremoniously dismantled into salvage and junk—consigned to oblivion without even the benefit of a wake.

Clientele

DURING THE first two years of full-scale operations, MRC's principal out-of-state customers were the publishers of the Iowa tests. For Science Research Associates it scored the *Iowa Tests of Educational Development* and an SRA edition of the *Iowa Tests of Basic Skills;* for the Houghton Mifflin Company, the Multilevel Edition of the *Iowa Tests of Basic Skills.* The services included complete test processing and the printing of answer sheets, for special standardization projects as well as regular sales. Other early users of the MRC services were the University of Illinois in its High School Guidance Program, which incorporated portions of the *Differential Aptitude Tests* in its battery; the Ohio State Department of Education in its scholarship programs for high school seniors and for eighth grade pupils; the Educational Testing Service on its *High School Guidance Battery* and in its National College Sophomore Testing Program materials.

In 1957–58 MRC's outreach widened considerably. Educational Testing Service subscribed for specialized services on the SCAT and STEP batteries in its National College Freshman Testing Program and in several others. SRA added the *Flanagan Aptitude Classification Tests* to its roster of machine scorable examinations, and purchased MRC scoring of the *Illinois State Scholarship Examination,* which it administered. The World Book Company introduced electronic scoring on the *Stanford Achievement Tests* and the *High School Entrance Examination.* A very bulky and important addition was the processing of the *National Merit Scholarship Qualifying Test,* for which Science Research Associates was the contractor. This extensive project enrolled half a million seniors annually. A companion program was added the following year by SRA: the *National Educational Development Tests* for high school freshmen and sophomores, which were taken by three to four hundred thousand annually. Scoring of the *Lorge Thorndike Intelligence Test,* perfected in 1958-59, zoomed to almost 240,000 in the first volume year.

The American College Testing Program, christened by board approval in early 1959 as a subsidiary of MRC, rocketed into motion the following autumn. Having origins in both Iowa Testing and Measurement Research Center, it may be considered a spin-off of both. Its rapid development ran parallel to that of MRC as ACT became a major client of MRC. A brief sketch of ACT's origin and relationship to ITP/MRC is given in chapter 9.

Other newcomers to the MRC orbit in 1959-60 were the diocesan elementary and high school programs conducted by Scholastic Testing Service, an arm of St. Louis University. SRA brought in the Achievement Series program in Virginia. The World Book Company launched service on the ubiquitous *Iowa Silent Reading Test.* This year, also, MRC carried out its first military assignment, a contract with the Rock Island Arsenal to supply answer sheets and scoring service for the *General Aptitude Test Battery* administered in an Ordnance Corps personnel research project at installations across the nation. (On a separate contract, Dr. Nathan Jaspen took charge of the intricate statistical analysis required in this project.)

By 1960 MRC had achieved a scoring *capacity* of 100,000 answer sheets per day. Maximum utilization of this capacity was unlikely during more than a few months of the year. However, lest overbooking at peak testing periods (particularly in the fall) lead to disappointments among customers, detailed procedures were adopted with each publisher-client to keep MRC informed of its sales and the scheduled testing dates in the schools. In wide-scale programs, such as ACT, very close communication was necessary between sponsor and service agency.

MRC's first venture into the complexities of multiple-factor scoring was a pilot run on the *Strong Vocational Interest Blank* administered in Illinois in conjunction with the 1961 American College Testing Program. From the experience thus gained, MRC was able in the spring of 1963 to initiate service on the SVIB directly to individual institutional users, by arrangement with the Stanford University Press. This was the corporation's first and only departure from its traditional marketing pattern. The venture occasioned a great deal of creative work by Lindquist's staff in the design of accessory materials, the development of a special handbook for users, and some promotional efforts, as well as the usual labors of initial set-up for electronic processing. Even so, MRC was able to offer the SVIB service at a phenomenally low price: 30-35 cents (depending on type of report) in contrast to the 55-85 cents charged by competitors using IBM and other types of machine scoring. Eventually MRC developed service on several other widely used personality, interest, and aptitude batteries, including the *Minnesota Multiphasic Personality Inventory*, the *General Aptitude Test Battery*, and the *Kuder Preference Record*.

Thus, year by year, MRC's sphere of influence expanded steadily. Its rapid growth demonstrated the ready and prevalent acceptance of electronics in measurement. This was spurred, no doubt, by lavish federal funding to schools and scholars in the fifties and sixties for measurement and research. Most of MRC's early customers became perennial clients. The roster included state departments of education administering wide-scale testing programs (as in California, Iowa, Ohio, Texas, Virginia, and in Canada) and metropolitan school districts (including Chicago, Los Angeles, New York City, and Philadelphia). Among the college level users were the Universities of California, Illinois, Iowa, Minnesota, Missouri, Southern Illinois, and the New York Regents. Federal agencies were represented by the Post Office Department, the Office of Education, the Office of Economic Opportunity, the Veterans Administration, and others. The first industrial application of the MRC scanner in 1960 led to a variety of assignments for business firms, particularly in the Iowa City area.

MRC's physical and financial growth fostered expansion of its service offerings, and vice versa. New applications tapped its facilities in different ways, not always fully anticipated. New procedures or adaptations of the old might be required, not only in the technical departments, but also in the clerical and accounting areas, and usually *at once!* Even engineering modifications were sometimes necessary to accommodate a client's needs.

The types of services offered clients increased steadily from simple lists of grade-equivalent scores, to percentile ranks, averages, and special types of scores, and eventually to a multiplicity of analyses and normative data. Results were reported in a variety of formats including punched cards, adhesive labels, and tapes. With developing technology, it was possible in some instances to increase services without extra charge. The production of new services for out-of-state test users often benefited Iowa schools as well.

One major advance was the development of answer cards of tabulating card size and shape, scorable on the MRC document scanner. Harcourt, Brace & World adopted this type of service for many of its standardized tests. The machine-readable response card became useful in nontest applications as well.

Another stride in services was the scoring of marked test booklets, men-

166 *The Iowa Testing Programs*

Plate 17. Illustrative views of test processing areas in the MRC Building, 321 E. Market (1964 photos). *(A)* Receiving and assembly check of answer sheets. *(B)* Scanning and scoring. *(C)* Quality control (editing). *(D)* Computer analysis and report production. *(E)* Reports assembly. *(F)* Systems analysis and programming.

D

E

F

tioned in chapter 5. This coup enabled ITP and the Houghton Mifflin Company to introduce the ITBS Primary Battery with full scoring service in 1971. When engineering improvements permitted less rigorous requirements in the printing of test booklets, MRC opened the booklet scoring service to the publishers of other tests.

Measurement Research Center was not in any sense a captive or "in-house" agency. It was free to negotiate with any suitable client, commercial or noncommercial. As has been indicated, its services were marketed through publishers, state agencies, or program sponsors. With the one limited exception (the SVIB), MRC did not deal *directly* with individual test users. It did not have the staff or the facilities to do business on a school-by-school basis, and the trustees had no inclination to alter its posture as a wholesaler. As such, it did not need a sales organization; the services were eagerly sought, and sometimes even had to be withheld by MRC. This occurred occasionally when the scoring service requested was part of a package too large or too complex for MRC to undertake. Grant projects and government proposals were sometimes rejected because of hobbling restrictions, red tape, or the inclusion of test construction, a task for which MRC was not staffed.

MRC's involvement in the establishment and/or successful conduct of several nationwide projects—most notably the National Merit Qualifying Test Program, Project TALENT, and the American College Testing Program—heightened its importance and influence. Its association with these programs again focused national attention on The University of Iowa and Iowa City, adding new luster to their reputation as *the* pioneering center for measurement.

The Sale of MRC

THE SUMMER of 1968 closed an era. Measurement Research Center came under new management. The board of trustees accepted an offer to exchange, for Westinghouse stock worth approximately $5 million, the name, the business, and all the physical assets of MRC. In its fifteen-year existence, the not-for-profit minicorporation had attained the status of world's largest processor of educational test results, scoring over 26 million documents per year. It grossed several million dollars annually; its annual payroll was roughly $1.5 million. It owned most of the land and buildings on two city blocks and was planning further construction.

Why, then, was it sold?

Dr. Lindquist sensed that the time was right for change, as he had in many past stages of the ITP/MRC development. Because of his impending

The Measurement Research Center (MRC)   169

Plate 18. Five models of MRC document readers developed during the sixties: *(A)* The Model 4 Scoring Machine. *(B)* The M7 Optical Document Scanner, the first entirely self-contained reader. *(C)* The MRC Document-to-Tape Scanner System. *(D)* The 801 Mark Scanner, high-speed card reader. *(E)* The 1501 Card Scanner, much faster and more sophisticated than the 801.

170 *The Iowa Testing Programs*

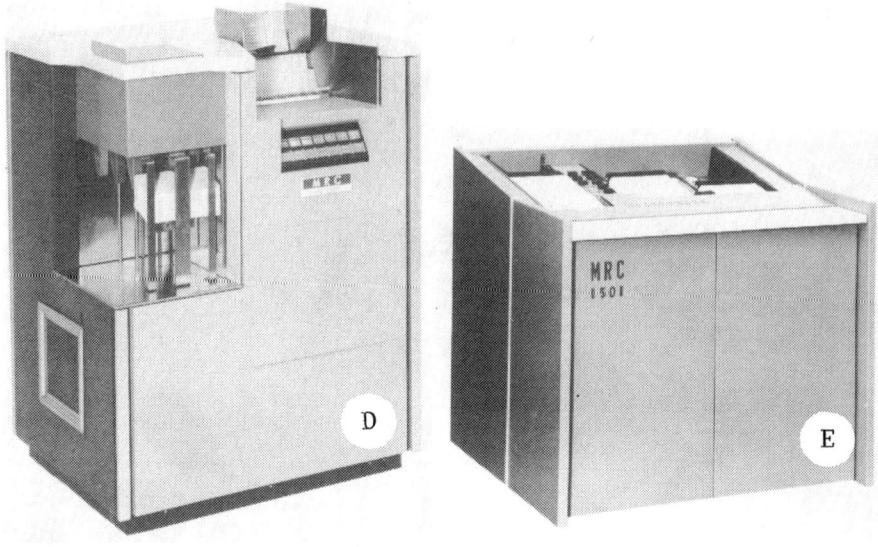

retirement the following year, the board also felt an urgency to define the direction of MRC's future. Yet the decision to sell was not easily made. Several courses of action were weighed.[98] The principal alternatives considered were: to continue MRC's existing structure and operations; to finance expansion by floating a loan; to "go public" and issue stock in the corporation; or to negotiate acquisition by a suitable outside firm.

The first alternative embodied serious uncertainties. MRC had risen on a surge of nationwide interest in educational testing and centralized electronic scoring. That wave appeared to be cresting, as resistance formed to the volume and character of testing in the schools. More immediately affecting MRC was the emergence of several relatively small electronic scoring machines—Digitek, IBM, and others—which schools of moderate-to-large size could afford. By 1968, at least twenty of the twenty-five largest school districts in the country had acquired Digiteks and were doing their own scoring. The vogue for in-house systems was growing steadily. Test publishers, too, showed interest in establishing their own test processing centers, from profit motives as well as the desire to reduce reliance on outside agencies. Some wanted MRC to build equipment for them; others were being courted by the newcomers to the market. MRC's contracts to supply scoring services for two major clients would be phased out in a couple of years. Those two accounted for a third of MRC's gross income from test processing. Science Research Associates already had acquired two MRC document readers, and Harcourt, Brace & Jovanovich had pressured MRC into an agreement to build them a scanner by mid-1969. Thus it appeared certain that these two *clients* would soon become *competitors* of MRC. How rapidly the American College Testing Program also might move toward self-sufficiency was unpredictable. Anticipated reductions in MRC's income from these and other sources would eventually dictate a shift away from costly hardware development and a corresponding cutback of the engineering division to a maintenance level. Of deep concern to Lindquist was the effect such a retrenchment would have on the welfare of MRC's dedicated engineering staff and on employee morale in general. The corporation itself undoubtedly would survive a change in the scope and direction of its operations. It could not hold its leadership position, however, unless new ventures were boldly undertaken.

Expansion and diversification would require outside capital. In particular, a large sum would be needed to support new production in the engineering services division and to offset deficits incurred in the development of the 1501 card reader. A loan (the second alternative) could be obtained readily in the money market, but the board was reluctant to mortgage MRC's future in this way. The investment of sizable borrowed funds in risk ventures was deemed inadvisable for a noncommercial organization. Furthermore, no qualified and willing candidate was available to assume the presidency on Lindquist's retirement, and the other board members did not wish to become more deeply and heavily involved themselves in the management of an expanded corporation.

The nature of MRC militated against the third alternative as well. A stock offering would not be consonant with the conditions and principles of the corporation's founding. MRC could hardly become a public corporation controlled by stockholders and at the same time remain an arm of the university. No doubt, it would have been quite easy to sell a new glamour stock in electronics, but the action would require restructuring MRC. The board neither favored such a move, nor wished to assume responsibility for it.

Acquisition by an appropriate buyer appeared the soundest course of action.

What was an appropriate buyer?

One already well established, highly respected, and committed to the support of educational values in its undertakings.

One that could make good use of MRC's engineering services division, its computers and programming staff, and its test processing facilities.

One that would continue to operate MRC in a manner that would be an asset and a credit to Iowa City, the university, and the state.

One that would bring new or additional business to Iowa City.

One that would insure continuing employment and improved opportunities for advancement to *all* MRC employees.

One that would continue to make available to the Iowa Testing Programs and other state units the services MRC had provided in the past, and at comparable rates.

One that commanded the large amounts of capital needed to make the most of certain engineering ideas that MRC had developed.

The Westinghouse Learning Corporation (a subsidiary of Westinghouse Electric Corporation) appeared to meet all these criteria as well as could be expected from any buyer. It was acceptable also to MRC's major clients. Acceptability was vital, especially by those with whom ITP had an author/publisher relationship and from whom it derived substantial royalties—revenue contingent partially upon the continuity of test processing services. Furthermore, Dr. Lindquist surmised that Westinghouse had ways of using the facilities that were open to no other possible buyer and yet were compatible with MRC's traditional goals. WLC's learning system PLAN was one of several educational projects already underway. In remarks to the MRC Board, the president stressed that the prime concern of the negotiating officers had been "not with how many dollars one can get for MRC, but with what will be the nature and quality of the on-going MRC in Iowa City." The board concurred unanimously in acceptance of the Westinghouse offer.

The transaction was announced by MRC president Lindquist and WLC president Verne S. Atwater at a press conference in the Iowa Memorial Union on June 27, 1968. At a special dinner that evening, local academic and business heads, representatives of the Board of Regents and the state legislature, and key staff members of MRC and WLC were briefed on the benefits of and reasons for the transaction. The sale was widely publicized in the press the following day. Active management of MRC shifted to Westinghouse in early July.

The Westinghouse offer was not for a cash payment, but for a transfer of stock worth roughly $5 million. Legalities dictated that the stock should not be placed on the market for at least two years. This requirement produced a windfall for the recipients. When marketed, the stock had risen in total value by about $2 million. Out of the $7 million proceeds from the sale of this stock, Iowa Testing Programs received approximately $2 million in settlement of the interest-bearing account owed by MRC at the time of the sale to WLC. The remainder of the proceeds became the assets of the Iowa Measurement Research Foundation, newly established to receive them.

With access to the Westinghouse engineering, manufacturing, production, and distribution facilities, and its education and training capabilities, MRC entered into a new phase of development that held promise of enhancing its stature and usefulness in the broad educational scene and in the Iowa City community as well.*

The Iowa Measurement Research Foundation

THE IOWA Measurement Research Foundation was heir to Measurement Research Center financially, administratively, and philosophically. It was formed to manage and expend the funds derived from the sale of MRC. Its officers and directors had served MRC in similar capacities.† It inherited the original MRC charter, amended to reflect the organization's change of name, its change of operations away from a service agency to a wholly nonprofit, tax-exempt, educational foundation, and its more restricted objectives.

The central purpose of the foundation was defined in the amended Articles of Incorporation as: "to advance, develop, increase and extend knowledge in the fields of testing and measurement" at The University of Iowa. The foundation dispenses no services, only financial support. Its assets are on deposit with a Chicago trust company, which acts also as its investment manager. The foundation board, meeting periodically in the Lindquist Center, monitors financial reports and considers requests for funds. Large grants are made only with full board approval. The funds are disbursed through the University Business Office, subject to the same administrative controls as are contributions from other outside organizations.

The first contribution of the new foundation to education on the Iowa campus was a very tangible one. Of the income from the sale of MRC, $2.8 million was earmarked immediately for the construction and furnishing of a new academic building, the Lindquist Center for Measurement.‡ This was the $2 million owed to ITP plus an additional $800,000.

---

*The name Measurement Research Center continued in use by Westinghouse until 1979, when it was changed to DataScore Systems.

†The composition of the initial IMRF Board of Directors was: E. F. Lindquist, president; Willard L. Boyd, vice president; Charles W. Davidson, secretary; Elwin T. Jolliffe, treasurer; William E. Coffman, registered agent; A. N. Hieronymus, Howard R. Jones, and Paul J. Blommers. Three of these (Lindquist, Davidson, and Hieronymus) had served continuously since MRC's founding in 1953. All the initial IMRF board members continued to serve through 1976. From 1977 on, there have been several replacements or additions, generally resulting from changes in the university faculty or staff. Among these board changes were Dr. Feldt's succession to the office of president and Dr. Coffman's designation as vice president for operations.

‡The Lindquist Center for Measurement was the first wing of the much larger structure completed in 1980 to house the College of Education. The entire building was then named the Lindquist Center.

174 The Iowa Testing Programs

Plate 19. The Lindquist Center for Measurement. (A) An exterior view. (B) Main foyer.

The Measurement Research Center (MRC)   175

The Iowa Testing Programs also contributed to the costs of this building approximately $740,000 from accumulated reserves it had earmarked for the joint structure planned earlier. Thus was fulfilled an intention twice mothballed during the previous decade. A building could now be constructed to house the Iowa Testing Programs; the Computer Center; the Division of Educational Psychology, Measurement and Statistics; and the Division of School Administration. The new edifice provided more adequate quarters for these units and freed space in East Hall badly needed for other departments. The two complete floors allocated to the Computer Center permitted enlargement of its facilities to serve users on and off the campus. A section of space on another floor was designed specifically to house a new center for the development and coordination of programs in computer-assisted instruction. The third floor included accommodations for a new departmental library devoted to the fields of statistics and measurement and an enlarged calculator laboratory for the use of graduate students and staff in education. The Lindquist Center for Measurement was completed and occupied in January 1973. Dedication ceremonies and an invitational conference focusing on the contemporary frontiers of measurement were held the following April.[99] (See Plate 22.) These events honored the man whose particular genius and drive had brought them about.

Income from the invested assets of IMRF has supported diverse activities directly or indirectly related to the advancement of research in

education. Considerable flexibility has been exercised by the board in interpreting the foundation's mission. Funds have been channeled, not only into specific research projects directed by education faculty members, but also into larger new developments at the university, such as the Center for Educational Experimentation, Development and Evaluation, and the Computer Assisted Instruction Laboratory. Distinguished visiting scholars-in-residence, American and foreign, have been brought to the campus; the measurement materials library has been wholly maintained from foundation funds; the creation of a new professional journal, the *Journal of Educational Statistics*, was underwritten; programs of research have been temporarily subsidized; and research assistantships exceeding $200,000 have been supported by the foundation to 1980. In all, IMRF has already dispensed nearly a million dollars for educational pursuits at The University of Iowa.

Thus another ITP spin-off, twice removed, continues to widen and enrich the "state of the art" of educational measurement in Iowa and in general, as well as advancing scholarship in related fields.

9 The American College Testing Program (ACT)

IN 1942 THE announcement of the first annual Fall Testing Program contained a prophetic marginal observation by Dr. Lindquist about the *Iowa Tests of Educational Development.*

> Tests of the type to be used in this program should constitute excellent entrance or placement examinations for use in public junior colleges of Iowa, as well as in private colleges and universities.[100]

Seventeen years later this early thought had matured into the American College Testing Program.

The influx of students into colleges following World War II had generated special need in higher education for comprehensive preadmissions information about potential registrants. After the launching of Sputnik the need became even more acute. Yet many large universities and most smaller colleges lacked the means to collect uniformly—especially from students in distant locations—the types of academic and personal information deemed useful for screening, prediction of college success, placement, and counseling. Dr. Lindquist recognized the desirability of establishing a national testing program that would thus assist colleges and universities across the country, public and private, particularly those not aligned with the programs of the College Entrance Examination Board. From his wide experience with ITP and other testing organizations, he understood well the essentials of such a national program: facilities for developing, publishing, distributing, and processing the test materials, risk capital for the launching and early support of the program, a legally responsible sponsor, and good channels of communication with prospective participants.[101] He explored at length with the president of SRA, Lyle Spencer, the possibilities of combining the resources and facilities of Science Research Associates, the Iowa Testing Programs, and Measurement Research Center in such a venture. A tentative organization and schedule of services were worked out and submitted to other measurement specialists. Their reactions were favorable. The plans were then broached to Ted McCarrel, registrar of The University of Iowa and nationally known in his profession. McCarrel, who had underway an experimental cooperative program with a group of Iowa colleges, enthusiastically espoused the proposed national project.

In March 1959, the Board of Trustees of Measurement Research Center authorized the establishment of the American College Testing Program (ACT) as a division within MRC. Thus a dream became a legal entity. Much remained to be done to give it substance.

On a part-time basis, McCarrel served as general director and Lindquist as director of research and development in that critical first year. Measurement Research Center, as corporate host of the program, paid the travel and other costs of the organizational meetings. It performed at less than cost the test scoring, the data processing, and special services requested by participating colleges. Science Research Associates supplied all publications, handled distribution and promotion, and furnished the necessary risk capital.[102] Many administrative tasks of that first program were accomplished in emergency fashion by ITP/MRC staff members. SRA also met crash schedules in its assigned operations. Lindquist and McCarrel traveled the country, laying the groundwork in meetings with regional coordinators and other educators. Under their guidance, the MRC technical staff designed systems for this complex undertaking, drawing heavily upon prototypes developed for ITP/MRC (Plate 20).

It had been decided, on Lindquist's recommendation, that a test battery patterned after the *Iowa Tests of Educational Development* would best serve the interests and purposes of the institutions and the program.* To meet the initial scheduled testing date of November 7, 1959, four ITED tests were employed as the first ACT battery, together with all pertinent normative and statistical data already accumulated by ITP. In the preparation of new subsequent editions under Dr. Lindquist's direction, ACT by arrangement employed ITP's unique channels and procedures for the tryout and analysis of test items.

Lindquist was instrumental also in fashioning the ACT Research Service, made available to all participating colleges for the collection

---

*See E. F. Lindquist, "Some Requirements of and Some Basic Considerations Concerning College Entrance and College Scholarship Examinations," paper prepared for the American Council on Education Subcommittee on Study of Higher Education, February 3, 1958; and "Achievement Testing for College Admission," paper for the American Educational Research Association symposium: The Coming Crisis in Selection for College Entrance, February 15–17, 1960. (EFL professional files.)

Plate 20. E. F. Lindquist and Ted McCarrel confer before one of the Iowa scoring machines used in the processing of ACT answer sheets. (1960 photo.)

and analysis of a wide variety of student information (test and nontest) bearing upon the transition from high school to college. From the outset, he considered this research function, detailed in talks at numerous conferences, to be as important as the preentrance testing itself.[103]

In the second year of the program, an independent ACT corporation was organized, to be governed as foreseen in the first ACT announcement.

> We had felt from the beginning that the ACT Program should be run by, as well as for, the colleges, and on a not-for-profit basis. As a first step in this direction, in 1960 we organized an independent ACT corporation, the members of which were the various state coordinators. MRC, without compensation, then gave up its title to ACT to this corporation. . . . ACT appointed a full-time president, and McCarrel and I [Lindquist] became members of the Board of Trustees.[104]

A 1966 reorganization implemented a resolution proposed two years earlier by Lindquist, which provided that the governing board should consist of members who had no other involvement with ACT.[105] Thus, the president of MRC disqualified himself from ACT board membership. Thereafter, Lindquist took no active part in ACT operations, retaining only a nominal link as senior consultant to the board.

The growth of the American College Testing Program, during and since Lindquist's association with it, has been phenomenal. ACT's influence upon educational practices has been strong and widespread. On the solid base of those first half-dozen years, the agency has expanded into new areas of student/college service, while continuing to fulfill the admissions purposes that brought it into being.

10 University Related Spin-offs

THE OPERATIONS of the Iowa Testing Programs and Dr. Lindquist's enterprise gave rise to several important entities within the university structure. The four new centers thus activated at The University of Iowa were, by their original names, the Statistical Service Bureau (1933), the Examinations Service (1943), The University Computer Center (1958), and the Iowa Educational Information Center (1963). The first three have operated continuously since their creation and at this writing are still vigorously evolving units. The fourth was merged eventually with another center in the university.

The Statistical Service Bureau

THE FIRST statistical center at The University of Iowa was created in 1933 largely through Lindquist's efforts to foster interest among colleagues in the immense possibilities of punched-card tabulating-machine methods for research and university accounting functions. He also enlisted from President Walter Jessup and the university business manager, William Cobb, support for his ideas of how the Iowa Testing Programs' needs and other university needs could balance one another nicely in the full-time use of a complete International Business Machines installation. The testing program work could be done with greater dispatch; the Business Office, the Registrar's Office, and other service divisions could convert to timesaving machine accounting and record keeping; and the statistical facilities would be a boon to research workers in all departments. Only cooperative use and financing could justify and meet the rental costs of the equipment.

Thus, the original three machines used by ITP in the basement of East Hall became the nucleus of a relatively sophisticated statistical center in University Hall (now Jessup Hall). An ITP brochure of that time could boast that "the University of Iowa has as complete an installation of tabulating equipment as can be found in any other institution in the country."[106] The new bureau was set up as a semi-autonomous division of the Business Office, supported partly out of the latter's operating funds and partly by charges to departmental and individual customers.

Karl Benson, an ITP statistical supervisor, was appointed the first manager of the Statistical Service Bureau. A few years later he was succeeded by Elwin T. Jolliffe, also formerly of ITP.

For many years, the Iowa Testing Programs was one of the bureau's most substantial customers. At peak periods, all-night sessions at the machines were common. Operators often worked shifts of twelve to fourteen hours. Dr. Lindquist worked closely with the staff in the formulation and improvement of procedures, and not infrequently was on hand himself in the midnight hours, bolstering morale. A succinct description by Mr. Jolliffe of the punched-card method used in analyzing the results of early Iowa programs appeared in the *Journal of Experimental Education*, March 1941.

ITP's use of the bureau fluctuated in the late forties and fifties with the swings of its own procedural developments, but continued to some degree until the University Computer Center came into being in late 1958. As the bureau's activities also shifted focus in the more recent years, its name was updated as well. It is now the Administrative Data Processing Service.

The University Examinations Service

THE PRESENT Evaluation and Examination Service, while not a direct spin-off of the Iowa Testing Programs, shares common origin in Professor Lindquist's measurement activities and concerns. It was partially an outgrowth of his involvement in test construction for the United States Armed Forces Institute and his engrossment with the whole wider problem of the granting of academic credit to returning servicemen for educational growth while in service. It stemmed also from Lindquist's concern for the maintenance of high standards in testing practices generally throughout the university. The specific actions taken in the spring of 1943 were precipitated by the awarding of a contract to The University of Iowa for the construction of certain examinations to be used in two military training programs on the Iowa campus: Pre-Meteorology and the Army Specialized Training Program.

On April 17, 1943, pursuant to previous conversations with Dr. Lindquist, President Hancher appointed a nine-member University Committee on Examinations, chaired by Lindquist. It was charged with taking ultimate responsibility for the military contract and related matters, and secondarily, with considering "the fields of testing and examination in relation to the University as a whole or to special areas in particular."[107] Lindquist's reply and his early memos to the Committee on Examinations elaborated upon this twin assignment and upon his proposal for the establishment of a permanent "Examinations Office." He spelled out an entire plan for such a unit, including organization, functions, staffing, and budgeting. Beyond its immediate responsibilities on the military contract, its long-term duties, in brief, would be to perform for the faculty the mechanical, clerical, and statistical tasks involved in test preparation and administration, and to give professional advice and technical assistance in matters of test construction and interpretation. Lindquist recommended that university departments not be asked to pay for the services, fearing that such charges might "defeat the most important purpose of the whole plan—to bring about a campus-wide improvement in examination practices, and, through them, in instructional procedures."[108]

The new service department was set up in University (now Jessup) Hall. It was headed by Dr. Lindquist, assisted by Dr. Paul Blommers, as part-time advisers to university instructors on examination problems. During 1943–44, under Lindquist's supervision, objective tests for the ASTP were constructed in geography, mathematics, physics, and engineering drawing, utilizing items composed by liberal arts faculty members in those fields.

About two years later, Blommers was named director, with full responsibility for the operations of the Examinations Service. Dr. Robert Ebel served as assistant director for a time, then succeeded Blommers as director in the late forties. Both of these men had conducted their doctoral research under Lindquist's direction, had served Iowa Testing Programs in technical capacities as research assistants, and were authors of tests for early forms of the ITED.

Dr. Lindquist continued as chairman of the Committee on Examinations for more than ten years. Blommers and Ebel in turn acted as secretary to that committee.

The purposes and goals envisioned for the new service by its originator apparently were well served from the outset. One early testimonial still in old files was addressed to E. T. Peterson, Dean of Education, by Professor Walter F. Loehwing. It expressed appreciation for the technical assistance received "in formulating adequate test devices," and for "objective information concerning . . . exactly what is being achieved by students in the lecture, laboratory and quiz work of the [biology core] course," information which "will enable us to improve materially the future content and method in the . . . course."[109]

The University Computer Center

THE FIRST move toward the acquisition of electronic computers at The University of Iowa appears to have been made in July 1956, when Graduate Dean Walter F. Loehwing appointed a six-member committee, including E. F. Lindquist, to explore the subject and offer recommendations.* This committee deliberated for two years. Lack of money hampered most of the alternatives considered.

At this time computer services were available to research workers of The University of Iowa only from distant facilities such as those at the Universities of Illinois and Wisconsin. The Collins Radio computer in Cedar Rapids was heavily scheduled for company work. In early 1957 Iowa State College at Ames installed an IBM 650 and began construction of its own "Cyclone," a digital computer duplicating the "Illiac," to specifications acquired *gratis* from the University of Illinois. In Iowa City, only traditional tabulating card equipment was available, mainly in the University Statistical Service.

Nonetheless, formal instruction in the theory and practice of machine computing was introduced at Iowa in the second semester of 1957–58.† It included actual computational work on the nearest available IBM computer, paid for partly by grant funds. An important outcome of this course offering was an allotment to the university from the International Business Machines Corporation of free computational time (fifteen hours per month through 1958) on the 704 computer at the Midwestern Universities Research Association in Madison, Wisconsin. The monetary value of this allotment was estimated at $80,000.

During development of the ITP scoring machine, Lindquist had studied all the angles of pairing it with an electronic computer. With the success of the scoring machine quite assured, by 1958 he was in a position to make concrete suggestions for merging research needs and test processing to bring about the creation of a university computer center without delay. In a letter to Provost Harvey Davis on July 10, he summarized his understanding of the outcome of numerous committee conferences:

---

*Members of the Graduate Council Committee on Electronic Computers were Professors J. A. Van Allen, N. C. Baenziger, E. N. Oberg, R. Beckett, E. F. Lindquist, and H. P. Bechtoldt, chairman. (EFL committee files.)

†This course (29:174) was scheduled on a trial basis in the Physics Department through the joint efforts of Provost Davis and Professor Van Allen, whose upper atmosphere and space researches were prime subjects for computer technology.

Plate 21. Two views of the University Computer Center in September 1961. *Above,* James Van Allen and E. F. Lindquist, standing; John Dolch seated at console.

The basic functions of the center would be "to provide instruction and training in computer applications, and to provide computing facilities for scientific and educational research and service agencies of the University of Iowa."[110] The report detailed anticipated equipment and staff needs, forecast probable early expenditures, and proposed an accounting and administrative system.* It was estimated that Iowa Testing Programs and Measurement Research Center together would need the facilities for a maximum of four hours a day on the average. The other sixteen hours of round-the-clock operation would be available to others for departmental and research work. During the first year of operation a major portion of the operating costs would be borne by ITP out of royalties on tests sold outside of Iowa. The Physics Department would contribute to the salary budget. It was hoped that within a year or so state funds might be appropriated for a large share of the support of the Computer Center, but it was understood that the Iowa Testing Programs would continue, if necessary, to give major support.

The agreements were implemented promptly. Site preparation in East Hall, which had already been predesigned by the director and engineers of ITP, was started at once.[111] Thanks to the special cooperation and effort of all departments and persons involved, by September of 1958 a new functioning unit had been added to the university structure.

Dr. John P. Dolch, who had served ITP as assistant engineer for three years, was appointed the first director of the University Computer Center (UCC). A course in computer programming and operation, required of all users, was scheduled that fall in the College of Education. A slate of faculty members in a dozen different departments who were knowledgeable in computer techniques served as departmental advisers, assisting individuals in the formulation of their computer problems.

Use of the facility increased rapidly. During the next few years, primarily at Lindquist's instigation, several changes to more advanced computers were made.† Repeated space revisions were necessary to

---

*The major items of equipment proposed as adequate for a year or two were: the computer console, an input-output machine that read and punched cards, a tabulator, a card reproducer, a card collator, a card sorter, and a printing keypunch. The initial staff would consist of director, instructor-programmer, and several machine operators. A separate budget would be set up within the College of Education accounts. An enlarged, broadly representative Computer Committee would set criteria for the allocation of computer time to departments and individuals, and would guide the development of the center in meeting educational and research needs. The director and staff of the center would otherwise be administratively responsible to the director of Iowa Testing Programs and through him to the dean of the College of Education.

†The IBM 650 was supplemented in the spring of 1960 by a Univac Solid State 80—not only to increase capacity but also, it was hoped, to reduce downtime. Expectations were not fulfilled. About a year later, these two systems were superseded by the IBM 7070 and 1401.

accommodate these expansions (Plate 21). The Department of Computer Sciences evolved concomitantly within the Division of Mathematical Sciences.

For many years ITP/MRC continued to shoulder a goodly chunk of the UCC operating expenses. In addition to payments for test processing services, ITP made direct subsidies to the center and at times assumed also a substantial portion of the machine rentals. For example, the 1958–59 Computer Center budget showed anticipated expenses of $47,000, to be balanced by $42,000 from ITP and MRC ($20,000 for MRC services and a $22,000 ITP subsidy) and only $5,000 from sponsored research. (At that time, all facilities and services of the center were cost-free to university personnel not receiving outside grants.)

In October 1961, Dr. Lindquist informed Dr. James Van Allen that Iowa Testing Programs was "in the position of underwriting the Computer Center [by] making up any difference between actual disbursements and actual receipts from resources other than the Iowa Testing Programs" to an upper limit of $94,815, in addition to payments to IBM of "over $100 an hour for all use that we [ITP/MRC] make of the 7070 [and] for overtime use on the 1401."[112]

During the first five years, the *direct subsidy* to UCC budgeted by ITP (apart from work charges and any extra computer equipment expenditures) ran: $22,000, $28,000, $40,000, $94,815, $106,000—in each case meeting more than half of UCC's total anticipated income needs. In the next two years, the subsidy dropped to $24,000 annually.[113] As ITP directed more of its resources to other educational research projects, particularly those of the Center for Research in School Administration and the Educational Information Center, UCC sought appropriations and other funds to fill the gap. ITP/MRC acquired its own computer as soon as housing for the installation became available in MRC property.

When the first wing of the Lindquist Center was constructed in the early seventies, an important element in Lindquist's own ideas throughout the planning stages was provision for a computer center of the future. Two entire floors in the building were allocated to and equipped for it—indirectly another gift from ITP/MRC via the Iowa Measurement Research Foundation.

The Iowa Educational Information Center

THE IOWA Educational Information Center (IEIC) was envisioned by E. F. Lindquist and colleagues as a vehicle to facilitate educational research requiring large quantities of information from many sources.

It would collect, organize, store, and disseminate vast amounts of scattered or hitherto uncollectible information useful to the advancement of education and the behavioral sciences. It would also supply related services not readily available elsewhere to Iowa schools. And it would be a model and a training facility for the development of similar regional data-collection centers in other parts of the country.[114]

Action upon this heady idea had to await the construction by Measurement Research Center of a general-purpose document-to-tape scanner. In December 1963, after completion of a successful pilot project, the IEIC was formally organized as a joint enterprise of the UI College of Education and the Iowa State Department of Public Instruction. It was governed by a coordinating board of three (State Superintendent Paul F. Johnston, Dean Howard R. Jones, and Professor Lindquist) and was headed initially by Professor Robert W. Marker.* The center was funded for the first several years by the United States Office of Education and the Ford Foundation. Data processing was done by MRC at or below cost.

Machine-scannable questionnaires and other forms for data collection and reporting were originated, including CardPac, a system of educational accounting adaptable to many uses in school administration. Computer programming and other data-processing procedures were developed. However, despite a promising beginning, the perceived potential of IEIC was never realized. Leonard Feldt recalls one unexpected obstacle to the coordination of gathered data. This was the center's inability to acquire a file of permanent pupil identification numbers from the schools. Some governmental officials were reluctant to release records even though it was legal to do so for educational purposes. Furthermore, it was found that many pupils had no social security numbers. Without permanent ID numbers for all pupils, test scores and other data could not readily be collated. For this and other reasons, no ITED or ITBS scores were ever transferred into IEIC files.

Apart from technical difficulties, the center's basic purpose fell victim to the times, loud with activist clamor against information gathering and computerization for any purpose. Some resentment among parents also was aroused by questionnaires relating to students' backgrounds and aspirations. Severe reductions in federal funding for educational research and development, as well as uncertainties about future leadership, mortally damaged IEIC's prospects for accomplishing its primary mission. Backing away from the data bank concept, it concentrated

---

*Subsequent directors were Drs. Ralph Van Dusseldorp, Walter Foley, and Gordon Harr.

rather upon developing systems for the coordination and analysis of information routinely collected by school districts and state agencies and on continuing services to subscriber schools.

In mid-1972, to avoid duplication of service activities and to utilize better the limited available subsidies, the IEIC was merged with the Iowa Center for Research in School Administration, which some years earlier had received financial support from ITP.[115] The combined unit was disbanded in 1976, but the influence and some functions of both centers are traceable in other programs of the College of Education.

PART FIVE:
THE IOWA PROGRAMS
IN RECENT DECADES
1960–1980

11 The Changing Environment

The General Climate

THE SIXTIES and seventies seethed with protest and confrontation on a variety of issues—social, political, and military, domestic and international. The two decades are considered here as one span, since the forces that churned the waters in the sixties roiled on well into the seventies.

Educational measurement was not unaffected by the general agitation. Positive and negative manifestations can be seen in: the onrushing development of computerized data processing; the tides of standardized testing throughout the country; the proliferation of examinations and survey documents for myriad purposes and of assorted size, type, and quality; eagerness for and resistance to evaluation; anxiety to outperform and resentment at the necessity; traditional standards versus allegations of bias; the clash of pundits; swings of public sentiment between friends and foes of "accountability" in education.

Sometimes in this heavy weather the whole testing movement seemed —but only seemed—awash. Iowa Testing Programs, for one, did not founder. Its skippers trimmed some sails and hoisted new ones as suited the winds of change, while steering on as steadily as possible in the main channel of sound educational practice.

Within ITP

CHANGES IN the ITP high command occurred also during this period. Most importantly, E. F. Lindquist retired from the directorship of the Iowa Testing Programs and his professorship in the College of Education. His retirement at age 68 became effective at the end of June 1969, a year after the sale of Measurement Research Center. Eschewing any further active role in the affairs of these organizations, he remained available for occasional consultation only. He retained the presidency of

Iowa Measurement Research Foundation until his death in May 1978.

Following Dr. Lindquist's retirement, Dr. William E. Coffman, formerly of the Educational Testing Service in Princeton, New Jersey, was appointed the first E. F. Lindquist Professor of Educational Measurement and general director of the Iowa Testing Programs. In this period of educational and societal unrest, a principal objective of his administration was to consolidate and manage ITP's resources with concern for future research and development potentials as well as for current stability and refinement. Many particular responsibilities of the first several years were related to the construction, furnishing, and dedication of the Lindquist Center for Measurement (phase I of the present building). Coffman also assumed executive duties for Iowa Measurement Research Foundation as board member and registered agent, and later, vice president for operations.

Dr. Leonard Feldt was named to succeed Dr. Lindquist as president of IMRF at the annual meeting of the board in October 1978.

Professors Hieronymus and Feldt continued to direct, respectively, the Iowa Basic Skills Testing Program and the Fall Testing Program in the thickening welter of changing demands from test users. Beginning in the late sixties and throughout this period, their chief assistants, particularly in test development, were Dr. H. D. Hoover on ITBS and Dr. Robert Forsyth on ITED, both of whom first became associated with ITP during their doctoral studies at The University of Iowa.

A succession of writers, editors, secretaries, statisticians, and other support staff have faithfully manned ITP stations in recent times and in circumstances quite different from those of earlier years. Perhaps only a veteran could sense a diminution of esprit in the diminished corps, as the feeling of oneness between ITP and MRC faded with the sale of the latter. Inevitably, the holding periods, however essential and important, offer less excitement than do those of discovery and creation.

The Changing Environment   195

Plate 22. Dedication of the Lindquist Center for Measurement, April 6–7, 1973. *(A)* Professor Robert Ebel addresses the assemblage. (Dr. Lindquist *second from left, front row;* Mrs. Lindquist *center front, in white blouse.*)

(B) Honoree E. F. Lindquist responds.

(C) Director-Emeritus Lindquist chats with ITP Director William E. Coffman.
(D) . . . with ITBS Director A. N. Hieronymus and visitor Harold Miller . . .

(E) with regent Stanley Redeker . . . *(F)* with UI President Willard L. Boyd and others . . .

198   *The Iowa Testing Programs*

(G, H) while other visitors tour the new building.

12 The ITED 1960–80

Overview

IN THE SIXTIES and seventies, advances in facilities and expertise made possible several new reporting services in the Fall Program. At the same time, construction of new test materials proceeded normally. An overview of the principal introductions and developments during the two decades is given in Table 1, followed by descriptions of the major new features.

TABLE 1

Overview of Developments in the Fall Testing Program (ITED)
1960–80

Program Date	Event
1960	*Local* norms and frequency distributions of pupil scores provided to all schools.
	Fourth edition of battery equated to third.
	Gummed label reports introduced.
	Consultant services made available on request.
1961	Forms X–4, Y–4 replaced X–3, Y–3 in Iowa program.
	Space for responses to ITED Experimental Units incorporated into regular answer sheet.
	System averages and frequency distributions, by grade, reported gratis to multibuilding districts.
	Pupil profile card redesigned for the plotting of standard scores on one side and percentile ranks on the reverse.
1962	New national and Iowa norms gathered on Forms X–4, Y–4.

Table 1 - Continued

Program Date	Event
1963	*Numeric grid* added to ITED answer sheet; related services supplied.
1966	*Item analysis* service introduced.
1967	Local percentile ranks reported on profile card in addition to pupil's state rankings for all subtests and the composite.
1969	Fifth edition of tests equated to fourth.
	Answer sheet design and spacing of response ovals improved.
1970	Testing of selected grades in Fall Program permitted.
	Questionnaire poll taken of teachers' attitudes toward the program and their uses of the test results.
	ITED fifth edition replaced fourth in state program.
1971	Sentiment of school officials for a shorter battery polled.
	National norms updated.
1972	Shortened ITED battery (Forms X–6, Y–6) published.
	Program schools given choice of long form (fifth edition) or short form (sixth edition) of ITED.
1974	Schools given choice of Iowa or national norms in all reports of results.
1975	Use of long ITED battery discontinued in state programs.
1976	First price increase in twenty-five years: from 35 cents to 40 cents per pupil.
1977	National norms for ITED revised.
1978	Two-level battery (seventh edition) completed; equated to sixth edition.
	Basic price increased to 45 cents per pupil.
1979	Forms X–7, Y–7 replaced previous edition.
	Basic charge raised to 50 cents.

Source: ITED annual files 1960–80.

Specifics of Service Improvements

The Local Norms and Distributions

The report of local norms and frequency distributions added another dimension to the possibilities of ITED test interpretation. For each test in the battery and for each grade in the district, it showed how many pupils earned each possible standard score and indicated the percentile rank of each score in that local distribution. A pupil's performance could thereby be evaluated in relation to that of classmates, as well as to state and national norms. This basis of comparison might be especially important to school systems experiencing unusual circumstances or located in atypical communities.

By 1967 it became electronically feasible to determine and to print on the pupil profile card the individual's local percentile ranks in addition to his/her state rankings on all subtests and composite. This gave teachers instant access to pupils' local standings. The full tabular report of local norms and frequencies was also provided as before.

The Consultant Services

The announcement in 1960 of an advisory service fulfilled a long-standing goal of the ITP administrators. Initiated in cooperation with the Division of Counseling and Guidance, since the first few years the service has been shouldered entirely by the ITP professional staff, generally by advanced graduate assistants well qualified in measurement and counseling. It brought directly to users on their home grounds expert assistance in the utilization of local ITED and ITBS data and in related guidance matters. A modest fee of twenty-five dollars per one-day visit helped (slightly) to defray travel expenses. By 1971 even that token charge was dropped.

This service has been quite widely used by both small and large school districts. The field consultants have traveled to all parts of the state and even out of state in response to calls for help, sometimes under grim winter conditions. Their mission is, of course, distinct from the ongoing top level ministry of faculty members in the dual capacities of ITP administrators and scholars in education. Over the years, Iowa school officials and organizations have not hesitated to seek up-to-date viewpoints and clarifications—by phone, correspondence, and in person —from Professors Lindquist, Hieronymus, Feldt, and (in the later years) Coffman, Forsyth, and Hoover.

The Numeric Grid

The numeric grid feature of the revised 1963 answer sheet extended its usefulness to other than current test purposes. Hitherto only the testee's name could be marked on the alphabetic grid, read by the scanner, and reproduced. In the four new fields of the enlarged grid (Fig. 26) numeric data or numerically coded information could be entered, to be transcribed in the test scoring process. Whatever the school official elected to have recorded on this grid would be printed out in marginal columns of the list report in line with the pupil's regular ITED scores. Use of all, some, or none of the fields was entirely optional, the service free of charge.

A special pamphlet explained proper use of the service and suggested some practical applications:[116]

The first (one-digit) field afforded a means of classifying the pupils in a grade into nine or fewer subgroups locally chosen. The classification might relate, for instance, to the pupil's post-high-school plans, general scholastic ability, or curriculum type.

> If Field 1 is used in this way, the Iowa test processing equipment will provide a separate report of ITED subtest averages *for each of the code groups*, as well as the usual report of averages for the class as a whole. In addition, if numerical information is recorded . . . in Fields 3 or 4, averages for these values will also be computed and reported for *each code group*.[117]

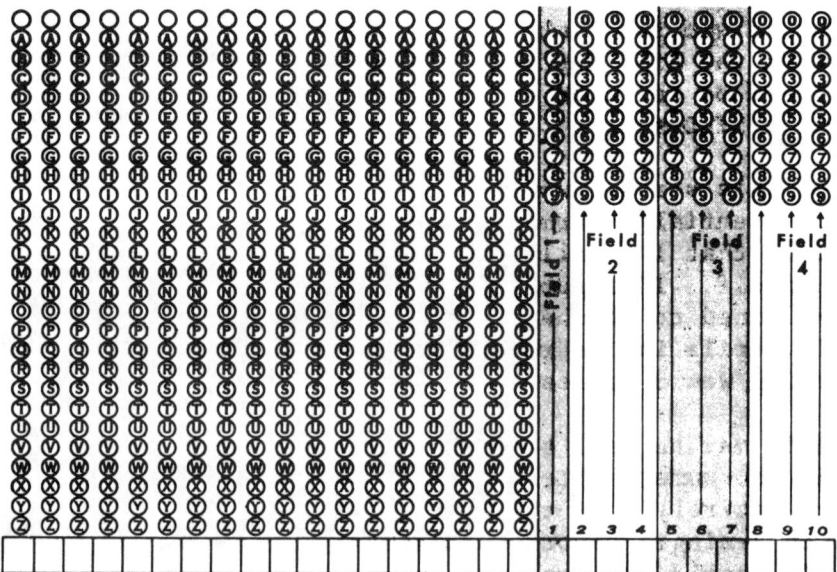

Fig. 26. The Numeric Grid. (*Source:* Simulated from 1963 ITED answer sheet.)

Field 2 could be used for an identification code, such as home room number, or for supplementary pupil information the school might want to have coded on the list report.

Any type of quantitative information that could be meaningfully averaged could be entered in Fields 3 and 4. Suggested uses included test scores, age recorded in months, grade-point averages. The range of possibilities was wide, including any information that could be expressed on a numerical scale.

Use of the numeric grid might entail considerable work for local personnel, particularly if the selected information could not be entered by the students themselves. Nonetheless, Dr. Feldt believed that supplemental information thus collected on the list report should make the ITED results more meaningful, and that its availability there might encourage and facilitate local research studies. In the year of its introduction, the grid was used in some way by about thirty percent of the high schools participating in the program. About a fourth of the schools used it in 1965. This general level of use has remained fairly constant.

A questionnaire study of the manner in which Iowa schools were utilizing the numeric grid was sponsored in 1966 by the Iowa Personnel and Guidance Association.[118] Analysis of the responses from users in the 1965 program indicated that the most frequently entered items of information were, in rank order, intelligence quotient, grade-point average, future plans, achievement battery score or percentile rank, type of curriculum followed, sex, instructional group number, junior high attendance area, class rank, and single subject achievement. The diversity of information gathered into the list reports included such items as automobile driving, rural/urban residence, various personal interests, even encyclopedia ownership.

Further services on specialized uses of the numeric grid were introduced in later programs. One relating to Field 2 permitted printouts of letter abbreviations indicating the student's tentative post-secondary plans, plus useful counselor information for low-performance individuals wishing to enroll in one of the three state universities. More recently another service relating to Field 1 produced item analyses (see next section) by coded groups within a grade, in addition to the test score averages of each group. An illustrative application suggested was a separate item analysis for persons in a remedial math course, in order to compare their performance on specific math items with that of the non-remedial students.

The Item Analysis Service

The optional item analysis service was intended as another tool for evaluation of the local program. It could yield useful clues to specific segments of a course or subject in need of instructional emphasis.

For each test in the ITED battery, the report showed what percent of local pupils in a given grade answered each item correctly and listed parallel percents for the state as a whole. A classification of the items in each test according to skills or content covered accompanied the report. A study of these two sets of information would draw attention to the kinds of skills in which local performance was above or below average. This knowledge in turn should improve awareness of possible causes for a generally high or low class standing on the test as a whole.

However, certain cautions were urged upon the users. One in particular was directed against improper classroom usage of the report. The dangers of pointing instruction toward specific test items, either purposely or inadvertently, were pointed out. The necessarily limited sampling of skills in any achievement test was stressed, as were the misleading effects on future test scores of drill on the test items in any skills category.

School officials also were warned not to draw unwarranted inferences from differences between the local and state percentages reported. They were cautioned to keep local factors in mind and to temper their conclusions or expectations with the realities of pupil population characteristics, academic philosophy, and school resources.[119]

ITP Adaptations to Changing Values

IN THE mid-sixties general dissatisfaction with the whole testing movement grew as the incidence of testing, for a variety of purposes, mounted across the country. Student disinterest was apparent in the increasing numbers of answer sheets returned with obviously random markings.

In ITP, efforts of various kinds were made to counter the ground swell of resistance to standardized testing without any sacrificial changes in the Fall Program. The problem of poor motivation among students was addressed frankly with Iowa educators, many of whom conceded disinterest among classroom teachers and a lack of local leadership in stimulating fruitful use of the test results. To improve teachers' understanding of the tests, a booklet of representative exercises from past editions was printed for distribution to teaching and guidance personnel. Counselors were urged to impress upon pupils the importance to them of accurate test scores, and to point out how their use in appraisals of the *total school program* benefits the entire student body. Procedures were instituted for segregation of casually marked answer sheets in the scoring process and exclusion of the resulting fictitious "scores" from a school's averages. To ease the strain on students and thus bolster flagging interest, schools were encouraged to spread the testing sessions over several days.

Changes in the rules for participation strengthened the voluntary aspect of the program and made local scheduling more flexible. From the beginning, whether to take part and how frequently was always a local decision, but each school had been expected to test all pupils *in all high school grades* whenever it did elect to use the ITED services. In 1970 this tight all-grades requirement was loosened to permit the testing of as few or as many grades as local circumstances warranted. If it wished, a school could stagger the testing of the various grades, so that any pupil would be tested no more often than every other year —or even less frequently. In order to protect the representativeness of the grade percentile norms for pupil scores, the every-pupil-within-grade rule was not waived. In any year, each participating school was asked to test all pupils enrolled in the grades chosen for testing. The number of schools that promptly took advantage of the relaxation in policy was substantial but not startling. Of the 432 school systems enrolled in the 1970 program, 360 continued to test all high school grades; 62 omitted one or more grades from the testing. Most often grade 12 was the one omitted. This fact caused the program director some concern that continuous lack of senior class results might distort a school's own evaluation of its total high school program. Some schools reduced annual testing to grades 9 and 11 only. Of those continuing to test all grades simultaneously, a sizable number planned to register only every other year.

While these deregulations within the program seemed welcome around the state, the length of the ITED battery remained, rightly or wrongly, the main butt of criticism.

The Shortened ITED Battery

For almost twenty-eight years Dr. Lindquist's original decision on battery length had stood firm. He believed that for pedagogical and statistical reasons almost eight hours of testing were necessary to fulfill the purposes of the *Iowa Tests of Educational Development.* The patience, concentration, and zeal of millions of students had been thus challenged annually. Their grumbling, while audible, did not become overriding in volume until well into the sixties. A steady erosion of Fall Program participation helped accelerate a crucial executive decision.

Another influence was the appearance of a shortened ITED battery on the national market.

The sentiments and effects visible in Iowa had developed as strongly among the nationwide clientele of Science Research Associates. Over the misgivings of the Iowa authors, SRA for some time had pressed for a short form of the ITED. Agreement to let SRA assemble a shortened version (named the *ITED Achievement Survey*) for its own trade was given reluctantly in 1970, provided that SRA continue to offer the full-length version as well.

But ITP did not immediately follow suit, despite inquiries from Iowa administrators. Dr. Feldt's response was candid.

> I firmly believe in the ITED as originally organized and feel the abbreviated battery would not be in the best interests of Iowa schools. I am sure many schools that adopt it are doing so with the full realization that they are giving up something by their choice. But others probably believe that they are getting everything the former ITED battery delivered in less than half the time. Obviously, this isn't true. The Chevrolet ads sound as if the car is equal to the Cadillac, but a sensible person knows that this isn't true. The analogy holds for ITED.[120]

The eight-hour battery was administered again by all participants in the 1971 Fall Program, despite an enrollment slide to 118,300 from over 157,000 the previous year. The following November a survey of a thousand Iowa high school principals and counselors revealed a majority preference for a shortened edition of the tests, with a strong minority still favoring the full-length battery. On this convincing evidence, it was decided that Iowa schools should be given a choice. With characteristic ITP dispatch, an Iowa short form, complete with all accessories and estimated norms, was readied for the next September program.

> The Sixth Edition was created out of the materials in the Fifth Edition. To shorten the battery, Test 1 (Social Studies Background) and Test 5 (Interpretation of Reading Materials in the Social Studies) have been reduced in length and combined. Greater emphasis is given the interpretation items than the background items. A similar change has been made in the science areas (Tests 2 and 6). All other tests have been shortened by about one-third. In the Sixth Edition the test on Uses of Sources of Information is included in the Composite. [See Table 2.]
> We have equated the two editions through a rescoring of all 1971 answer sheets. This should result in a high degree of comparability of scores, assuming comparable conditions of administration. However, the combining of Test 1 with 5 and 2 with 6 will affect the results, as will the inclusion of the Sources subtest in the Composite. We shall report Iowa norms and offer the same array of services with both editions.[121]

TABLE 2. Relationship of the Sixth Edition (Forms X–6 and Y–6) to Earlier Editions of ITED

	Sixth Edition				Earlier Editions		
	Title	Working Time (Minutes)	Number of Items		Title	Working Time (Minutes)	Number of Items
Test E:	Correctness and Appropriateness of Expression	35	69	Test 3:	Correctness and Appropriateness of Expression	60	99
Test Q:	Quantitative Thinking	40	36	Test 4:	Quantitative Thinking	65	53
Test SS:	Concepts and Reading Materials in the Social Studies	45	60	Test 1:	Basic Social Concepts	55	90
				Test 5:	Interpretation of Reading Materials in the Social Studies	60	80
Test NS:	Background and Reading Materials in the Natural Sciences	45	60	Test 2:	Background in the Natural Sciences	60	90
				Test 6:	Interpretation of Reading Materials in the Natural Sciences	60	80
Test L:	Interpretation of Literary Materials	35	46	Test 7:	Interpretation of Literary Materials	55	80
Test V:	General Vocabulary	15	40	Test 8:	General Vocabulary	22	58
Test SI:	Use of Sources of Information	20	46	[Composite]			
[Composite] [Reading Total]				Test 9:	Use of Sources of Information	27	65

Source: *Manual for Administrators and Testing Directors*, ITED Forms X–6 and Y–6, 1972.

One new type of score was introduced with the sixth edition. This was called a reading total score (RT), derived from the reading passages in the social studies, natural science, and literature subtests. This was expressed as a standard score, and percentile norms were provided. It was not considered in arriving at the composite score, being already represented there through the student's scores on Tests SS, NS, and L.

The act of providing a shortened edition did not concede equal merits with the longer battery.

> It is a measurement absurdity to claim a test of 30 items can have a reliability and validity identical to that of a test which contains these 30 and 60 others. It is absurd to argue that achievement in an area can be covered as well with 18 exercises as it can with 80. No two items ever overlap completely. The entire concept of reliability of measurement is concerned with neutralizing errors of measurement through the averaging of many assessments (exercises). The heart of the concept of content validity is the suitability and comprehensiveness of behavior sampling. So it is untrue that no sacrifice in validity and reliability occurs with reductions in length.
>
> In one sense, however, [such a] claim has some justification. You can take several areas for which individual scores were formerly reported and combine them, redefining the area more broadly than before. The single score then reported can be comparable in reliability to each of the several scores formerly obtained. The issue now is not entirely one of reliability. It will become one, however, if someone suddenly asks, "How about getting a score on just the science reading passages in the reading test?" Or, "Can we get a score on the literary-type passages?"
>
> But I realize that the most overriding consideration at this point in time is not the relative merits of tests taking 20 or 60 minutes. If students and staff reject a longer battery but will accept a shorter one, potential comparative advantages become irrelevant. Student willingness to cooperate becomes the key, whether one likes it or not.[122]

The rush to the short form in Iowa surprised even its sponsors. In the year of introduction, 1972, it was administered by 80 percent of the participating systems, including all but one of the largest districts. Approximately 125,800 pupils took the short form and 21,600 took the long, a definite rise in *total* number of pupils tested from the previous year. The registrations represented about 87 percent of Iowa public schools, plus some thirty-seven parochial and private schools. In 1973 even more participants switched to the sixth edition. The following year only four systems still persevered with the long form. It was then withdrawn.

The price per pupil on both editions had been held at 35 cents for the time being. This was quite a feat. While the programming and procedural changes required for the new form had been minimal, it was necessary to process the sixth edition answer sheets separately from the fifth, slowing down the schedule. The printing and maintenance of dual stocks of materials was more expensive, and greater clerical care was required in handling to avoid confusion. The extra costs and care could hardly be justified for so few users, nor could defensible norms be calculated on the results. Clearly, it was wiser to concentrate all resources on a single offering as in the past.

With the 1975 Fall Program, the long ITED battery became historical in Iowa. Forms X-4, Y-4 of the long battery remained available from the national publisher to a dwindling number of users outside the state. Quite possibly, in the shifts of societal melding and educational practice, the full-length battery may one day be seen again as superior and essential.

The Two-Level Battery

The second structural change in the *Iowa Tests of Educational Development* was a limited effort at fitting difficulty of content to individual ability in the manner of the *Iowa Tests of Basic Skills*. In the latter, six different segments of each test were designated as appropriate, respectively, to grades 3 through 8. In the ITED the split was two-way: Level I for grades 9 and 10, Level II for grades 11 and 12. The sections overlapped, as did those in the ITBS. This seventh edition was completed and equated in 1978; it replaced the sixth edition in the statewide program the following year.

In general, the new edition sampled the same content areas as did X-6, Y-6, with the easiest and simplest exercises for each area gathered into Level I. In each test, roughly the first two-thirds formed Level I and the last two-thirds formed Level II, the middle third being common to both levels. The total length of battery and the time limits were alike for both levels, and the subtest timings were similar to those of the sixth edition. The changes in the battery did not disturb the ITED profiles or the longitudinal comparability of standard scores and averages on the two editions.

In a pamphlet for the 1979 program users, Dr. Feldt elaborated on the rationale for the change.

> From its inception, the guiding philosophy of ITED has been to present in the test many of the intellectual tasks faced by adults. In the first six editions the same exercises were taken by all students. The use of a single set of exercises by all grades had several advantages. A major virtue was that it avoided the technical problems which arise when we measure student growth via tests that increase in difficulty from grade to grade. But the

> simplicity and measurement accuracy of the same-tests-for-all-grades approach was achieved at a price. Many younger students found the tests quite difficult—significantly more difficult than the typical materials they had been exposed to in grades 7-8.
>
> In the 1970s the effect of this factor on lower-ability students seemed to become more serious than it had ever been before. In some cases it may have had a negative effect on student motivation. Teachers speculated that some younger students may have had difficulty in relating test content to their own life activities. The ITED provided too abrupt a transition, perhaps, between the experiences and concerns of younger students and the challenges faced by young adults out of school.
>
> In the Seventh Edition, . . . Level I, which will be given in grades 9-10, contains easier and less sophisticated exercises than Level II, and is oriented as much as possible toward the activities of young adolescents. Level II, which will be given in grades 11-12, is somewhat harder and oriented more directly toward the tasks which older students will soon face in adult life. In general, the reading passages of Level I are shorter, the language situations more directly related to in-school and out-of-school activities of students, the mathematical problems less complex, and the vocabulary words less difficult. . . . The Level I social studies reading test, for example, includes samples of magazine advertisements and short newspaper articles. The science test contains passages patterned after newspaper stories or articles in popular magazines. The language test includes specimens of student writing such as a bulletin board announcement, an informal note from one student to another, and a description of the responsibilities of a part-time job. Level II of each test contains more advanced material, generally comparable to previous editions of ITED.[123]

During the development of the tests, efforts were redoubled in the writing, editing, and reviewing to detect and eliminate possible racial or other bias in the content. In addition, the final manuscripts were reviewed by black and Mexican-American teachers and administrators in two large Iowa school districts. The success of these precautions seems demonstrated in the results of a study in which Form X-7 was administered in a large southeastern school system to approximately equal groups of white and black students in each of grades 9-12. An index was calculated to indicate whether an item tended to favor one group or the other. An item was judged to be unfairly biased if the index was unfavorable in at least two grades. On this basis, 12 of the 357 items in Form X-7 might be called biased in favor of whites and 14 in favor of blacks. These items were scattered throughout the battery. Their fewness and the near balance in their numbers further support the opinion of the test authors that the battery is not seriously biased in either direction.

In view of the importance of reading comprehension to performance on the tests, particularly on the passages involved in the RT score, the "readability" of these passages was tested before publication of the seventh edition. The formulas and interpretive procedures used were those employed by Robert Forsyth in his 1976 study of the readability of the sixth edition, detailed in Iowa Testing Programs Research Report Number 6. On the basis of these calculations and comparisons, the seventh edition reading passages were judged no harder (and in some instances a bit easier) than the criterion materials (high school textbooks, a newspaper, and selected periodicals).

The bias and readability information, along with extensive other technical data and research references, are supplied to test users in the *Manual for Administrators and Testing Directors* accompanying the seventh edition of the battery.

One hazard to the progress of standardized testing in the commotion of the seventies was the upsurge of opposition to normative interpretations of test scores. The calculation and use of norms, it was claimed by some, was at least passé, probably detrimental, and undoubtedly suspect. The critics would discard norms of achievement in favor of other less objective, judgmental types of criteria. Skirting this reef, the ITP directors continued to recommend the norm-referenced approach as being the most practicable and satisfactory way of assessing advancement toward developmental objectives. They also continued to supply a classification of exercises by skills or areas, for whatever use the local staff might wish to make of it in setting limited class standards or goals.

Comment on this "minicontroversy" is coupled with a mild chiding in a 1977 program circular.

> Many of the proponents of criterion-referenced tests seem to find it necessary to try to discredit norm-referenced tests. We regret this attempt to belittle the value of norms. Scores on tests like ITBS or ITED can be interpreted in either the criterion-referenced or the norm-referenced sense. We have tended to emphasize norm-referenced interpretations, however, because the derivation of reasonable expectations—independent of norms—is generally very difficult. Almost every teacher uses "homemade" tests in ways that closely resemble the criterion-referenced approach. But most teachers also welcome data that help them compare local students to a broader population not available for direct observation. The two types of tests nicely complement each other, as teachers discovered long ago.
>
> We hope the advertising literature for criterion-referenced tests that occasionally floods the state has not misled Iowa teachers. A new or rediscovered idea is not always a better idea. Many practices have survived for decades because they are sound practices. We believe the use of the Iowa tests is one of these.[124]

In order to establish dependable norms for the new edition, it was necessary at the outset to tie each level strictly to the two specified grades. But a promise was made to Iowa educators that the concept of individualized testing would soon become substantive at the high school level.

> Eventually, we will permit "out-of-level" testing. By 1981 we will be ready to permit schools to assign pupils to levels on the basis of ability or other characteristics. For the present, however, Level I must be given in grades 9 and 10 and Level II in grades 11 and 12.[125]

The immediacy of subject matter and the pragmatic slant prevalent in the seventh edition test exercises are qualities that may displease some while delighting many. The social studies sections, particularly, more than ever center upon current topics, including conservation, political and social activism, civic problems, and personal understanding of or reaction to them. It recognizes often hard-fought issues that should be of concern to all citizens. It is a test battery for the times, but one which the authors insist does not downgrade intellectual achievement.

> Level I should answer some of the problems which educators have observed in previous editions. . . . However, [it] is not intended as a test of *minimum competencies* only. It is not intended as a test of "survival skills." Though easier than former editions, Level I will require honest intellectual effort. It will reliably measure achievement at levels well above that which most educators would consider minimum competency.[126]

The Slide in Student Performance

CONCERN FOR the quality of intellectual achievement in the schools had been rising with the mounting evidence of a downtrend in scores on standardized tests. This was true in Iowa as well as countrywide. Hitherto there had been a steady uptrend. During the fifties, in any one grade and year the median composite score of Iowa pupils on the ITED was substantially higher than the median for the same grade the previous year. In the early sixties the year-to-year rise leveled off. Then a long decline set in.

The ITP directors kept close watch over this worrisome situation. In correspondence with participating schools, the downward drift was illustrated by comparisons of the median composite scores (as in Table 3) and of the *mean* composites (Fig. 27) over extended periods. Accompanying comments grappled with their implications.

> Evidence of declining average achievement nationwide continues to accumulate. The National Assessment of Educational Progress (NAEP) has confirmed the trend that we have been aware of in Iowa for years and has recently been acknowledged by the American College Testing Program and the College Board. The NAEP investigators have found a decline in science achievement in the relatively brief three-year period

since the last science assessment. In another NAEP study the consumer math skills of 17-year-olds were found to average significantly below that of adults. The NAEP director attributes this in part to the abrupt shift to "new math" several years ago. The report concludes that the young adults learn more from practical experience in the marketplace than from school mathematics instruction.

The consistent evidence from these several independent sources contradicts the hypothesis that the trends we have observed may have been unique to the content of ITED or ITBS. It would also seem to rule out the possibility that poor student motivation during school-wide testing programs is the primary factor in the state decline. Very few students who take the ACT and College Board tests mark answers randomly, and yet averages have gone down. The NAEP testing is done in small groups or individually, with great concern for examinee motivation. It seems clear the causal factors lie elsewhere. Reversing the trend of the last ten years constitutes a major challenge to educators—in Iowa as well as the nation as a whole.[127]

The mean composite scores for the years 1976-79 inclusive are expressed numerically in Table 4. The data support some cautious optimism. Average performance on the ITED, as indicated by the mean composite score, appears to have stabilized in all grades and risen slightly in some. Dr. Feldt construes the evidence to show that the turn in the tide occurred when the 1979 grade 10 entered high school in 1978, no consistent improvement from year to year by other grades being apparent before that time.

Continuation of organized testing in the schools was vigorously defended in ITP communiqués of that unsettled time. In 1972, for instance:

> The fundamental purpose of all testing is to gather needed facts. Without objective information about student achievement, it would be much more difficult to evaluate and improve programs or to individualize the process of education. In a period that emphasizes experimentation, innovation, and individualization, we feel the need for measurement is unusually great.[128]

And four years later:

> We do not believe elimination of standardized tests, even on a temporary basis, would be in the best interests of Iowa schools. In times of declining test scores the temptation is strong to eliminate the sources of disturbing data. But the goal of providing high quality education for all Iowa children is not served, in our opinion, by denying educators one of their important evaluation and guidance tools. . . .
> . . . On the national level we believe the problems have been greatly exaggerated in many published articles. Where a local problem does exist, the solution lies in in-service training and better programs of communication with the local citizens, not in the elimination of potentially valuable programs.[129]

214   The Iowa Testing Programs

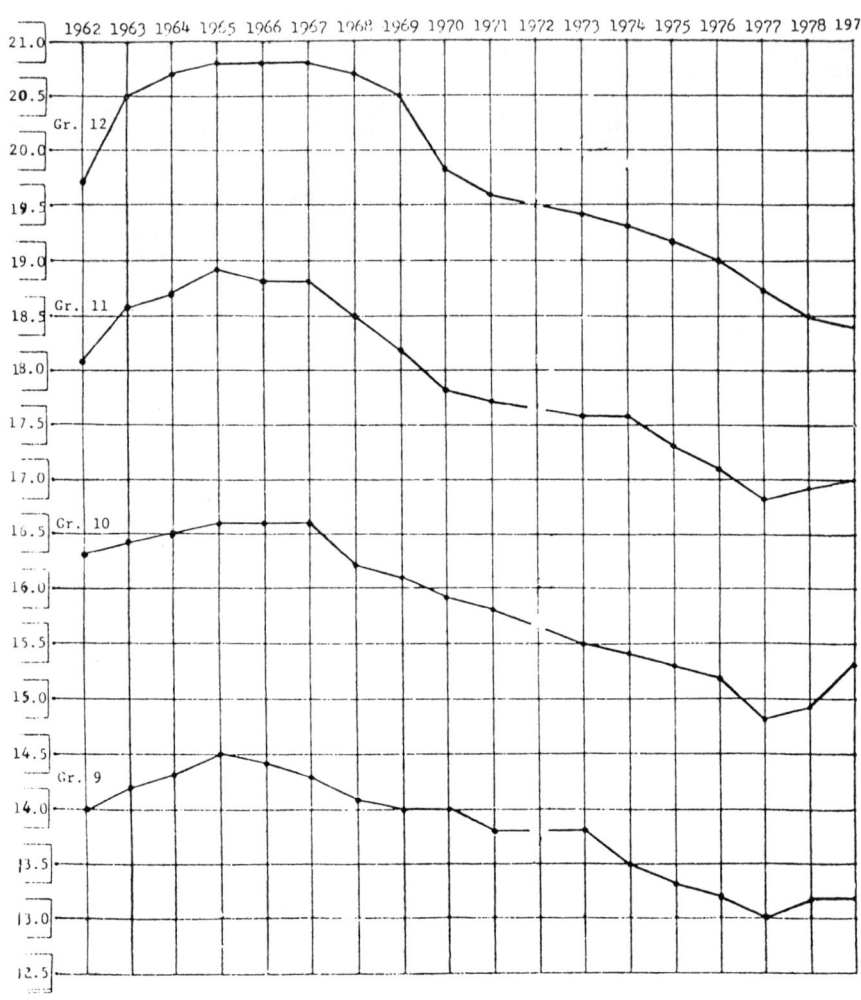

Fig. 27. Mean Composite Scores of Iowa Pupils on the ITED in Grades 9–12, 1962–79. (*Source:* 1980 Fall Program files.)

TABLE 3

Median Composite Scores of Iowa Pupils on the
Fourth and Fifth Editions of ITED, 1962–71

Year	Grade 9	Grade 10	Grade 11	Grade 12
1971	13.5	15.5	17.6	19.1
1970	13.7	15.7	17.8	19.5
1969	13.7	15.8	18.1	20.1
1968	13.8	16.0	18.4	20.5
1967	14.0	16.3	18.7	20.6
1966	14.1	16.4	18.7	20.7
1965	14.2	16.3	18.8	20.6
1964	14.0	16.3	18.7	20.7
1963	13.8	16.2	18.7	20.3
1962	13.7	16.2	18.0	19.4

Source: Letters to participants, 1964 and 1972 Fall Programs.

TABLE 4

Mean Composite Scores of Iowa Pupils
on the ITED, 1976–79

Grade	1976	1977	1978	1979
9	13.2	13.0	13.2	13.2
10	15.2	14.8	14.9	15.3
11	17.1	16.8	16.9	17.0
12	19.0	18.7	18.5	18.4

Source: Graphs in Figure 27.

The Test Results and "Accountability"

DURING THE seventies, while standardized test results were being assailed in certain quarters, other groups sought to exploit test scores in support of their own particular contentions concerning the academic productivity of present educational systems. Perhaps the two phenomena were opposite sides of the same coin. In the flurry of investigations into how well the schools were doing their job, long-established testing programs were seen as uniquely rich sources of dependable data gathered over an extended period of time. The Iowa Testing Programs was one of these. As publicity on the subject of educational "accountability" increased, so also did the requests from investigators and researchers for access to the ITP files.

In response to these pressures, the ITP directors publicly reiterated the policy of confidentiality which had been scrupulously observed in the administration of the state testing programs since their inception. As early as September 1970, a joint circular signed by directors William Coffman, Leonard Feldt, and A. N. Hieronymus reaffirmed the policy.

> We will not make available the pupil scores or grade averages of any particular system to any unauthorized individual without the written consent of the system superintendent. Furthermore, whenever the files of the Iowa Testing Programs are used for research purposes, the investigator must guarantee that the schools will remain anonymous and unidentifiable in all published reports.[130]

It was pointed out further that when access to a school's test scores was granted by a local authority for a specific purpose, the school's records could be used only under supervision in the ITP offices. Professional advice would be offered about the complexities of measurement and the ever-present pitfalls of dubious interpretations and unwarranted conclusions. The directors expressed mild skepticism about the usefulness of "cost-effectiveness" studies, but did not directly recommend either for or against participation in them.

> The Iowa Testing Programs were organized to meet *selected* measurement needs of the schools of Iowa, and their operation is guided by our perceptions of those needs. The Programs do not exist to make possible the evaluation of local organizational structure, operating procedures, or instructional practices by any outside authority. These principles constitute the foundation of the Iowa Testing Programs policy of local control over the dissemination of results.[131]

The Fall Program at 1980

IN THE aftermath of the storm—or is it merely a lull—Dr. Feldt acknowledged some possibly permanent damage to the Fall Testing Program. This despite the many efforts made to adapt the ITED battery to changing educational needs, to modernize certain elements of the program, to meet critical challenges, and sometimes in turn to challenge the critics. But Feldt believes that the program has retained a faithful following among Iowa educators, although the extent and frequency of testing has decreased in many schools.

He assessed the situation thus in a recent statement to the author:

> The wave of student opposition to the establishment in the 1960s and early 1970s did not leave us unscarred. Tests were a focal point of many student "revolts." Even today, the bias issues and anti-IQ concerns have generalized to achievement tests. In recent years they have taken their toll. Our annual Fall Program enrollment has stabilized at about 120,000 students. Our *school* participation is still about ninety percent of Iowa schools.

Plate 23. Leonard S. Feldt, *left*, and Robert A. Forsyth.

13 The ITBS 1960-80

Overview

THE SURGE of development in the Iowa Testing Programs during the last two decades has been particularly marked at the elementary grade levels. Although somewhat affected by the changing social environment, ITP accomplishments in the basic skills area were rather a maturing of aims cherished by Professors Lindquist and Hieronymus from the early years of the program. Certain of these had remained unattainable until the necessary electronic ware had been perfected.

Three entirely new and improved editions of the Basic Skills Tests for grades 3–9 were completed and placed in use during this period. A separate test measuring directly the newer mathematics concepts and terminology of the late sixties was prepared to supplement the math tests in the earlier regular batteries. The idea of individualized testing of academic skills development became a reality. Tables of relationships between the ITBS and several standardized tests of cognitive abilities or scholastic aptitude were formulated and published. Preliminary research, item construction, and standardization were completed for new six-level supplemental tests in the social studies and science. With the cooperation of ITP, large print and Braille editions of the ITBS were published under the auspices of the Iowa Department of Public Instruction.

Two important extensions of the program occurred. The first was the publication of the Primary Battery (in two editions) for grades 1.7 to 3.5. More recently, the Early Primary Battery for kindergarten and first grade was introduced.

A filmstrip/cassette duo, "Those Tests Again," and an illustrated booklet, *Test Results in Perspective*, were new self-help interpretative materials executed under Dr. Coffman's direction.

In the midst of all this developmental activity, plus additional editorial and statistical projects for the national and Canadian markets, it was decided that year-round processing of the ITBS should be opened to Iowa schools. This action afforded significant new local options to Iowa users. It also had an explosive effect upon the complexities of program administration in Iowa City!

Table 5 chronicles the principal year-to-year changes in the state program.

TABLE 5

Overview of Developments in the Iowa Basic Skills Testing Program 1960 – 80

Program Date	Event
(January)	
1960	Consultant service initiated.
1962	*Local* frequency distributions and percentile norms provided. Estimated norms for item performance on Forms 1 and 2 issued.
1964	ITBS Forms 3 and 4 replaced Forms 1 and 2 in Iowa program. School average norms based on data from *current* year (1964 – 72).
1965	Numeric grid reporting added to standard service. New extra services offered at cost: Adhesive label reports of pupil scores. Item performance analyses for groups and individuals. Punched card reports. Extra list reports.
1966	Percentile norms for Lorge-Thorndike IQ levels developed for Iowa users.
1969	Modern Mathematics Supplement to ITBS battery published.
1971	ITBS Forms 5 and 6, Levels 9–14, adopted in Iowa; grade labeling on tests eliminated. Modern Math Supplement discontinued.
1972	Optional out-of-level testing initiated in grades 3-9. Tables of *national* grade-equivalents and percentile norms *for averages* supplied to Iowa schools.
1972–73	Year-round ITBS service to Iowa schools initiated. Primary Battery Forms 5 and 6, Levels 7 and 8, introduced for grades 1.7 – 3.5. Iowa schools given option of national or Iowa norms in pupil and school reports.

Table 5 - Continued

Program Date	Event
1974–75	Individualized (out-of-level) testing option extended to Primary Battery. ITBS filmstrip with taped commentary issued. Percentile norms for *Cognitive Abilities Test* IQ levels developed for Iowa users. Option allowed of receiving reports in terms of *both* state and national norms.
1975–76	Interpretive booklet, *Test Results in Perspective*, published.
1976–77	First increase since 1955 levied in basic service charges: to 40 cents (Multilevel Battery) and 75 cents (Primary Battery).
1978–79	Multilevel Forms 7 and 8 and Primary Form 7 replaced earlier forms in Iowa program. Prices increased to 45 cents and 85 cents, respectively.
1979–80	Early Primary Battery for kindergarten and grade 1 introduced. Multilevel Battery charge raised to 50 cents.
Fall 1980	*Social Studies and Science Supplement*, Forms 7/8, Levels 9 – 14, published for optional use.

Source: ITBS annual files, 1960–80.

Individualized Testing With the ITBS

THE HOPE for eventual individualized testing had strongly influenced the original structure of the battery for grades 3 – 9. From the outset the sponsors would have preferred not to tie the achievement stages in the tests strictly to particular grades. They wanted to permit each school to decide which level of test content and difficulty was most appropriate for a given class or for atypical individuals within a grade. However, the mechanics of test processing at that time were less advanced than the thinking of the test originators. It was not then possible to score the answer sheets, compute averages, and assign appropriate percentile rankings unless all youngsters in the group tested had taken the same tests, the tests designated for their grade.

About 1970, a technological breakthrough at MRC/Westinghouse broke this barrier. Means were found to control automatically rapid changes of scoring keys and conversion tables from sheet to sheet in a stack of differing answer sheets, and, from a combination of certain scanned information, to determine and apply instantaneously the grade-equivalent scales and grade norms appropriate to each sheet. This electronic development was essential to fast processing of mixed answer sheets, which in turn was essential to unrestricted out-of-level testing.

Since the breakthrough was achieved during the assembly of the third ITBS edition, the test authors promptly and happily banished grade designations from Forms 5 and 6, supplanting them with levels designations that corresponded roughly to chronological age. The six levels of the battery were coded 9 to 14, representing the typical ages of pupils in grades 3 to 8. (The level appropriate for typical grade 6 groups, for example, was coded level 12.) In the late sixties, letter designations (A, B, and so on) had been tried experimentally by Houghton Mifflin Company on special editions of Form 3 prepared for limited use in a few metropolitan districts comprising large numbers of disadvantaged pupils. The success of that effort to measure their abilities more accurately but unobtrusively with simpler, more appropriate materials was encouraging. It supported the decision to forgo grade labeling in all future editions of the Iowa battery.

Plate 24. Conference of test authors and publishers in E. F. Lindquist's office, April 1962. *From left around table:* Lindquist, Leonard S. Feldt, Dale P. Scannell, A. N. Hieronymus, Harold T. Miller, Stanley W. Osgood, and Robert L. Thorndike.

These developments immediately facilitated individualized testing in out-of-state schools. The home folks had to wait a little longer, but only until procedural snags peculiar to the state program could be remedied. Revisions had to be made in various Iowa manuals and forms. Modifications were necessary in the mechanics of handling and processing the answer sheets and reports. By 1972 Iowa schools, too, could test out of level, to whatever extent they saw fit. A gradual transition based on experience was recommended. Schools were advised to begin by administering tests out-of-level only to markedly retarded or accelerated *groups*, and then to move on to testing selected *pupils* in this manner.

The choice of level to be used in any given situation was, of course, left to school officials; however, help was offered.

> The first consideration should be the objectives of instruction represented by the various levels of the tests. The level assigned to each pupil should be relevant to his needs, abilities, and stage of development. This is especially important in the area of mathematics concepts, in which grade placement tends to be more rigid.
>
> A second consideration is item difficulty. The level of test selected should present tasks which are challenging but attainable.
>
> If a more objective basis for assigning levels is desired, achievement test results from the previous year may be used as a partial guide. [To] the grade level of performance attained that year [add] an increment representing estimated growth.[132]

Any administrators who feared (or hoped) that out-of-level testing would lower (or raise) the school's standing were disabused. The program director had frequent occasion to explain that only the raw scores vary according to level of test taken. The grade-equivalent scores (into which the raw scores are converted) remain comparable from level to level. It is the grade-equivalents that are averaged and assigned percentile ranks.

This push toward individualizing measurement via the ITBS predated by six years the simpler two-level scheme adopted for the ITED. The Basic Skills Program was the proving ground. There the possibilities were richer. The range of behavior involved was very broad, and a commonly accepted continuum of development from grade to grade was specifiable in each skills area. Dr. Hieronymus had long contended that individualization was as important in measurement as in instruction. In his conception of accurate, valid testing, it is essential that each child be called upon to *exercise and stretch* acquired skills in reasonably familiar situations. This optimum may not often be reached, even given the best of tests and the most favorable conditions for out-of-level testing, but the effort toward it continues.

The pairing of challenge and attainability in this described ideal is vital, not incidental. To careless contentions that testing, per se, is virtual child abuse, the usually mild-mannered director has retorted that one cannot wipe frustration out of life simply by eliminating tests. One could single out other "threatening" experiences in a child's life: competition in games, class recitations, parental discipline, and so on, possibly even trips to the dentist. On the other hand, many pupils enjoy pitting their skills in test taking, and learn in doing so. In most instances, Hieronymus would insist, the positive, long-range benefits far outweigh any temporary discomforts if the testing and the results are properly handled.

Most Iowa school administrators initially took a fairly cautious approach to out-of-level testing, though a few virtually "went overboard" from the start. The number taking advantage of this option increased rapidly, until by 1980 at least a third of the participants in any one program adopted it. Some rarely or never do, probably for pragmatic reasons—it does complicate somewhat the ordering and distribution of answer sheets. Some schools that are especially concerned with curriculum studies and revisions forgo individualized testing in order to be able to obtain local item analyses of the test responses of all pupils in each grade. Such a trade-off is not uncommon.

Early on, Lindquist and Hieronymus had foreseen greater possibilities for out-of-level testing—not merely across the battery, but from test to test and part to part within the battery. Thus, a pupil might be tested at one level in reading, at another in spelling, and at still different levels in other skills.

> To achieve complete individualization, it remains only to provide a single comprehensive answer sheet or folder for all levels combined, corresponding to the complete test booklet. Each pupil could then be provided with typed individual instructions, telling him with which items he should begin and end in each test. . . . Each pupil in a large group conceivably [might be taking] a different combination of levels in the eleven tests. . . . In a computer-monitored system the individual instructions would be computer-prepared, and the combination of test levels most appropriate to each individual would be selected on the basis of past test performance and other available data in the computer's information bank.[133]

So far, it has not been deemed practical or warranted in the Iowa Program to refine individualized testing to that extent. However, the present capability significantly enlarges the usefulness of the program in the measurement of differences and improves its local option characteristics.

The Latest Multilevel Edition

BESIDES signifying developmental stages as levels rather than grades, the authors made substantive changes in the fourth edition (1978) of the Multilevel Battery for grades 3–9 which improved the suitability of the battery for out-of-level administration. Two subtests, Visual Materials and Reference Materials, replaced the former three subtests of work-study skills. A separate test of mathematics computation skills was added—a reluctant bow to current sentiment among test users. Other content revisions reflected recent instructional changes in skills objectives, curricular sequences, and emphasis. The system of classifying skills objectives was reorganized to be of greater aid in the determination of pupil needs as well as in criterion-referenced interpretations of the test results. The level-to-level overlap of content in each area was overhauled to insure appropriate difficulty and efficiency in the subtests. All subtests except Spelling were shortened, and their work times were reduced correspondingly. The total time for the battery was thus decreased by thirty-five minutes.

This new edition was standardized nationally and prenormed for Iowa during the term preceding its appearance in the Iowa program. The tentative Iowa norms were later reexamined and adjustments made on the basis of actual data from the first Iowa administration. This has been typical procedure in the norming of all new ITBS batteries for some time.

Work on a fifth edition for levels 9–14 is underway.

The Tests for Primary Grades

THE PRIMARY BATTERY (1972) and the Early Primary Battery (1979) extended downward through kindergarten the means and the opportunity of doing what had been possible in grades 3–9 since 1955. They completed a slate of Iowa tests that afforded continuous assessment of individual development from kindergarten through high school. Scholastic progress and needs could now be monitored without interruption by means of coordinated Iowa-built tests, administered either within level or out of level according to local circumstances. The average developmental stage for which each level of the current Iowa Basic Skills series was designed is shown in Table 6.

The objectives of measurement underlying the Primary and Early Primary batteries are similar to those of the Multilevel Battery, with particular attention to determining the young child's readiness to begin instruction in each area or to proceed to the next step. The skills coverage is similar also but includes two new categories, listening and word

TABLE 6

Normal Intended Usage of the ITBS

	Level	Average Developmental Level	
		Age	Grade
Early Primary Battery	5	5	K.1–1.5
	6	6	K.8–1.9
Primary Battery	7	7	1.7–2.6
	8	8	2.7–3.5
Multilevel Battery	9	9	3
	10	10	4
	11	11	5
	12	12	6
	13	13	7
	14	14	8–9

Source: Teacher's Guide, Primary Battery, Form 7, *Iowa Tests of Basic Skills*, 1980, p. 1.

analysis. There is no reading test in the level intended mainly for use in kindergarten.

The approaches used with beginning and primary pupils differ, of course, from those in the battery for the higher grades. Understanding of pictures is an important element in the tests of listening, vocabulary, and reading skills. Oral administration is employed in some subtests, considerably more assistance is given to the younger pupils throughout the testing, and the use of cardboard place markers by the pupils is recommended. The manuals for teachers detail an imposing array of skills analyses and developmental objectives. The Primary Listening Test, for example, is described as measuring nine subskills: literal meaning, inferential meaning, concept development, following directions, linguistic relationships, numerical and spatial relationships, understanding sequence, predicting outcomes, and attention span. Suggestions are offered on how to improve pupil mastery of these elements.

Nine of the fifteen Primary subtests and all but one of the Early Primary are orally administered. The Primary and Early Primary tests are not timed; the director recommends that all but exceptionally slow pupils be allowed to finish. Working time per testing session may range from 15 to 30 minutes on the Primary and from 20 to 40 on the Early Primary. Both batteries are entirely machine scorable.

As in all other ITP tests issued during the last two decades, particular attention was paid during construction to possible ethnic and cultural influences upon pupil responses, avoidance of stereotyping, and exclusion of sexist or racist implications in item situations and vocabulary.[134] Generally, in all aspects of test content, the authors and editors earnestly sought to reflect contemporary social concerns.

The Supplementary Tests in Social Studies and Science

THE MOST RECENT (1980) addition to the slate of tests offered through the Basic Skills Program is not *in series* with the others but *supplementary* to them. The *Social Studies and Science Supplement* is available for purchase by participants in the regular program at their option. Users generally administer it at about the same time as the other Basic Skills Tests. In one sense narrower in focus, being concerned with only the social studies and science fields, within these fields the Supplement touches a broader range and variety of achievement than can appropriately be tested in the Multilevel Battery. Since the Supplement was designed in part as an instrument for program evaluation, more attention is given to the content and the objectives of contemporary curricula in these areas of instruction.

In the accompanying manual for teachers, the tests are described as measuring "outcomes not covered in the regular [Multilevel ITBS] battery." While devoted mainly to background information, the tests measure the "generalization and application of social and scientific principles, and the extent [to which] the particular course of study contributes to the attainment of the ultimate objectives of the social studies and science programs." Being "vertically articulated" with the ITBS and the *Tests of Achievement and Proficiency*, they contribute to making possible a complete assessment program in the major elementary fields of study.[135]

Each of the two tests in the Supplement employs the familiar ITBS pattern of six overlapping levels (9–14). The social studies items fall into two broad categories—historical perspective, and knowledge of contemporary patterns and systems. The spread of item difficulty and sophistication ranges from a simple "Which is part of a plumber's job?" for third graders to questions about foreign governments for eighth graders to ponder. Content objectives represented in the science items include: nature of science, life science, earth and space science, physics, chemistry, and health and safety.

The types of scores, norms, and services available with the Supplement are similar to those provided with the other Basic Skills Tests. This kinship, of course, is preserved to facilitate interpretation and the interweaving of results from battery to battery.

Iowa Performance on the Tests

Achievement Trends in Iowa

Between 1955 and 1972, the Iowa norms on the ITBS were reestablished annually by revising the raw-score-to-grade-equivalent conversion tables on the basis of results from the January program. This basis remained stable from year to year because all testing was done in midyear under uniform conditions. That traditional stability was forfeited when in 1972 – 73 the schools were given the privilege of testing at any time of the year. For the next three years, until a reservoir of data from the new testing patterns was collected, provisional, broader-based conversion tables were employed that combined the results of January 1971 and 1972. Percentile norms for fall and spring were interpolated. New conversion tables subsequently were calculated on the three-year period (1972 – 73, 1973 – 74, and 1974 – 75), and new Iowa percentile norms were established for October 30, January 30, and April 30. (The most appropriate set—that is, the closest to time of testing—was applied in ranking a school's scores and averages.) Thereafter, it was again feasible to update the norms by making annual adjustments.

The very large accumulation of normative data on the *Iowa Tests of Basic Skills* has yielded significant indicators of trends in performance on the tests, in Iowa and nationwide. A pamphlet distributed to participants in the 1977–78 program briefly summarized achievement trends in Iowa.

> The first Multilevel Edition was used in the 1955 Iowa Basic Skills Testing Program. The period between 1955 and 1960 was a time of extensive reorganization in Iowa schools, and achievement in the basic skills improved markedly. Achievement continued to improve at a somewhat slower rate between 1960 and 1965.
>
> Between 1965 and 1970 there was a general decline in all areas except work-study. Losses were most pronounced in language usage and mathematics. Between 1970 and 1975 there were further substantial losses, particularly in the language skills. During the past two years there were small improvements in most test areas and an overall decline in only two areas, language usage and math concepts.[136]

Table 7 summarizes the extent of change in performance on each part of the battery during each five-year interval from 1955 to 1977. Each entry is an average of the changes in midyear grade-equivalent (GE) medians in all grades in all years of the interval, expressed in GE units ("months").

Table 8 shows changes in the composite by grade for each of the years 1970 – 80, as well as for five-year intervals, 1955 – 80.

TABLE 7

Average Changes in Median Grade-Equivalents of
Iowa Pupils in Grades 3–8 on the ITBS, 1955–77

	Test V: Vocabulary V	Test R: Reading R	Test L: Language Skills					Test W: Work-Study Skills				Test M: Mathematics Skills			Composite C
			Spelling L-1	Capitalization L-2	Punctuation L-3	Usage L-4	Total L	Maps W-1	Graphs W-2	References W-3	Total W	Concepts M-1	Problems M-2	Total M	
1955–60	3.5	3.9	4.2	8.3	3.3	5.6	5.4	4.2	4.6	4.1	4.3	4.5	3.0	3.8	4.2
1960–65	.9	.9	1.5	3.1	1.9	1.7	2.0	1.4	.7	1.5	1.2	2.4	1.1	1.8	1.3
1965–70	−.7	−1.1	−.7	−1.6	−1.3	−2.2	−1.4	.4	.3	.4	.4	−1.6	−2.6	−2.1	−1.0
1970–75	−1.0	−1.4	−1.7	−3.6	−3.0	−2.5	−2.7	−1.3	−.6	−1.2	−1.0	−2.0	−1.3	−1.6	−1.5
1975–77	.1	0.0	.1	.7	.6	−.2	.3	.3	.5	.2	.3	−.4	.2	−.2	.1

Source: "New Iowa Norms," 1977–78 Iowa Basic Skills Testing Program, Table 2, p. 2.

TABLE 8

Changes in ITBS Composite Scores, Grades 3–8,
Iowa Basic Skills Testing Program, 1955–80

	Differences Expressed in Grade-Equivalent Units ("Months")						
	Grade 3	Grade 4	Grade 5	Grade 6	Grade 7	Grade 8	Average Grades 3–8
				1970–80			
1970–71	–.1	–.2	–.2	.2	.0	.2	–.0
1971–72	.3	.4	.0	–.3	.0	–.2	.0
1972–73	.1	–.1	–.4	–.6	–1.0	–1.0	–.5
1973–74	.0	–.1	–.4	–.6	–1.0	–1.0	–.5
1974–75	.0	–.2	–.4	–.6	–1.0	–1.0	–.5
1975–76	.4	.2	.2	.3	–.3	–.2	.1
1976–77	.5	.3	.2	–.2	.0	–.5	.1
1977–78	.4	.3	.4	.4	.4	.0	.3
1978–79	.3	.4	.6	.9	.9	.6	.6
1979–80	.3	.3	.4	.6	.7	.5	.5
				1955–80			
1955–60	3.0	3.6	3.7	4.3	5.7	4.8	4.2
1960–65	1.3	1.2	1.6	1.3	1.4	1.2	1.3
1965–70	.1	–.3	–.5	–.8	–2.3	–2.2	–1.0
1970–75	–.3	–.2	–1.4	–1.9	–3.0	–3.0	–1.6
1975–80	1.9	1.5	2.3	2.0	1.7	.4	1.6

Source: Analysis by A. N. Hieronymus et al.

The 1970–75 period appears to be the trough of the decline/rise cycle evidenced in these tables. On the ITBS composite score (Table 8) some declines continued in the upper grades during the next two years, but at a much slower rate. During 1977–80 the downward trend was reversed in all grades.

The general decline in 1965–75 on the ITBS (as on the ITED) reflected a national pattern in standardized test performance. Speculation about this widely noted phenomenon has ranged over many possible causes. Dr. Hieronymus cited as those most frequently blamed:

(1) changes in priorities which have resulted in decreased instructional emphasis in the basic skills;
(2) changes in attitudes of pupils, teachers, parents, and the lay public toward the importance of school, the basic skills, and tests;
(3) changes in the character of instructional materials, particularly in mathematics and the language skills.

In addition some critics blame organizational innovations in the school, lack of "discipline" in the schools, decreasing teacher competence, the effects of television, or parental permissiveness. On the other hand, it is contended by some that the evidence of decreasing achievement is unconvincing or faulty; that the tests used to measure change are lacking in relevance, are biased, or are measuring the wrong outcomes.[137]

He believed it simplistic to try to pinpoint one or a few of these possible reasons as overriding causes.

Different factors are involved in differing degrees in different situations. In some situations pupil attitude and motivation may be serious factors; in others instructional emphasis should probably be reexamined. Recent losses have not taken away the substantial gains of the previous years, but they should be evaluated seriously if the trend is to be reversed.[138]

Comparisons With National Performance

The Iowa norms on the Basic Skills Tests have consistently differed from norms of performance in general across the nation. Because of this difference, information drawn from the national standardizations of the tests has been provided regularly to Iowa administrators, so that they might be informed periodically about levels and changing trends of basic skills development in the country as a whole, and might compare ITP data with similar types of information from other sources.

The differences between national and Iowa norms on the ITBS have long been in Iowa's favor. Hieronymus observed in early 1970 that "through the years we have seen performance in Iowa grow from a mediocre position in relation to that in other states, to a highly superior position."[139] The latter relationship was again demonstrated in the national standardizations of 1970–71 and 1977–78. Results from the former, when compared with Iowa norms, revealed differences in median grade-equivalent scores on the various subtests ranging from three to seventeen months.[140] Iowa performance was superior on all tests in all grades, and at all levels in the score distributions except at the very top, where little difference was noted. Differences for school averages, reflecting the greater heterogeneity of schools in the national standardization sample, were even more striking. For example, in grade 4 on the Composite, half of the Iowa schools exceeded the average performance of 90 percent of buildings nationwide.[141]

In comments accompanying the 1972 report of national norms, Dr. Hieronymus drew attention to the many factors to be considered in state versus national comparisons, including population characteristics, educational resources, and cultural traditions. He pointed out also that in performance on IQ tests, Iowa pupils outdistanced national averages.

He further admonished that "while Iowans can take a great deal of pride in the superiority of the results for their schools, caution should be exercised against becoming self-satisfied or complacent." Citing the decline in test scores already in motion at that time, he observed that "in view of other demands . . . being made of schools, it is getting increasingly difficult to maintain the present level of performance in the basic skills."[142]

Nonetheless, in subsequent studies based on the 1977–78 Multilevel Battery standardization, Iowa retained its lead. Differences in median pupil performance, expressed as grade-equivalent units or "months" in a ten-month year, are given in Table 9. On the Vocabulary Test, for example, the Iowa median in grade 3 is 7.1 "months" above the national median.

TABLE 9

Differences Between Iowa and National Medians on the ITBS

	Differences Stated as "Months"					
Grade	Test V	Test R	Test L	Test W	Test M	C
3	7.1	7.6	9.6	7.6	4.4	7.2
4	7.5	8.9	9.6	9.6	5.6	8.2
5	8.0	8.8	12.1	11.3	7.0	9.9
6	7.2	9.3	12.0	11.4	8.0	10.5
7	5.0	8.8	11.5	11.6	8.5	9.3
8	7.5	11.5	13.5	14.9	10.7	11.3

Source: Data supplied by Dr. Hieronymus.
Note: V = Vocabulary; R = Reading; L = Language; W = Work-Study; M = Mathematics; C = Composite.

In the annual programs from 1974–75 on, it has been possible to prepare a school's reports in terms of *both* state and national norms as an extra service. This option was requested for about half of the more than 239,000 pupils tested in 1980. Some administrators, especially those in the larger school districts and the border cities, have felt that the national norms are representative of their particular school populations. Others have found the state norms more appropriate for certain uses and national norms for others. With national, state, local, and sometimes regional or other group norms available on the Basic Skills Tests, Iowa educators are well equipped for wisely interpreting and applying the test results.

Growth in Program Services

VIRTUALLY ALL of the new or improved services developed by ITP in the sixties and seventies were incorporated into both the ITBS and ITED programs, though not always at the same time. The most important of the newer common services include: the local norms and frequency distributions; adhesive label reports of pupil scores; the numeric grid for including other local data in the score reports; item performance analyses; the option of state or national rankings (or both); and local consultation. These services have been described in the preceding chapter with reference to the ITED. Differences of application in the elementary program are occasioned mainly by its greater complexity. The Basic Skills batteries involve a much larger number of tests, levels, and scores. The elementary program is less wieldy than the high school program in size and scope, serves more diverse educational entities, allows more autonomy to school officials in the selection and scheduling of the tests, and must be adaptable to more substantial variation in the utilization of the results. These factors, of course, affect the manner in which each service is rendered, the technical production difficulties encountered, and the cost of supplying it.

The norms for ability levels (see page 233) further enriched the amount and variety of normative data on basic skills performance available through the ITBS program. Large city norms and parochial school norms have been gathered periodically. Particular types of reports have been furnished in increasing numbers on request from individual urban districts and other educational agencies. Special information has been compiled when needed by Iowa schools in meeting increased requirements for evaluation data, particularly those of federal acts concerned with programs for the educationally disadvantaged. Consultation and related service have been supplied, not only to local school systems, but also to some of the Area Education Agencies that were organized by statute in the early 1970s (officially designated by number but colorfully subtitled "Loess Hills," "Northern Trail," "Heartland," "Mississippi Bend," and so on).

Certain special services on the Basic Skills Tests have been developed for out-of-state users only, at the behest of the national distributors. At present these include: reporting in terms of standard scores and stanines, narrative reporting, student criterion-referenced skills analysis, and services resulting from the use of a combined answer folder for concurrent administration of the ITBS and the *Cognitive Abilities Test*.[143] These services have not been offered in the Iowa Program for a number of reasons, including: the excessive cost of programming for the smaller number of probable buyers; the risks of overextending local facilities; the more restrictive requirements of the state program; and, occasionally, differences in measurement philosophy.

Technical and procedural advances made it possible from 1964 to 1972 to calculate school average norms on the basis of *current* ITBS results rather than on those from the previous year. As long as all participants were testing within about five weeks in January/February, this was an appropriate method of calculating annual norms. With the advent of year-round testing, other methods had to be devised for establishing and updating separate norms for fall, midyear, and spring.

Achievement Versus Ability Data

The publication in 1966 of special Iowa percentile norms for IQ levels was a boon to ITBS user schools that had also purchased (elsewhere) and administered the *Lorge-Thorndike Intelligence Tests* (1963 edition).[144] This service widened the possible interpretations of ITBS scores to include a comparison of an individual's ranking on the ITBS among pupils in the same grade and his/her ranking among pupils of similar measured intelligence. The two ratings might differ considerably. Such information could be another important tool in follow-up work on the basic skills. As usual, however, test users were cautioned to exercise judgment and to recognize the many factors other than measured intelligence that bear upon academic achievement. It was pointed out, also, that the educational significance of differences between the two rankings was related to whether the two testing instruments measured *unlike* elements of behavior. Correlations and reliability data were supplied to guide and augment the user's subjective appraisals and conclusions.

Further assistance along these lines was given the schools with the publication in 1969 of the Iowa Testing Programs Research Report Number 2, *Comparability of IQ Scores on Five Widely Used Intelligence Tests*. It contained tables for converting IQs on one test to those on another. These would be especially useful with respect to transfer students whose records showed scores on intelligence tests different from those administered locally. The report was of value also for use in conjunction with the Iowa percentile norms for Lorge-Thorndike IQ levels. Other data given made possible direct comparisons between ITP achievement results expressed in terms of Iowa norms and IQs reflecting national norms. The means of making such comparisons gains importance from the fact that Iowa pupils exceed national averages on tests of mental as well as academic ability.

In 1974–75, data were developed making possible comparisons between achievement scores on the *Iowa Tests of Basic Skills* and ability scores on the *Cognitive Abilities Test*. The two batteries had been standardized on the same population of pupils and at approximately the same time. Thus, the new data were gathered from a nationwide sample highly representative in factors relevant to the characteristics measured. Three types of comparisons were made available.

For the first type, voluminous tables of percentile norms were provided for eight ability levels, three *Cognitive Abilities Test* scores, and six grades. These permitted comparisons of ability test results with basic skills achievement test results at any cognitive ability level, but were fully appropriate only for pupils tested in the fall.

A second approach involved the use of prediction equations, computed at scoring headquarters, to reveal discrepancies in performance. This method, however, necessitated concurrent testing of achievement and ability and the use of an oversized answer folder accommodating both sets of responses; hence, it could not be employed in the state program.

The third and simplest comparison, which could be accomplished quickly, was the one recommended to Iowa users. It involved identifying, from a single appropriate table, which pupils in a class "achieved" (on any ITBS subtest) in the bottom 20 percent among pupils having the same standard age score on the *Cognitive Abilities Test*. While not conclusive, this evidence would at least point up that something might be amiss and should lead to further investigation.

After publication of Multilevel Forms 7 and 8, similar but expanded tables were compiled for results on those forms. These supplied achievement figures at the 20th, 50th, and 80th percentiles of ability scores, enabling the teacher to identify pupils in four segments of the distribution, not merely the lowest. A simple flagging system (+ +, +, −, − −) was suggested to indicate on the record the apparent quality of a pupil's achievement (in relation to measured ability) on each Basic Skills Test.

Incidentally, the 1966 norms for IQ levels had been determined empirically and arduously by the hand method of plotting scores, drawing curves, and reading off and recording into tables the thousands of values reported. Ten years later the comparable data relating to scores on the *Cognitive Abilities Test* were computer generated from the processed reports of test results. Computer programming was now the critical task.

The State of the Program

Recent Volume of Testing

The buffetings of the sixties did not shrink user interest in the Basic Skills Tests. On the contrary, during that decade annual administrations of the Multilevel Battery in Iowa rose from about 206,500 to some 307,800. In the following decade, however, this trend was gradually reversed (with minor fluctuations) to approximately 230,700, but by other causes than confrontation.

Usage of the Primary Battery, which began at roughly 17,250 in 1972-73, increased to 29,500 by 1978-79. With the introduction of the Early Primary Tests in 1979-80, pupil participation at the primary and kindergarten levels totaled approximately 40,350.

The reduction during the seventies in number of Iowa pupils tested with the Multilevel Battery in grades 3-9 seems attributable to a new combination of circumstances. Relentless inflation pushed up the cost of the ITBS service to the schools. The same financial pressure affected allocations of school funds, including expenditures for standardized testing. Local school administrators enjoyed greater freedom in the selection of tests and the rotation of test schedules. The strongest factor, however, appears to have been the decrease in the elementary school population. Viewed in this light, the gradual decline in number of Multilevel tests administered annually does not signal a real lessening in the popularity of the battery. Exact comparisons between school population and test administrations at the start and the end of the decade are difficult to make because of differences in methods of compilation. Furthermore, the availability in 1980 of the Primary and Early Primary batteries and out-of-level testing would tend to dilute grade-by-grade comparisons of Multilevel Battery usage that year and in 1970. To generalize, during the decade the number of Multilevel batteries (only) administered annually, principally in grades 3-8, decreased by about 22.5 percent. According to the State Department of Public Instruction, the *total* school enrollment in Iowa (public and nonpublic, *all* grades) declined by approximately 19 percent from 1970 to 1980.

Moreover, *school* participation in this program has been remarkably stable. Over the past ten years, each annual program has served approximately 95 percent of Iowa school districts—public, private, and parochial. The school registration figures (by categories) for 1979-80 are shown in Table 10. Incomplete figures for 1980-81 showed a similar pattern.

TABLE 10

Participation by Iowa Schools in the 1979–80 Basic Skills Testing Program

Total public school districts in Iowa	445
Public school participants	424
Private school participants	225
Catholic	142
Lutheran	23
Christian	36
Other	24
Total participants	649

Source: Registration data in ITBS files.

The out-of-state market for the *Iowa Tests of Basic Skills* remained strong throughout the twenty-year period. It draws heavily upon large urban areas, less subject to population fluctuations. Furthermore, the many combinations of service and a virtual plethora of special services available from the national publishers have undoubtedly stimulated sales of the tests, despite rising prices. As is usual, a surge in sales across the country accompanied the introduction of new tests and the issue of new editions near the end of the last decade.

Increasing Complexities of Program Operations

Administration of the statewide program has steadily become more complicated, more demanding of time, care, talent, and money. Some of the complications have developed out of changes in educational structures and policies. Reorganizations of school districts and county systems have changed many local procedures, from planning to follow-up, as well as central procedures, from registration to reporting to billing. Increased autonomy of individual schools within certain districts often produces variations in the testing activities from building to building. Such differences, in turn, may necessitate special instructions for processing; they also make the preparation and reporting of *system* data more difficult. A mounting number of requests flows into the director's office for special services and analyses to meet a peculiar local need or to satisfy some external requirement, often tied to the disbursement of federal funds to education. Split payments for test services tangle the invoicing; within a single district, tests for some grades (or even classes) may be charged to a town superintendent's budget, some to county funds, and some to federal or state subsidies. Year-round testing leaves no breathing space in program operations to be devoted to rehabilitation and planning, such as had long been enjoyed with a six-week January/February testing period. No time is reserved exclusively for development. Yet continuing attention must be, and is, paid to the results of ongoing research in educational and psychological measurement at The University of Iowa and elsewhere.*

Test construction has, of course, been made more painstaking by commitment to the avoidance of stereotyping, discrimination, and other sociological blemishes, and by shifts of favor or emphasis in curricula. In batteries measuring the broad range of elementary school instruction, contemporary attitudes and directives appreciably complicate the technical specifications for test building. A distant and unexpected action may devastate the progress and peace of a whole editorial team. In one such case, virtually on the eve of publication, several parts of a new ITBS Multilevel Battery had to be ripped apart, rewritten or redrawn, because a populous western state decided to ban the sale of "junk foods" on all school properties. Some of the original test items and illustrations had measured the pupil's understanding of choices, quantities, weights, prices, and so on, of just such fare—so commonly available to kids everywhere. The arithmetic test was expurgated (in double time!) by wholesale replacement of hitherto innocuous art work depicting a food vending machine and the related items.

Standardization of new forms has been affected by changes in the composition of school populations in many areas. Obtaining the necessary cooperation and insuring against bias in the test administration are not easily accomplished.

Thus, the supplying of standardized tests has become ever more challenging over the last twenty years. At the same time, the notion has bloomed (especially in national channels of test distribution) that it is, or should be, possible to provide limitless combinations of tests and services virtually tailor-made for Eagleville or Surf City. The rapid growth in electronic capabilities undoubtedly has fostered this expectation. Such ambitions seem to have outrun the realities of theory/practice gaps, staggering costs, and perhaps even educational good sense. Within the Iowa Testing Programs, which operates on narrow margins and strives to give its participants as much as possible for as little money as possible, spiraling production costs could limit future innovations.

Meanwhile, Dr. Hieronymus' faith in the power and effectiveness of parents and surrogates as guardians of the educational welfare remains

---

*One important example (and a subject of current debate) is item response theory. Though propounded as new by certain specialists, it actually was an element of Professor Lindquist's measurement courses in the forties and has been a topic of many studies at Iowa during the past two decades.

unshaken. As he affirmed in a recent conversation, he sees their steady insistence upon good education for their children as ballast against its capsizing in the currents of change.

NOTE

In 1981 a series of administrative changes occurred in the Iowa Testing Programs. Director William Coffman retired in June. Thereupon, Professor Leonard Feldt was appointed General Director of the Iowa Testing Programs and E. F. Lindquist Professor of Educational Measurement. Professor Robert Forsyth was then named Director of the ITED Fall Testing Program.

POSTWORD

And at the same time . . .

While the Iowa Testing Programs and satellite projects were evolving, E. F. Lindquist was also engaged in:

teaching . . .
During the thirties, forties, and early fifties he taught a regular schedule of graduate courses in statistical methods, educational measurement, and the design of experiments.

directing research . . .
Particularly during the thirties and forties, he served as principal advisor to many candidates for advanced degrees—fully 150 during the thirties, and as many as 23 M.A. recipients at a single convocation. His advice on experimental designs was widely sought by colleagues as well.

consulting and advising . . .
He participated as a member of or consultant to numerous committees, boards, and agencies, intramural to international, collegiate, governmental, military. One educational mission took him to West Berlin in 1947; another, in 1967.

writing . . .
He was the author of three textbooks, the coauthor of two, and the editor as well as a coauthor of two others. The dates of first publication were 1936, '38, '40, '50, '51, '53, and '60. Three of his works on statistical methods were issued in foreign editions also: British, Turkish, Indian, and Czechoslovakian. His writings over the years from 1929 to 1970 also included some forty articles published in professional journals and many more informal papers and addresses.

and inventing . . .
Even after his retirement in 1969 he continued to invent, designing two simulators for indoor golf practice which have been patented through The University of Iowa Research Foundation.

For such intense achievement, the record itself is tribute.

APPENDIX

TABLE A

Authors of Early Iowa High School Achievement Tests, 1929 and 1930

1929

English	M. F. Carpenter, E. F. Lindquist, Henning Larsen, John Fellows
History	G. G. Andrews, E. F. Lindquist, B. L. Pierce, H. R. Anderson, Elmer Ellis
Mathematics	H. L. Rietz, E. F. Lindquist, Ruth Lane, F. D. Austin, L. W. Miller, E. W. Chittenden
Science	C. J. Lapp, E. F. Lindquist, P. M. Bail, C. B. Yager, P. C. Norvell, C. S. Trachsel
Commerce	E. G. Blackstone, E. F. Lindquist, Frances Botsford, Robert La Dow, Mary McLaughlin

1930

Economics	George D. Haskell, Walter F. Crowden, E. F. Lindquist
English	M. F. Carpenter, Henning Larsen, Agnella Gunn, E. F. Lindquist
Government	George F. Robeson, Hilda Watters, E. F. Lindquist
History	G. G. Andrews, H. R. Anderson, Elmer Ellis, Thyra Carter, Denzil Nelson, E. F. Lindquist
Mathematics	H. L. Rietz, E. W. Chittenden, Ruth Lane, Harold Lundholm, E. F. Lindquist
Science	C. J. Lapp, P. M. Bail, C. B. Yager, Winifred Gilbert, E. F. Lindquist

Sources: 1929 University of Iowa Extension Bulletin No. 203 (Arch. I–1929–7B) and 1930 "Convocation, Iowa Academic Meet, State Contest" (Arch. I–1930–7H).

Note: In each subject, the chairman of the test committee is listed first. E. F. Lindquist was general editor in all subjects.

TABLE B

Authors/Editors of Iowa Every-Pupil High School Achievement Tests 1931–42

Author/Editor	'31	'32	'33	'34	'35	'36	'37	'38	'39	'40	'41	'42
Algebra												
H. Vernon Price								A	A	A	A	E
Harold Lundholm	A	A	A	A	A	A	A					
Ruth Lane												A
Plane Geometry												
Ruth Lane	A							A	A	A	A	A
Harold Lundholm		A	A	A	A	A	A					
H. Vernon Price												E
American Government												
John H. Haefner								A	A	A	A	E
John E. Briggs						E	E	E	E	E	E	E
H. R. Anderson	A	E	A	A			A					
Ethan P. Allen		A										
Erma B. Plaehn					A	A						
Leslie Miller												A
Economics												
H. R. Anderson		A	A	A	A	A	A					
J. E. Partington		E	E	E	E	E	E					
G. W. Haskell	A	E			E							
U. S. History												
H. R. Anderson	A	A	A	A	A	A						
G. G. Andrews	A	E	E	E	E	E	E					
Harry Berg								A	A	A		A
H. J. Thornton									E		E	E
John H. Haefner												E
Louis Pelzer									E			
Wallace Taylor										A		
Ryland W. Crary										A		
C. W. de Kiewiet										E		
World History												
H. R. Anderson	A	A	A	A	A	A	A					
G. G. Andrews	E	E	E	E	E		E	E				
Wallace Taylor								A	A	A		
C. W. de Kiewiet										E	E	
Harry Berg											A	A
Goldwin Smith												E
John H. Haefner												E

Note: A = author or co-author; E = editor. E. F. Lindquist was general editor of all tests.

Table B - Continued

Author/Editor	'31	'32	'33	'34	'35	'36	'37	'38	'39	'40	'41	'42
Biology												
Paul E. Kambly				A	A	A	A	A	A	A	E	E
Willard Unsicker											A	A
Willis R. Boss			A									
Kenneth L. Cochran		A										
General Science												
Paul E. Kambly												A
C. J. Lapp		E	E	E	E	E	E	E	E	E	E	E
Alvin W. Schindler		A	A	A	A	A	A	A	A	A		
Paul H. Lahr									E	E		
Donald Petit											A	
Willard Unsicker											A	
Charles B. Yager	A											
Physics												
Alvin Schindler		A	A	A	A	A	A	A	A			
C. J. Lapp		E	E	E	E	E	E	E	E	E	E	E
Donald Petit								E	E	E	A	
Armin Graber												A
P. M. Bail	A											
Latin												
Helen M. Eddy			A	A	A	A	A	A	A	A	A	A
F. H. Potter			A	A	A	A	A	A	A	E	E	E
H. R. Butts										A	A	A
Marguirette Struble		A	A	A	A							
American Literature												
M. F. Carpenter	A	A	A	A								
English Literature												
M. F. Carpenter	A	A	A	A								
Reading Comprehension of Literature												
M. F. Carpenter							A	A	A	A	A	A
Julia Peterson									A			
William R. Wood					A	A	A					
English Correctness												
M. F. Carpenter	A	A	A	A	A	A	A	A	A	A	A	A

Table B -Continued

Author/Editor	Editions of Test (Year)											
	'31	'32	'33	'34	'35	'36	'37	'38	'39	'40	'41	'42
*Contemporary Affairs**												
T. H. Roberts											A	A
E. F. Lindquist					A	A	A	A	A	A	A	A
Harry Berg												A
C. W. de Kiewiet											A	A
E. T. Peterson											A	A
Ethan P. Allen									A	A	A	
H. R. Anderson				A	A	A						
Jack Johnson								A				

Sources: Tests in ITP Archives, 1931–42.

*Other University of Iowa faculty members who collaborated as editors of contemporary affairs items in their respective fields for various editions between 1935 and 1940 were G. G. Andrews, Harry Berg, J. E. Briggs, G. R. Davies, J. H. Haefner, C. W. Hart, K. E. Leib, E. T. Peterson, Wallace Taylor, and H. J. Thornton.

TABLE C

Editions of *Iowa Tests of Basic Skills*, 1935–39

Year	Authors/Collaborators
1935	J. Lloyd Rogers and H. A. Greene
1936 1937 1938 1939	Under dir. of Ernest Horn, Maude McBroom, H. A. Greene, F. B. Knight, E. F. Lindquist (gen. ed.); with (on various editions) Ruth Clendenen, G. V. Lannholm, Thelma Lewis, William Maucker, R. F. Netzer, J. L. Rogers, H. F. Spitzer; and faculty of University Experimental Schools

Sources: Tests in ITP archives.

TABLE D
Editions of *Iowa Tests of Basic Skills*, Forms L – T, 1940 – 54

Form	Years Used in Iowa Program	Author(s)/Collaborators	
L	1940	H. F. Spitzer	
M	1941		
N	1942, 1945	H. F. Spitzer, Ruth Fridell	with Ernest Horn
			Maude McBroom
O	1943, 1946	H. F. Spitzer	H. A. Greene
P	1944, 1948		E. F. Lindquist (gen. ed.)
Q	1947, 1952	H. F. Spitzer, Katherine Hunt, Julia Peterson	
R	1949, 1953	Under dir. of E. F. Lindquist with E. Horn, H. F. Spitzer, M. McBroom, H. A. Greene, Robert Ebel, K. Hunt, J. Peterson	
S	1950, 1954	Under dir. of E. F. Lindquist with R. Ebel, A. N. Hieronymus, J. Peterson, Gordon Rhum, H. A. Greene, E. Horn, H. F. Spitzer	
T	1951		

Sources: Tests in ITP archives.

TABLE E

Editions of *Iowa Tests of Educational Development*, 1942–80

Forms	Years Used in Iowa Program	Authors/Collaborators
X–1, Y–1	1942–47	Paul Blommers, William Maucker, Julia Peterson, Kenneth Vaughn; under dir. of E. F. Lindquist
X–2, Y–2	1948–52	P. Blommers, Robert Ebel, John Gerber, J. Peterson, W. Maucker, K. Vaughn; under dir. of E. F. Lindquist
X–3, Y–3	1953–60	Janet Afflerbach, Howard Anderson, P. Blommers, Miriam Bryan, Paul Burke, A. T. Clarke, R. Ebel, J. Gerber, John Haefner, T. J. Kallsen, Jerry Kollros, W. Maucker, Ruth Miller, Bernice Orshansky, Vernon Price, Rolland Ray, Geraldine Spaulding; under dir. of E. F. Lindquist, with M. Bryan and J. Peterson
X–4, Y–4	1961–69	Harry Berg, Richard Braddock, P. Burke, Mary Alice Burmester, Earle Eley, Alfred Hall, Victor Harris, David Heenan, Benjamin Hickok, George Morgan, Clarence Nelson, Reginald Porter, G. Spaulding, Harriet Stull, John Warner; under dir. of E. F. Lindquist and Leonard S. Feldt
X–5, Y–5	1970–74*	Under dir. of E. F. Lindquist and L. Feldt, with Robert A. Forsyth and Esther Neckere
X–6, Y–6	1972–78*	Under dir. of E. F. Lindquist and L. Feldt, with R. Forsyth and E. Neckere
X–7, Y–7	1979–	Under dir. of L. Feldt, R. Forsyth, and E. F. Lindquist, with Stephanie D. Alnot and Paul S. Belgrade

Sources: Tests in ITP archives.

Note: In repetitions of names in this table, initials only are used in place of first names.

*In 1972, '73, and '74 the long Fifth Edition and the short Sixth Edition were both available to participating schools.

TABLE F
Editions of *Iowa Tests of Basic Skills*, 1955 – 80

Form(s)	Years Used in Iowa Program	Principal Authors/Editors	Collaborators on Various Editions
Multilevel Battery			
1	1955 ⎫		
2	1956 ⎬ E. F. Lindquist and		
1, 2	1957–63 ⎬ A. N. Hieronymus		
3, 4	1964–70 ⎭		
5, 6	1971–77	A. N. Hieronymus and E. F. Lindquist	Janet Afflerbach, Rex Billington, Miriam Bryan, Allan Cohen,
7, 8	1978–	A. N. Hieronymus E. F. Lindquist H. D. Hoover	Susan Eberly, Leonard Feldt, Maurine Fry, Nathan Goldstein, Theresa Hagemann, H.D. Hoover Kathy Humphrey, Betty
Primary Battery			Humphry, Thelma Lewis, Pat Lohmann, Barbara Long,
5, 6	1972–77	A. N. Hieronymus and E. F. Lindquist	Brenda Loyd, Mavis Martin, Ruth Miller, Virginia Monroe,
7	1978–	A. N. Hieronymus E. F. Lindquist H. D. Hoover	Esther Neckere, Kathleen Oberley, Julia Peterson, Barbara Plake, Rolland Ray, Robert Renk, Beatriz Santos, Gunnar
Early Primary Battery			Sausjord, Geraldine Spaulding, Faye Strayer, Mary Vermillion,
7	1979–	A. N. Hieronymus E. F. Lindquist H. D. Hoover	Virginia Vial, Marcia Whitney
Social Studies and Science Supplement	1980–	A. N. Hieronymus E. F. Lindquist H. D. Hoover	

Sources: Tests in ITBS files.

TABLE G

Principal MRC Publications, 1956–69

"Comprehensive Test Processing Service," first announcement, 1956; enlarged edition, 1958.

The Measurement Research Center Way! descriptive booklet, April 1964.
Reprinted in June 1964 for distribution by major client publishers; third printing in April 1966; fourth printing in June 1967.

"Guide to the Selection of Scoring Machines and Optical Scanners," by Robert A. Edberg et al., published by MRC in 1964; reprinted in the *Journal of Educational Data Processing*, vol. 2, nos. 2 and 3, 1965; reprinted by MRC in January 1966; translated into Swedish by Lars-Magnus Bjorquist, October 1965.

"MRC Employee's Handbook," 1964; reprinted in 1966.

Special equipment brochures:
"MRC M7 Optical Document Scanner"
"MRC 801 High Speed Mark Scanner"
"MRC 1501 Optical Card Scanner"

Source: ITP/MRC files.

NOTES

Note: All program documents cited are currently located in the Lindquist Center. Early sources coded by a number in parentheses—for example, (IV–III–2A)—are filed in the Iowa Testing Programs Archives, Room 304. Later ITBS and ITED sources dating from about 1965 are filed in the ITBS or ITED laboratories adjacent to the directors' offices. Other sources cited are in relevant special files as indicated.

1. Thomas J. Kirby to school superintendents, 2 November 1928. (I–1929–3)
2. I–1930–5F.
3. Kirby to superintendents, 4 March 1930. (I–1930–3)
4. University of Iowa Extension Bulletin no. 203, (I–1929–7B); E. F. Lindquist letter to Eric Wilson, University News Service, 5 February 1931. (I–1931–7L)
5. "Scope of the Tests." (I–1930–3)
6. [E. F. Lindquist], "The Iowa Academic Contest (A Preliminary Copy of an Explanatory Bulletin)," p. 5. (I–1930–3)
7. Statement in I–1930–5F.
8. The point systems of selection are detailed in a February 1929 mimeographed bulletin, "The Iowa Academic Meet," pp. 3–5. (I–1929–3)
9. Ibid., p. 4.
10. E. F. Lindquist, *The Iowa Academic Contest: Its Purposes and Possibilities*, Bulletin of the State University of Iowa, n.s. no. 577, 15 December 1930, pp. 24–25. (I–1931–2)
11. Ibid., pp. 17–37.
12. Ibid., pp. 17–23.
13. E. F. Lindquist, *The Iowa Academic Contest*, Bulletin of the State University of Iowa, n.s. no. 667, 23 December 1932, pp. 6–10. (I–1933–2)
14. Ibid., p. 10.
15. Ibid., p. 11.
16. E. F. Lindquist, "Announcements for 1931–32," p. 5. (I–1932–2)
17. Bulletin No. 826, 11 January 1936, p. 8. (I–1936–2)
18. Pp. 17–18. (I–1935–5A)
19. E. F. Lindquist, *The Fourteenth Annual Iowa Every-Pupil High School Testing Program*, University of Iowa Publication, n.s. no. 1228, 17 January 1942, p. 15. (I–1942–2)
20. E. F. Lindquist, "The Iowa Testing Programs—A Retrospective View," *Education* 91, no. 1 (September-October 1970): 9 (hereafter cited as "A Retrospective View").
21. E. F. Lindquist, "Special Report of Norms on the 1934 *Iowa Every-Pupil Achievement Tests* for Pupils at Different Levels of Intelligence." (VII–1934–3A)
22. E. F. Lindquist, *Iowa Every-Pupil Intelligence Testing Program*, Bulletin of the State University of Iowa, n.s. no. 712, 4 November 1933, pp. 15–16. (VII–1934–2A)
23. (II–1 to II–7 incl.)
24. Lindquist, "A Retrospective View," p. 8.
25. E. F. Lindquist, *A Cooperative Testing Program for Iowa Elementary Schools*, Bulletin of the State University of Iowa, n.s. no. 760, 6 October 1934, pp. 5–6. (IV–1935–2A)
26. Ibid., p. 6.
27. Ibid., p. 7.
28. Ibid., p. 12.
29. Ibid., p. 13.

30. E. F. Lindquist, *The 1937 Iowa Every-Pupil Basic Skills Testing Program*, Bulletin of the State University of Iowa, n.s. no. 873, 21 November 1936, p. 12. (IV-1937-2A)
31. Lindquist, *Cooperative Testing Program*, p. 13.
32. [Lindquist], *Manual for Administration and Interpretation of Iowa Every-Pupil Tests of Basic Skills*, 1937, pp. 21-23. (IV-1937-1E)
33. E. F. Lindquist, *The 1936 Every-Pupil Testing Program for Grades Six, Seven, and Eight*, Bulletin of the State University of Iowa, n.s. no. 808, 7 September 1935, p. 14. (IV-1936-2A)
34. [Lindquist], *Manual for Administration and Interpretation of Iowa Every-Pupil Tests of Basic Skills*, 1936, pp. 14-15. (IV-1936-1E)
35. E. F. Lindquist, "Progress in Educational Measurement in Iowa Schools," 6-7 October 1938, pp. 2-4. (EFL professional files, The University of Iowa, Iowa City)
36. "Norms for Iowa Every-Pupil Tests, Form L." (IV-1940-2E)
37. "Approximate Age Norms for the Iowa Every-Pupil Tests of Basic Skills, Form L." (IV-1940-2E)
38. For equating procedures followed in the forties see IV-1947-4A, IV-1948-4A, IV-1949-3A, and IV-1949-4A.
39. Procedure described in IV-1945-3A and IV-1948-3A.
40. E. F. Lindquist, "A Retrospective View," *Education* 91, no. 1 (September-October 1970): 13.
41. Lindquist to Iowa superintendents, 7 September 1948. (IV-1949-2B)
42. Lindquist to William E. Spaulding, 2 April 1940. (ITP correspondence files)
43. Lindquist to G. M. Fenollosa, 6 August 1949. (ITP correspondence files)
44. Lindquist to Fenollosa, 22 February 1950. (ITP correspondence files)
45. E. F. Lindquist, "A New Program of Testing for Guidance and Evaluation in Iowa High Schools," *Epsilon Bulletin* of Phi Delta Kappa 21, no. 1 (21 October 1941): 14.
46. Ibid., pp. 14-15.
47. E. F. Lindquist, *Fall Testing Program for Iowa High Schools*, University of Iowa Bulletin, n.s. no. 1242, 11 April 1942, pp. 19-20. (III-1942-2A)
48. E. F. Lindquist, "A New and Vital Testing Program for Iowa High Schools," supplement to University of Iowa Bulletin no. 1242, p. 1. (III-1942-2A)
49. Lindquist, *Fall Testing Program*, 1942, pp. 9-17.
50. Ibid., p. 24.
51. Ibid., pp. 20-22.
52. [Lindquist], "The Nature and Purposes of the *Iowa Tests of Educational Development*," 1948, p. 8. (III-1948-2A)
53. E. F. Lindquist, "A Retrospective View," *Education* 91, no. 1 (September-October 1970): 12.
54. Lindquist to school superintendents, 16 April 1948. (III-1948-5A)
55. [Lindquist], "Nature and Purposes of ITED," 1948, p. 17.
56. E. F. Lindquist, "Curriculum Revision in English," North Central Division Conference, Fort Dodge, Iowa, 25 March 1938. (Professional papers)
57. Lindquist, *Fall Testing Program*, 1942, p. 10.
58. Ibid., p. 30.
59. Major steps are analyzed in Part Two of *Educational Measurement* by E. F. Lindquist et al. (Washington, D.C.: American Council on Education, 1951), pp. 119-454.
60. "Scoring the *Iowa Tests of Educational Development*." (III-1942-IV)
61. Lindquist to Iowa school administrators, 27 September 1948 and 19 April 1949. (III-1948-2E and III-1949-2B)
62. E. F. Lindquist, Lauren A. Van Dyke, and John R. Yale, *What good is high school?* and *Instructors' Guide* to same, Life Adjustment Booklet (Chicago: Science Research Associates, 1948). (III-1948-2A) [Note: No author's royalties or sales commissions were paid on sales to Iowa program schools. (Lindquist to Iowa school administrators, 27 September 1948.)]

63. Lindquist to Iowa school administrators, 8 April 1948. (III-1948-2B)
64. Participating Schools, 1944-48. (III-1948-2C)
65. William F. McDermott, "Prospecting for Brain Power," *National Parent-Teacher* (June 1954); and "They Spotlight Hidden Talent," *Reader's Digest* (October 1954).
66. "Sound Educational Credit for Military Experience" (Washington, D.C.: American Council on Education, 1943).
67. [Lindquist], "A Nationwide High School Testing Program," Cooperative Test Service of the American Council on Education, 1946. (V-1946-2A)
68. Lindquist to V. A. Hines, 21 June 1947. (V-1947-4)
69. Study sponsored by *The New York Times*, summarized in article by Benjamin Fine, 23 January 1950.
70. [Lindquist], "Seventh Annual Contemporary Affairs Testing Program for Iowa High Schools . . . 1952," ITP Bulletin. (V-1952-2A)
71. Lindquist to Lehan Tunks, 16 July 1953. (ITP/MRC files)
72. Ibid.
73. E. F. Lindquist, "The Iowa Electronic Test Processing Equipment," *Proceedings, 1953 Invitational Conference on Testing Problems* (Princeton, N. J.: Educational Testing Service), pp. 160-68.
74. A. N. Hieronymus to school administrators, 1956. (IV-1956-2B)
75. Lindquist to Rulon, 30 April 1956.
76. Lindquist to Rulon, 9 October 1957.
77. Lindquist to Rulon, 2 October 1958.
78. Lindquist to George Hite, 28 June 1955. (MRC files)
79. ITED *Manual for the School Administrator*, rev. for 1959, p. 30. (III-1959-2D)
80. Ibid.
81. Lindquist to school administrators, 1959. (III-1959-2B)
82. *How to Use the Test Results*, ITED, 1959 State of Iowa Edition, p. 4. (III-1959-2D)
83. A. N. Hieronymus, "The New *Iowa Tests of Basic Skills*," address to the Annual Conference on Administration and Supervision, Iowa City, Iowa, 29 November 1955 (hereafter cited as 1955 Conference address). (ANH professional files) Summarized in *Epsilon Bulletin* of Phi Delta Kappa 31 (1956): 5-6.
84. Ibid., p. 4.
85. Ibid., p. 5.
86. Ibid., p. 6.
87. Ibid., p. 12.
88. Ibid.
89. National Council for the Social Studies. *Skills in the Social Studies*. Twenty-fourth Yearbook.
90. Leonard Feldt, "Measurement of Skills in Capitalization, Punctuation, and Usage," 1954; Rolland Ray, "Some Problems in the Measurement of Arithmetic," 1951; Gunnar Sausjord, "Problems in Measurement of Work-Study Skills," 1951; Betty Humphry, "The Development of the Work-Study Skills in Selected Elementary School Textbooks," 1954. Ph.D. theses, The University of Iowa.
91. Hieronymus, 1955 Conference address, p. 7.
92. *Manual for Administrators, Supervisors, and Counselors, Iowa Tests of Basic Skills*, Iowa Testing Programs, 1956, p. 82. (IV-1957-1B)
93. Hieronymus, 1955 Conference address, p. 18.
94. Ibid.
95. Ibid., p. 20.
96. E. F. Lindquist, "The Iowa Electronic Test Processing Equipment," *Proceedings, 1953 Invitational Conference on Testing Problems* (Princeton, N.J.: Educational Testing Service), p. 167.
97. E. F. Lindquist, "A Retrospective View," *Education* 91, no. 1, (September-October 1970): 15.
98. Lindquist's report to the MRC board, 7 June 1968, and oral recollections of Dr. Lindquist and Dr. Hieronymus to the author.

99. William E. Coffman, ed., *Frontiers of Educational Measurement and Information Systems—1973*. Proceedings of conference. (Boston: Houghton Mifflin Company, 1973). Available from Iowa Testing Programs, 334 Lindquist Center, Iowa City, Iowa 52242.
100. E. F. Lindquist, *Fall Testing Program for Iowa High Schools*, **University of Iowa Bulletin**, n.s. no. 1242, 11 April 1942, p. 33 (III – 1942 – 2A).
101. E. F. Lindquist, "A Retrospective View," *Education* 91, no. 1 (September-October 1970): 18.
102. Lindquist to Lyle Spencer, 31 March 1959. (Early ACT records in ITP files)
103. E. F. Lindquist, "Recent and Possible Future Developments in ACT Services to Schools and Colleges," paper presented at the Annual Meeting of the ACT Membership, Chicago, 7 May 1962. (EFL professional files)
104. Lindquist, "A Retrospective View," p. 19; and records in ACT/ITP files.
105. Ibid.
106. E. F. Lindquist, *A Cooperative Testing Program for Iowa Elementary Schools*, Bulletin of the State University of Iowa, n.s. no. 760, 6 October 1934, p. 8. (IV–1935–2A)
107. Virgil M. Hancher to Lindquist, 17 April 1943. (EFL committee files)
108. Lindquist to Hancher, 20 April 1943.
109. Loehwing to Peterson, 24 February 1945.
110. Lindquist to Davis, 10 July 1958. (Professional files)
111. Robert A. Edberg to E. F. Lindquist and John Dolch, notes of conference on 11 July 1958 concerning technical specifications for the center.
112. Lindquist to Van Allen, 5 October 1961. (EFL files)
113. Early UCC records in ITP accounting files.
114. "Iowa Educational Information Center," announcement brochure issued jointly by the Department of Public Instruction and the College of Education, University of Iowa [1964]; and E. F. Lindquist, "A Proposed Information Center for Iowa Schools," paper presented at the Forty-eighth Annual Conference on School Administration and Supervision, The University of Iowa, 4 December 1963. (IEIC/ITP files)
115. ITP contributions of $3,500 and $7,500 to ICRSA are acknowledged by John W. Harold to Lindquist, 2 February 1960 and 26 January 1961. (ITP files)
116. [Feldt], "Use of the Numeric Grid," *Supplement to the Manual for the School Administrator*, ITED, 1963. (III–1963–3A)
117. Ibid., p. 4.
118. Robert Savereide, "Use of the ITED Numeric Grid by Iowa Secondary Schools in the 1965 Fall Testing Program." (III–1966–3A)
119. [Feldt], "The Nature and Use of the ITED Item Analysis Report," 1966 Fall Program. (III–1966–3A)
120. Feldt to Gary Johnson, 18 February 1971. (Fall Program files)
121. Feldt to school administrators, 15 March 1972.
122. Feldt to Glenn E. Fear, 10 November 1971.
123. [Feldt], "A Brief Description of the Seventh Edition of the *Iowa Tests of Educational Development*," 1979, pp. 1 – 2.
124. Feldt to school administrators, 15 March 1977.
125. [Feldt], "Description of Seventh Edition," p. 3.
126. [Feldt], *Manual for Teachers, Counselors, and Examiners*, ITED Forms X-7 and Y-7, 1980, p. 2.
127. Feldt to school administrators, Fall 1975.
128. Feldt to school administrators, August 1972.
129. Feldt to school administrators, 15 March 1976.
130. Coffman, Feldt, and Hieronymus to school administrators, September 1970. (Fall Program files)
131. Ibid.

132. [Hieronymus], "How to Register for Out-of-Level or Individualized Testing," p. 2. (1972–73 ITBS files)
133. E. F. Lindquist, "A Retrospective View," *Education* 91, no. 1 (September-October 1970): 23.
134. *Teacher's Guide*, Primary Battery, Form 7, *Iowa Tests of Basic Skills*, 1980, p. 2.
135. *Teacher's Guide* for the ITBS *Social Studies and Science Supplement*, 1980, p. 2.
136. [Hieronymus], "New Iowa Norms," 1977–78 Iowa Basic Skills Testing Program, p. 2.
137. [Hieronymus], "Achievement Trends in Iowa: 1955–76," Iowa Basic Skills Testing Program.
138. Ibid.
139. Hieronymus to Sister Janita Curae, 17 March 1970.
140. "Tables of National Grade-Equivalent and Percentile Norms for Pupil Scores," 1971 Iowa Basic Skills Testing Program.
141. "Tables of National Norms for School Averages," 1972 Iowa Basic Skills Testing Program.
142. Ibid.
143. "Special Iowa Supplement to *Manual for Administrators*," 1980–81 Iowa Basic Skills Testing Program, p. 2.
144. "Special Percentile Norms for IQ Levels," 1966 Iowa Basic Skills Testing Program.

INDEX

Accountability, 216
Achievement trends in Iowa, 227 – 31. See also Test score decline
ACT, 177 – 80
Administrative Data Processing Service, 182. See also Statistical Service Bureau
Ambrose, Fred, 106
American College Testing Program. See ACT
American Council on Education, 82 – 83
Answer sheets, printing of, 109, 111. See also Separate answer sheet
Application for knowledge: testing of, 15
Area Education Agencies, 232
Atwater, Verne S., 172
Automatic punching of scores, 118
Automation, first appearance, 11 – 12

Basic Skills Program, advanced battery, 43; characteristics of, 27 – 31, 44 – 45; comparability of forms, 44; cost, 37, 44, 49; cumulative record form, 46; elementary battery, 43; first machine scoring, 115 – 19; format, 28 – 29; improved service systems, 35 – 37; item analyses, 44; need for, 26; new series, 43 – 45; participation in, 38, 50; printing, 44; purposes, 30 – 31; scoring, 29; statistical services, 32 – 37
Basic Skills Testing Program, 218 – 20; recent volume, 235 – 36; *Social Studies and Science Supplement*, 226. See also *Iowa Tests of Basic Skills*
Benson, Karl, 182
Blommers, Paul, 183
Bowen, Howard, 152
Brain Derby. See Iowa Academic Meet
Bureau of Educational Research and Service, 11, 23, 35

CardPac, 188
Card Scanner, 158
Carsner, George, 159
Chaloux, L. Y., 102 – 03
Cobb, William, 181
Coffman, William E., 194, 239
Cognitive Abilities Test, 234
Communication with users, 12 – 14
Compagnie des Machines Bull, 95
Comparisons between achievement and ability scores, 233 – 34
Comprehension of Literature Test, 18
Computers at MRC, 159
Consultant services, 201
Contemporary Affairs Test, 15, 18 – 20
Cooperative Test on Recent Social and Scientific Developments, 83 – 85
Correction for guessing, 20 – 21
Cranium Contest. See Iowa Academic Meet
Criterion-referenced tests, 211
Cumulative record, 45
Curricula, influences of tests on, 14

Davidson, Charles W., 145
Davidson offset press, 94
Davis, Harvey, 184
Dolch, John P., 186
Do You Know Your Skills? See *How are Your Skills?*

Early Elementary School Program, 26 – 39. See also Basic Skills Program
Ebel, Robert L., 81, 183
Edberg, Robert A., 95, 102, 108
Educational Records Bureau, 1
Educational Research Corporation, 90, 102
Educational Testing Service, 106 – 07
Electronic test processing: significance of, 107 – 08

Engineers Northwest, 107
English Correctness Test, 16–18
Evaluation and Examination Service, 182–83.
Every-Pupil Program, 16. *See also* Iowa Academic Meet
Extension Division, 11

Fall Testing Program: booklet of representative exercises, 204; cost of, 208–09; developments 1960–80, 199–200; in 1980, 217; new services, 124–25, 201–04; opinion about, 78–79; organization of, 64–77; participation in, 77–78, 125–26. *See also* ITED
Feldt, Leonard: director, Fall Testing Program, 124; E. F. Lindquist Professor of Educational Measurement, 239; research in language testing, 135; president of IMRF, 194
Forsyth, Robert, 194, 239

GED. See *Tests of General Educational Development*
George, Richard, 159
Greene, Harry, 27, 44

Hancher, Virgil M., 91, 108
Hand scoring, 68–75
Hieronymus, Albert N.: director, ITBS Program, 49–50; 114–15, 229–31.
Hoover, H. D., 194
Horn, Ernest, 27, 44
Houghton Mifflin Company, 51, 102
How Are Your Skills? 127–28
Humidity control, 111
Humphrey, Betty, 135
Hunter Manufacturing Company, 154

IEIC. See Iowa Educational Information Center
IMRF. See Iowa Measurement Research Foundation
Individualized testing, 211–12. *See also* Out-of-level testing
Intelligence Testing Program, 22–23
Invitational Conference on Testing Problems 1953, 107
Iowa Academic Contest, 24. *See also* Iowa Academic Meet

Iowa Academic Meet, 1–15; awards, 9; cost of, 4, 11; effects of, 5–6; objectives of, 2, 10; participation in, 3; printing of, 10–11; questions: types of, 3; recognition for pupils, 5; reports, 10–12; research, 14, 24; scoring of, 5; subjects tested, 3
Iowa Center for Research in School Administration, 189
Iowa Educational Information Center, 187–89
Iowa Every-Pupil Achievement Testing Program, 24. *See also* Iowa Academic Meet
Iowa Every-Pupil Elementary School Testing Program. *See* Basic Skills Program
Iowa Every-Pupil High School Testing Program, 24. *See also* Iowa Academic Meet
Iowa Every-Pupil Tests, 9, 16, 23
Iowa Measurement Research Foundation, 173–76
Iowa State Department of Public Instruction and Iowa Testing Programs, 50
Iowa Tests of Basic Skills: commercial distribution, 50–51; developments 1960–80, 219–20; features of, 51; multilevel edition, 129–39; norms, 52; specifications, 130–36
Iowa Tests of Educational Development: rationale, 53–54; two-level battery, 209–12. *See also* Fall Testing Program
ITBS: Early Primary Battery, 224–26; fourth edition, 224; Primary Battery, 224–26; program services, 232–34. See also *Iowa Tests of Basic Skills*
ITED: Achievement Survey, 206; characteristics, 56–64; commercial marketing of, 80–81; criteria, 55; development of, 64–65; English Test, 59–61; features, 54; Forms X–3 and Y–3, 123; local norms, 201; Manual for Administrators and Testing Directors, 211; military service by, 82; Forms X–4 and Y–4, 123–26; Reading Tests, 57–59;

reading total score, 208; scoring and reporting services, 61 – 62; seventh edition, 209; shortened battery, 205 – 09; sixth edition, 206; standard score scale, 62 – 64. See also *Iowa Tests of Educational Development*
Item analysis, 15, 204

Jaspen, Nathan, 164
Jessup, Walter, 181
Johnston, Paul F., 188
Jolliffe, Elwin T., 182
Jones, Howard R., 188

Kirby, Thomas J., 2
Knight, F. B., 27
Krohn, Earl, 95, 101
Krohn-Hite Instrument Company, 91, 102

Latin Test, 15
Lindquist Center for Measurement, 173 – 75
Lindquist, E. F.: ACT director of research and development, 178; activities of, 241; design of scoring machine, 90 – 91; director, Iowa Academic Meet, 6; general editor, 16; idea for measure of contemporary affairs, 83; inventions, summary of, 122; inventor, 114; Iowa Educational Information Center, 187; philosophy of testing, 53; procedures, formulation of, 182; procedures, improvement of, 182; retirement of, 193; scoring machine 89 – 122; University Committee on Examinations, 182 – 83; values of, 38 – 39; writing of, 4
Lindquist Professor of Educational Measurement, 194, 239
Loehwing, Walter F., 183, 184
Lorge-Thorndike Intelligence Tests, 233
Lundquist, Elmer, 45

Mahan, Bruce E., 2
Manual for Administration and Interpretation, 35 – 36
Marker, Robert W., 188
Martin, C. W., 23
Mast Development Company, 94

Mast, Clifford, 94
McBroom, Maude, 27, 44
McCall, W. C., 38
McCarrel, Ted, 178
McMillin, John, 159
Measurement Research Center. See MRC
Mental Measurements Yearbook, 52
Military Training Programs: Army Specialized Training Program, 182; pre-meteorology, 176
Missouri Achievement Testing Program, 23
MRC: board of trustees, 145; customers, 163 – 65; engineering developments, 153 – 63; establishment of, 143 – 47; financial structure, 147 – 50; plant and personnel, 150 – 53; purposes of, 143 – 44; sale of, 168 – 73; scoring capacity, 164; services, types of, 165, 168
Multilevel edition of ITBS, 129 – 39

National Merit Scholarship Program, 49
Nimtz, Albert E., 23
Norm-referenced tests, 211
Norms: Basic Skills Program, 44; by IQ levels, 233; differences between national and Iowa, 230; ITED, 124; large city, 232; multilevel edition, 136 – 37; parochial school, 232
Numeric grid, 202 – 03

Ohio Eighth Grade Test, 118
Optical scanners for "export," 159
Original Iowa high school testing program. See Iowa Academic Meet
Out-of-level testing, 221. See also Individualized testing

Packer, Paul C., 2
Peterson, Elmer T., 91, 183
Physics Test, 15
PLAN, 172
Primary and Early Primary tests, 224 – 26
Printing, quality control of, 158
Profile leaflet. See "Your Scores on the ITED . . . and What They Mean"
Psychological Examination for Grades 9 – 12, 22
Pupil Profile Chart, 32 – 34, 45

Ray, Rolland, 81, 135
Readability, study of, 211
Reading Comprehension of Literature Tests, 15
Rental of Test Booklets, 65
Research studies: comparing IQ scores on different tests, 233; in arithmetic, 135; in language, 135; in work-study, 135; new type of item, 133–35; separate answer sheets, 133
Royalties, 107
RSSD. See *Cooperative Test on Recent Social and Scientific Developments*
Rulon, Phillip J., 90, 102, 108

Sausjord, Gunnar, 135
Scaling of multilevel edition, 136–37
School averages, 48
Science Research Associates: contract with, 79–80; contributors to ACT, 178; MRC scanner installed, 159; short form of the ITED, 206
Score reporting: exclusion of fictitious "scores," 205; mark-sense card, 47
Scoring machines: components of, 94; cost of development, 102–06; functions of, 118–19; fundamental design for, 90–91; installation, 111; item analysis unit, 94–95; Mod 1, 94; Mod 2, 153–54; Mod 3, Mod 4, Mod 5, 154–155; Mod 7, 155, 158; Mod 9, 158; principal features of, 107; procurement complications, 108–14; shakedown, 111; technical problems, 108–14
Self-interpreting profiles: ITBS, 127–28; ITED, 76–77.
Separate answer sheet, 21–22
Spaulding, William, 106
Special services, 236–38; for out-of-state users, 232–33

Spencer, Lyle M., 81, 177
Spitzer, H. F., 44
SRA. See Science Research Associates
State Scholarship Contest. See Iowa Academic Meet
Statistical Service Bureau, 181–82

Test analyses, 15
Test bias, 210
Test score decline 212–13. See also Achievement trends in Iowa
Test security, 63–69
Tests of General Educational Development, 82
Thurstone, L. L., 22
Thurstone, Thelma Gwinn, 22
Tryout of items, 48–49
Tyler, Ralph W., 82

UCC, 187. See also University Computer Center
United States Armed Forces Institute. See USAFI
University Committee on Examinations, 182–83
University Computer Center, 184–87; support from Iowa Testing Programs, 186–87
University Examinations Service. See Evaluation and Examination Service
University Experimental Schools, 27
USAFI, 52

Van Allen, James, 187
Varenais, Andrejs, 95, 101

Wartime problems, 45–49
Williamson, E. G., 82
Work-Study Skills Test, 134–35

"Your Scores on the ITED . . . and What They Mean," 76–77